Voyage into Savage Europe
A Declining Civilization

Avigdor
Hameiri

Voyage into Savage Europe
A Declining Civilization

Translated
and Edited
by Peter
C. Appelbaum

BOSTON
2020

Library of Congress Cataloging-in-Publication Data

Names: Hameiri, Avigdor, 1890-1970, author. | Appelbaum, Peter C., translator, editor.
Title: Voyage into savage Europe : a declining civilization / Avigdor Hameiri ; translated and edited by Peter C. Appelbaum.
Other titles: Masaʻ be-Eropah ha-peraʼit. English
Description: [Brookline, MA] : [Academic Studies Press], [2020] | Originally published in 1938 as "Masa Be'eropa Haperait. Rishmei Derech Anakroniyim" (Journey to Savage Europe. Anachronistic Travel Notes).
Identifiers: LCCN 2020009946 (print) | LCCN 2020009947 (ebook) | ISBN 9781644693360 (hardback) | ISBN 9781644693377 (paperback) | ISBN 9781644693384 (adobe pdf)
Subjects: LCSH: Europe, Central--Description and travel. | Jews--Europe, Central. | Europe, Central--Politics and government--20th century.
Classification: LCC DAW1014 .H3613 2020 (print) | LCC DAW1014 (ebook) | DDC 943.703/2--dc23
LC record available at https://lccn.loc.gov/2020009946
LC ebook record available at https://lccn.loc.gov/2020009947

ISBN 9781644693360 (hardback)
ISBN 9781644693377 (paperback)
ISBN 9781644693384 (adobe pdf)
ISBN 9781644693391 (Epub)

Copyright, English translation © 2020 Academic Studies Press
All rights reserved.

Book design by Lapiz Digital Services.

Cover design by Ivan Grave.

On the cover: the cover of the original Hebrew edition of the book (*Masa Be"eropa Haperait. Rishmei Derech Anakroniyim*, 1938), courtesy of Yoni, Joel, and Gideon Shapira.

Published by Cherry Orchard Books, an imprint of Academic Studies Press
1577 Beacon Street
Brookline, MA 02446, USA
press@academicstudiespress.com
www.academicstudiespress.com

*For our murdered millions who didn't
or couldn't heed the warning.*

Contents

Acknowledgements		ix
Introduction		xiii
Translator's Introduction		xxii
Prologue		xxvii
Publisher's Introduction		xxxi
Chapter 1.	Drama	1
Chapter 2.	A Scattering of Exiles	6
Chapter 3.	A Telegram on Credit	10
Chapter 4.	The Dawn of Europe	17
Chapter 5.	The Viennese Smile	22
Chapter 6.	The Eye and the Ear	29
Chapter 7.	The Prisoner	33
Chapter 8.	Our Two Faces	39
Chapter 9.	With the Almighty's Help	43
Chapter 10.	The Dust of Criticism	48
Chapter 11.	Sicarii	51
Chapter 12.	Journey to Ruin	60
Chapter 13.	Blond is Beautiful	66
Chapter 14.	The Costume Party	71
Chapter 15.	A Hebrew Novel	81
Chapter 16.	Frozen in Time	86
Chapter 17.	The Baptists	93
Chapter 18.	Mosaic	102
Chapter 19.	My Two Souls	108
Chapter 20.	The Living Scarecrow	116
Chapter 21.	The Messiah's Entreaty	123
Chapter 22.	My Birthplace's Agony	128
Chapter 23.	The Holy Operetta	138

Chapter 24.	The Canaanite Servant	144
Chapter 25.	Spain the Healer	145
Chapter 26.	Charoset	147
Chapter 27.	The Legend of Alliance	154
Chapter 28.	The Rear Echelon	160
Chapter 29.	The Beacon of Light	167
Chapter 30.	The Intoxicating Darkness	171
Chapter 31.	Conscience	177
Chapter 32.	Homeward Bound	181

Notes 189

Acknowledgements

The publication of this book is supported in part by brothers Yoni Shapira, Joel Shapira, and Gideon Shapira, Avigdor Hameiri's grandsons.

1 Vienna (Austria)
2 Prague (Czechoslovakia), now in Czech Republic
3 Munkács (Czechoslovakia), now Mukachevo in western Ukraine
4 Prešov (Czechoslovakia), now in Slovak Republic
5 Budapest (Hungary)
6 Trieste (Italy), part of the Austro-Hungarian Empire before the First World War
7 Brindisi (Italy)
8 Cluj Napoca (Romania), Klausenberg, Hungarian Transylvania before the First World War
9 Bucharest (Romania)
10 Sighetu Marmației (Northern Romania); Sighet (part of Hungary) before the First World War
11 Bratislava/Pressburg (Czechoslovakia); Pressburg, Austro-Hungary before the First World War, now Bratislava (Slovak Republic)

Introduction
Dan Hecht[1]

On Thursday 8 October 1931, an announcement informed readers of the Hebrew daily *Doar Hayom* that the next day's issue would contain the first in a series of articles by the author and poet Avigdor Hameiri. They would, in the words of the newspaper, provide readers with "a true and honest reflection of postwar Europe. Not stories, table scraps, images of horror, but the brushstrokes of an artist, who, with G-d's help, does wonders. All the articles have one central theme—the relationship between an author/poet from the Land of Israel and the Diaspora. A pleasant tune is played hereby from a member of the homeland visiting the Diaspora."

The collection of articles more than fulfilled their pledge, above and beyond what was expected. The credible, disturbing articles provided an honest reflection of Europe's life and mindset between the wars. They not only allowed the reader to gain insight into the relationship "between the homeland and the Diaspora," but also to observe the return of a prodigal son to his country of birth, his original homeland.

Caught between two homelands, Avigdor Hameiri is unique in Hebrew literature—the spiritual Hebrew Zionist, a connection which gradually weakened during the course of the 1920s, and the Hungarian, which informed his *Weltanschauung* from a young age.

He was born Avigdor Feuerstein in a small village in the eastern part of the Austro-Hungarian Empire, and grew up in his grandfather's home. His grandfather planted in him the seeds of love for the Hebrew language. He was educated in Hungarian *yeshivot*, became captivated by the magic of Zionism, and after moving to Hungary's largest city Budapest, found himself caught between the two poles of Hungarian Jewry—strict

Orthodoxy in the region of his birth and assimilatory Neolog Judaism, both of which rejected Zionism.

By 1912, he had already made a name for himself with the publication of his first book of poetry *Mishirei Avigdor Feuerstein* in Budapest. The passion in this young man's poetry drew much attention, with critiques ranging from positive to negative. Two years later, he volunteered to serve in the First World War and fought in the Austro-Hungarian Army on the Eastern Front, first as a noncommissioned, then as a commissioned, officer. In 1916, during the Brusilov Offensive, he was taken prisoner by the Russians. Upon his release, Hameiri joined the circle of Hebrew writers in Odessa. With Bialik's help, he was finally able to emigrate to his spiritual homeland, the Land of Israel, in August 1921.[2]

The 1920s in the Land of Israel were very productive years for Avigdor Hameiri, albeit difficult and stressful. During this time, he reached the pinnacle of his creative ability and importance in the area of prose writing. His first war novel *Hashigaon Hagadol* (The Great Madness) was an artistic and financial success. However, his expectations of realizing the dreams of his youth were not in keeping with the daily realities of life in Israel. Hameiri did not become integrated with the local literary establishment. His position as head of the literary section of *Doar Hayom*, as well as his journalism itself, made him many enemies in workers' newspapers, which denounced him and made him a political outcast. His fiery temperament was also an obstacle and in his periodicals *Lev Hadash* and *Hamahar* and his satirical theater *Hakumkum*, he returned fire at his critics. By doing so, he increasingly excluded himself and acquired more and more rivals. He published many poems expressing disillusionment and disappointment, and even began to express a desire to leave the Land of Israel and return to Europe. This was Hameiri's state of mind when he embarked on a lecture tour of Europe at the behest of *Keren Hayesod* in 1930.[3]

From a practical point of view, *Masa Be'eropa Haperait* (Voyage into Savage Europe) is a travelogue consisting of newspaper reports and is, therefore, in effect, reportage. Nevertheless, when the articles are woven together as a consolidated, coherent, chronological whole, they acquire a literary value much greater than that of mere travel reports and present Hameiri's journey to his deepest being. At its center stands his multilayered personality—an author and poet filled with disappointment, bitter, and fiery. He is not an objective journalist who is studying Europe; rather, he is a man filled with negative feelings about the Land of Israel, who makes a renewed visit to the country of his birth and experiences a kind of purification and reaffirmation of his Zionist ideals. On the other hand, the book describes patriotism, mixed sometimes with extreme nationalism on Hameiri's part, sentiments which were widespread in large portions of Hungarian society, coinciding with Hameiri's own strengthening Zionism. His trip is a kind of journey into the "heart of darkness," in which wild animals dress like urban bohemians who frequent cafés and are cordial and well mannered. Hameiri uses terms like "Bushmen," "Hottentots," and "jungle" to describe the violence crawling under the apparent order of European cleanliness and politeness. Having graduated from the killing fields of the First World War Eastern Front, Hameiri regards himself as a universal-pacifist author and poet. He recognizes the small drops of repressed violence, those harbingers of the awful flood to come, but—of course—he does not imagine the depths of depravity into which Europe will eventually fall in the years to come.

"Europe is calling." At the start of the trip, a woman is parting from her husband on the deck. Europe is pulling Hameiri back.

> And now, oh now when we have arrived,
> When there is everything, when there is nothing:
> How good it would be to return backwards
> Just a little backwards.
> To the Edges of Hell.
> (from Hameiri, "Halom Hamidbara" [Desert Dream])

This poem from 1923, a scant two years after Hameiri finally reached the Land of Israel, portrays deep disappointment and pain. Hameiri yearns for the place of hope that existed before the realization of his Zionist dream, a perfect place in Europe in the form of a long-awaited dream, not grim routine. While on the deck of the ship sailing to Europe, he hears a mixture of voices—some pioneers imbued with the dream of Zionism, others completely clear-eyed as to reality. These contradictory voices stem from what Hameiri calls his "two souls," his two identities—Hebrew and Hungarian.

When he first reaches Europe, he is impressed, repeatedly comparing people, soldiers, post office staff, the cleanliness of Italian streets, to their equivalents in Tel Aviv. In Vienna, he describes at length and in detail a series of positive gestures and characteristics in the inhabitants of the city: kind hearts, patience, fairness, honesty, respectful officials, and respect for the law. He writes his impressions down in his notebook, as if he were a stranger. But, simultaneously, reservations appear when he suddenly longs for Israel's sun in the midst of a fog-enshrouded Vienna.

In Vienna, the reader is also introduced for the first time to the dark side of the writer's journey. Hameiri observes the first signs of the savage beast within civilized man—he spots swastika flags waving on the outskirts of Vienna. In retrospect, one may see the polished pavements in Fascist Trieste and the Austrian politeness and courtesy that Hameiri so appreciates as an expression of the desire to clean and rid Europe of unwelcome people. There is an ugly and terrifying side to the hygiene and good manners, which cancels all the comparisons Hameiri makes between them and the Land of Israel. He is sufficiently insightful to find in Vienna "a Europe that is wild, full of life, dancing with the latest fashions, whose motto is: 'Eat, drink and be merry for tomorrow we die. Tomorrow there will be a new world war, so we might as well enjoy the present'" (chapter 8).

And yet, "Europe is calling." Hameiri is drawn to Europe, but also temporarily appalled by it. This duality increases the nearer he gets to his Hungarian homeland, for which he fought and was taken captive. When he sees the Hungarian flag flying outside the Hungarian consulate in Trieste, Hameiri's feelings of patriotism border on ultra-nationalism: "My heart convulses with the tragedy of poor, mutilated, postwar Hungary" (chapter 3).

Several times during the course of this book, Hameiri grieves over Hungary's hard fate in the wake of the First World War, with the redrawing of its borders after the Treaty of Trianon. Two-thirds of its territory was taken and one-third of its total Hungarian population was left outside their homeland. Suddenly, Hungarians became a minority in another country. Hungary shrank from being part of the Imperial Dual Monarchy to a small, weak, landlocked state. Hameiri mourns like a true patriot at what he regards as a "tragedy" and likens Hungary's loss with the destruction of the Second Temple in Jerusalem.

This mourning and lamentation continues when he visits the regions of his homeland which were "stolen," including the village of his birth which was at the time of his visit part of Czechoslovakia (but is now in Western Ukraine). While visiting Transylvania (then, as now, Romanian), he writes: "Hungary has ruled this land of wonders for about 1,000 years—how many wars were fought in this region, in how many causes? But now, only one war (not even between Hungary and Romania) has been enough to change the long historical status quo" (chapter 19). When he visits Southern Slovakia (now the Slovak Republic), he writes in great pain: "How is it possible that Hungary, after a thousand years of rule, has lost all these ancient regions, including Slovakia? . . . Not one of the countries defeated in the Great War has been punished so cruelly and terribly as Hungary. . . . And yet, this same nation was forced to pay for a lost war by national destruction on a scale unlike anything previously seen in European history" (chapter 27).

Hameiri's sentiments about the mutilating annexations of his homeland echo the poisoned passions of the Nazis demanding back the territories of Alsace-Lorraine from France, the Sudetenland from Czechoslovakia, and Danzig and the Polish Corridor from Poland, after the Versailles Treaty. Hameiri finds the Duce's clean and ordered Italy attractive, identifying himself with the antisemitic nationalists' feelings of theft. Again, he draws a parallel between the nationalists, comparing his feelings to the destruction of the Temple. Hameiri repeatedly mentions the "1,000 years" during which Hungary ruled over the now lost provinces, as if embracing the image of his Zionist poems about the Jews' 2,000-years exile after the destruction of the Second Temple. As a Hungarian patriot, however, he contrasts the 1,000-year-long Hungarian conquest with the Jews' 2,000-years exile from the homeland. His loyalty has two opposite faces—one as a ruler who was robbed, the other as a son of a conquered people. While he feels love and a sense of national loyalty to both—two nations that have both experienced tragedy and destruction—he sees one with fading hope, the other with hope for renewal. Hameiri wants to help his Hungarian homeland, to overcome its loss: "As a sign of eternal thanks to the country of my birth, I want to share with them what I myself have learned, as a member of the world's most tragic nation" (chapter 27).

Awareness of the dispositions of the Treaty of Trianon still lives in Hungarian communal awareness. Between the world wars, Hungary underwent several difficult upheavals. By the time the Treaty of Trianon was concluded, the country had already experienced nationalist and Communist revolutions, as well as a war with its neighbors which ended in Romanian occupation of Eastern Hungary within six months. After that, Admiral Miklós Horthy, a controversial figure to this day, became regent of Hungary and changed the situation to what it was during Hameiri's visit.[4] A wave of anti-Communist, socialist, and Jewish persecution began, and the Hungary which Hameiri encountered during his trip was less tolerant to Jews than the country of his youth.

Hameiri's opinions about the political climate in Israel after bloody clashes between Jews and Arabs in 1929 must be taken into consideration when evaluating his comparisons between Europe and Tel Aviv. The violence led to a breach of trust between the *yishuv* and the British Mandate authorities. It also led to a growing belief, particularly among the youth, in the need for a Jewish army. In his role as a pacifist author and poet, Hameiri took an unambiguous position against the militarization of the Jews in Israel

During his trip to Europe, Hameiri makes an unflattering comparison between the Israel nationalist *Brit Habiryonim* (Alliance of Strong Men or Alliance of Thugs)—founded by Uri Zvi Greenberg, Abba Ahimeir, and others—and the Hungarian nationalist-fascist movement Association of Awakening Magyars (*Ebredő Magyarok Egyesülete*).[5] He encounters two young men from this movement, which has made the exclusion of Jews from society central to its political platform, in a train car. Their conversation is cordial and polite. The youths are portrayed as eloquent and seeking justice for their people—and they consider their stance to be legitimate in every detail. Hameiri seems to find more in common with these Hungarian antisemites than with his anti-Zionist Hungarian Jewish brothers, at the same time shaking off his earlier revelation of Jewish extreme nationalism in Israel. One of the Awakening Magyars even says to Hameiri: "When you talk, as a Jew, about your 'homeland' it changes our way of thinking pleasantly and completely" (chapter 11).

It seems that Hameiri and the Hungarian antisemites think the same way about all aspects of Zionism. They both look with hostility at assimilated Hungarian Jews who oppose Zionism. In light of the anti-Jewish pogroms of the previous decade (as well as the *numerus clausus* introduced by Horthy soon after he took power, which limited the registration of Jewish students in Hungarian universities to six percent), his positive portrayal of these two antisemites inevitably arouses feelings of discomfort in the reader.⁶ Yet, at the same time, Hameiri writes: "I think about the issue of work exclusion by Jews (*numerus clausus*) and the poem 'Sikarikin' (Zealots) by Uri Zvi Greenberg" (chapter 11).

As modernist poets of the 1920s, Hameiri and Greenberg initially stood shoulder to shoulder on political matters, but during the 1930s they grew apart ideologically. At the end of the novel, which appeared six years after the above had been written, Hameiri stated: "I don't believe that Hungary can descend into barbarism: I know it too well. In any event, no worse than our own situation at the moment, which, to say the least, leaves a great deal to be desired" (prologue). The passage of events proved this to be untrue. However, during this stage of the journey, Hameiri's bitter disappointment with Israel had not waned and the pendulum had not yet swung in a Zionist direction, when he returned to Hungary in 1930.

From a literary point of view, *Voyage into Savage Europe* cannot be classified as an objective travel diary, free of artistic impressions and sentiments. According to Avner Holtzman, Hameiri was "a pioneer whose style of writing—the documentary novel—had not existed before, sensu stricto, in Hebrew literature. The principle on which this type of novel is based is use of factual raw material, screened out and then recombined according to artistic, organizational principles."⁷ This literary approach is most powerfully expressed in *Hashigaon Hagadol* and in his second novel about his time in Russian captivity *Bagehinom shel Mata* (Hell on Earth).⁸ It is also present in his short stories describing the Russian Civil War and anti-Jewish pogroms in Odessa.⁹ Another feature of Hameiri's writing combines supernatural elements with factual historical connections. A moving example of this is the peak of intensity reached when he visits his birth village Ó-Dávidháza. Seeing an abandoned pear tree whose top is swaying, he intermixes the literalness of a newspaper report with personification: "The thick, prickly top of the wild pear tree in the garden, whose small sour fruit only ripen around Rosh Hashanah, waves to me. Oh—Oh—Oh—since you left me, there is no one to follow your grandfather's directive to pronounce the blessing on new fruit" (chapter 22).

The house yard is also abandoned and Hector the dog is not there anymore. Instead of Hector, an impudent Canaanite puppy barks at

Hameiri. In the complete novel, published in 1938, Hameiri added some details not reported in the periodical *Doar Hayom*. The reason, apparently, was that relevant poems from *Halomot shel Beit Raban*, in which the images of Hector, Yossi the parrot, Peter, etc., are described had not yet been published:[10]

> What wonderful eternal life has nourished us all—myself, grandfather, Hector, Yossi the parrot, Maria girl of my dreams, Peter, the family of storks living on top of our cowshed, and the wild pear tree—all of us together?! Now only two of us are left: the tree and myself. Old man pear tree is gradually losing his hair and becoming blind—he hardly recognizes me, but still hears my voice. And I—I? A few futile springs have passed.—I am not—I am not "sentimental." Where is Hector? Don't you hear that you have a visitor? Where are you, Hector?! Where are my other friends? You don't even allow me the compassionate untruth of an immortal soul after death! Wicked people? Where is Hector? Maria! Peter! Yossi! Yossi!! (chapter 22).

Although Hameiri wishes to enter the house where he was born, and in which a *Prezzite* now lives, the semi-miraculous (and its disturbance of the general narrative) takes the novel elsewhere. The shadow of his late grandfather appears and forbids Hameiri to enter the house, which does not have a *mezuza* on the doorpost: "Quick March! Go home to the Land of Israel, whence you came! Quick as you can, little boy!" (chapter 22).

His grandfather's warning is instrumental in revealing to Hameiri his true homeland—the Land of Israel. This is a key moment in the journey and the novel: Zionism returns to its original place in Hameiri's heart. After all, his grandfather instilled into him the writer's love of Hebrew. This love of Hebrew is fundamental because it is synonymous with Hameiri's love of Israel.

The series of articles "Voyage into Savage Europe," published in book form in 1938 as *Masa Be"eropa Haperait. Rishmei Derech Anakroniyim* (Voyage into Savage Europe: Anachronistic Travel Notes) are presented here for the first time in English. This novel is uniquely important for understanding the extent of Hameiri's dual sense of belonging to two parallel but geographically different cultures. He was sent to Europe by *Keren Hayesod* as a Hebrew and Zionist poet and author. He visits the Mediterranean, the component parts of the old Austro-Hungarian Empire (Italy, Austria, Hungary, Romania, Slovakia) and passes through the stations of his life in his homeland, which he has not visited for seventeen years. The picture that emerges is sometimes confused, even to Hameiri himself, alternating between past and present, with tension between his metaphysical and national worlds, and the intrigues, upheavals, and disappointments of 1920s Israel. In addition to his physical journey, the book also reflects an inner journey through the very fibers of Hameiri's being, and should be read as an important document of warning in a stormy area fluctuating between two World Wars. A world which is sharpening its swords in preparation for a new world of violence, far greater than that which preceded it, pregnant with catastrophe for the Jewish people of Eastern Europe. After the initial disappointment and disdain which he embarked on his voyage, Hameiri finally realizes that the Land of Israel is his answer to savage Europe and that Zionism is more than an ideology, but the Jewish People's escape from annihilation. His journey was in fact a farewell to a Jewish world which, in a few short years, was to disappear without a trace.

Translator's Introduction

This book follows Avigdor Hameiri's three books on the First World War and its aftermath—*Hashiga'on Hagadol* (The Great Madness), *Bagehinom Shel mata* (Hell on Earth) and *Ben Shinei Ha'adam* (Of Human Carnage)—and documents the only postwar trip that he took to Europe, during 1930. Its last chapter states that he made several "slight but important changes" during the years that followed. Because the book was ultimately published in 1938, not all the events described could have been experienced personally because of differences in dates.[1] Where necessary, this is pointed out in the text. However, most of his experiences are current and powerfully evocative of a Europe teetering on the edge of a yet unknown catastrophe. Parts of this book were published in thirty-three articles in *Doar Hayom* between 9 October 1930 and 20 May 1932.

Hameiri arrives by boat via Brindisi in Trieste and then travels to points further afield. As with all his other books, his perception of his fellow travelers is often acerbic: he couldn't have been an easy traveling companion. He has a good impression of the order and cleanliness of Mussolini's Italy: Trieste is incomparably cleaner than it was under Austria-Hungary: the streets are clean, children begging for money are absent, and post office personnel are ordered and courteous.

Courtesy and consideration permeate every aspect of Viennese life; one is left wondering how this could have changed so radically overnight after the *Anschluss*. The Jewish population of Vienna are described as directionless. Hilda, the spoiled young girl with peasant clothes, a rich background, and confused ideas about Zionism is a case in point. The noxious racial ideas of Nazism have already begun to seep in, but Jews do not understand that extreme nationalism, as espoused by Adolf Hitler, is much more dangerous for them than Communism. In Hungary, Hameiri finds the large Jewish community sharply divided. At one end are Orthodox Jews, on the other are Jews who, assimilated and some even converted, try in vain to escape from their own Jewishness and inherent Hungarian antisemitism, thereby experiencing varying degrees of alienation. The community is split along Zionist and non-Zionist lines. In Hungary as well, the unseen enemy is approaching. The country is traumatized due to loss of two-thirds of its territory following the Treaty of Trianon in 1920.

During his visit to Romania, Hameiri visits Cluj Napoca (Klausenberg), capital of Transylvania, and several other towns in the region. Transylvania and the Banat had been annexed by Romania after the war, leaving Hungary severely truncated. His citation of poetry by Endre Ady—a turn of the century poet known and beloved inside, but almost entirely unknown outside, Hungary—is very moving. In 1905, strangely and presciently, Ady predicted the ruinous loss of Hungarian Transylvania. Here and elsewhere in the novel, Ady's lines toll like a mourning bell predicting terrible events. Like many Hungarians (especially after the war), Hameiri has a low opinion of Romanians. Bribery and corruption prevail at railway stations and everywhere else during visits to towns such as Sighet (the birthplace of Eli Wiesel); Hameiri observes antisemitism, which did not exist when Transylvania belonged to Hungary. Romanians have acquired the rich farmlands of Transylvania, but the harvest lies rotting in the fields because Romanians have no idea how to apportion the land and harvest the crops.

The description of his visit to the village of his birth (now in the Eastern Slovak portion of the newly formed Czechoslovak state) is very moving. He stands outside his old house and it is as if an Old Testament prophet in the form of his beloved grandfather's spirit is standing on the hill opposite, telling him: "Do not enter! Leave this place and go back where you came from!" Even the old pear tree whose fruit he had so enjoyed as a boy is old and holds no more attraction for him. He feels a premonition of coming terrible events in which the Jews will suffer. The Messianic vision of the 100-year-old Transylvanian village woman—"Leave at once: emigrate to the Land of Israel!"—is almost unbearably prophetic.

Hameiri's description of Hungarian chauvinism may be at times exaggerated and irritating, but it reflects his love for Magyar culture. As befits an educated writer, poet, and former boulevardier, he is a bit of a snob, needlessly looking down on the poor people of Carpatho-Ruthenia. Both he and his interlocutors are incorrect when they boast of Hungary's special martial prowess. There is no evidence that Hungarian soldiers were more willing to die in battle than others in the region. That said, he shows a deep understanding of Budapest culture, which was often inspired by Jews.

Hameiri comments scathingly about Rabbi Elazar Spira, leader of one of the Hasidic schools in Carpatho-Ruthenia. He compares him with other rabbis, and in the process gives us a picture of a vanished world destroyed during the Holocaust. His description of the ostentatious nature of Rabbi Spira's daughter's wedding in Munkács seemed ridiculous until I discovered a movie that had been made of the event. Difficult as it may be to believe today, borders were opened to let people stream to the event and police were necessary to keep back the crowds. Needless to say, Hameiri's disdain for the hypocrisy of such a showy event knows no bounds. He has no patience for ultra-Orthodox rabbis who anathemize Zionists and Zionism and insist that Israel can only be redeemed by the Messiah and not by human efforts. He grasps the potential propagandistic power of motion pictures over the masses, and doesn't think much of modern inventions such as jazz and cocktails. Although he has little time for American black artists like Josephine Baker, he excoriates American lynchings.

In all this chaos, Hameiri does find a few worthy people: the Czech statesman Tomáš Masaryk (who mercifully died before Hitler occupied Czechoslovakia) embodies everything good in a modern statesman. He holds up Albert Einstein and Bronisław Huberman as the consciences of a Europe gone wild and hurtling towards catastrophe—Einstein because of his steadfast pacifism and God-given ability to reduce the divine order of the universe into seemingly simple physics equations; Huberman because of his good deeds. It must be emphasized that Hameiri's trip took place in 1930, but that the book was published in 1938, so interim events (such as the Spira wedding in 1933 and Huberman's almost superhuman efforts in the mid-1930s to save Jewish musicians from the Nazis by helping them to emigrate to Palestine and found the Palestine Philharmonic

Orchestra) also helped shape this work. The book must have been written over a period of time and revised several times, but we have no accurate information on this.

The last chapter (written four or five years after his trip)—presented here as a prologue—is especially compelling: "One more war and Europe will resemble a slaughterhouse." Tragically, his prediction was all too true. In the final lines of the novel, he describes his book as joining many others on the bonfires of the auto-da-fé—a tragic, if unconscious, prophecy of Nazi book burning. Hameiri's comments on the necessity of a European economic union to prevent war and promote conciliation are decades ahead of their time.

The timing of *Voyage into Savage Europe* prevented it from being read widely. It may have had a greater impact in the early 1930s, but, appearing as it did in 1938, the year of the *Anschluss*, the Sudetenland crisis and *Kristallnacht*, the Jews of Europe had other more pressing things to do than read a Hebrew book that was (ostensibly) about a trip in 1930, before Hitler had come to power. With the ability of hindsight, however, this is a great novel of warning. Hameiri is saying to the Jews of Europe, as God said to Abraham: *Lech lecha*.[2] Emigrate to Palestine. Leave Europe by whatever means, catastrophe awaits you here!

Unlike *The Great Madness* and *Hell on Earth*, *Voyage into Savage Europe* has relatively little dialogue, making it more difficult to read. As if on purpose, it's full of small factual errors about people (hair color, marital status, etc.). There is very little unabashed comedy, but a great deal of implied tragedy. The section about the living scarecrow who chases birds away for a living is symbolic of a disordered Europe that has lost its way.

The number of endnotes that I felt needed inclusion is very high because few readers will be cognizant of all the citations, people, and places mentioned in this book. This is particularly the case with Hungarians: I learned more about Hungarian history and culture while translating this book than I ever thought possible, given the impossible nature of the language. I was struck by the poetry of Endre Ady, whose weighty words, written in 1905, sound like those of an Old Testament Jeremiah. It seems to me that his poetry is the axle around which the book turns, and I thank Miriam Neiger with help translating his emotionally profound work. The reader is reminded of the huge Hungarian Jewish contribution to the arts and sciences during the period before the Second World War.

The many instances of Hebrew puns and wordplay, as well as Biblical and Talmud quotes, also required clarification in the endnotes. This book is essential reading for anyone who wishes a deeper understanding of the Jewish situation in Central Europe during the fateful 1930s.

I thank my Hebrew teacher Siegbert Silbermann z'l for his wise counsel and guidance that has shaped my lifelong love of the Hebrew language. I thank Dan Hecht for his excellent introduction, János Köbányai for help with Hungarian names, the Shapira brothers for their approval to translate another of their grandfather's novels, also for the photograph and original book cover, and Avner Holtzman and Glenda Abramson for patient translation and other advice. Hillel Halkin provided invaluable and patient guidance when I had the chutzpah to embark on translating Hebrew novels. István Deák provided insightful comments on the text and endnotes. Benton Arnovitz kept faith with me, providing invaluable encouragement and advice in finding a publisher. Esther Dell (Hershey Medical Center Library) provided me with a copy of Hameiri's original manuscript, stained with age, from which to work; and Heather Ross (Donald W. Hamer Center for Maps and Geospatial Information, Penn State University Libraries) did yeoman service providing the map. Alessandra Anzani, Stuart Allen, Jenna Colozza, Matthew Charlton, and Kira Nemirovsky at Academic Studies Press were a pleasure to work with at every stage of the publication process. As always, my wife and partner in all things, Addie, cast a critical eye on the manuscript. Both she and my daughter Madeleine helped provide the loving background which enables me to work, mumbling uninterruptedly in several languages at once. Any translation or annotation errors are mine alone.

Peter C. Appelbaum
Land O'Lakes, Florida, March 2020

Prologue

These notes were written four to five years ago. The fate of my writings has been put on hold for the moment, like so many thousands of words written by other Hebrew writers awaiting official approval before they can reach the awaiting literature-hungry reading public.

I am not to blame.

I do not consider this any better or worse than my other books. I had not seen Europe for seventeen years and am not to blame for the continent's drastic interim changes. I arrived at the edge of the precipice, but did not fall into it. What I saw then was a Europe returning straight to the jungle. As soon as I left, the gorilla appeared in all its glory, a natural and necessary result of existing conditions. One more war and Europe will resemble a slaughterhouse—sanctioned by law. First, the flesh of foreign races will be fed to the dogs, and then the enemy's flesh to the soldiers at the front. Is this fantasy? Wasn't Shneur's poem twenty years ago "The Middle Ages Approach" also regarded as fantasy?[1]

Several "heroes" of this book have since passed away. Amongst them the "Great Gaon, Holy Light, Ethereal Holiness, Coachman of Israel and all its horses, Holy King, Rabbi of Rabbis, His Holiness Elazar Spira," whose purulent body rose up like a suppurating abscess stinking up the environment for miles around with noxious, leaking bodily fluids. There has never been a greater moral hypocrite in the history of human ethics. To show the difference between his impurity and a righteous non-Jew, destiny placed the great Tomáš Masaryk together in Munkács with this plague of Israel: the director of the Heavenly Orchestra has a very evil sense of humor.

"Spain the Redeemer" has changed its tune as well. The few Jewish families, with whom Spain was said to begin to heal and be healed, will soon fall prey to the new inquisition. After one of my talks on Spain in Tel Aviv, a bearded man comes up to me and whispers burning words in my ear: "I am not rich, but if they would accept it I would inscribe Franco into the golden book of the Jewish National Fund."

The lamb has become used to the slaughter and does honor to the butcher.[2]

Pure, celibate Greta Garbo has gotten married (for the second or third time?) to a very talented artist, like her first husband. If she tires of him, they'll write: "What a tragedy: she just doesn't have any luck with men!"

She has no luck. Poor Morris Stiller had the better part of the deal![3]

Before the great movies of democratic Weimar ceased, there was still time for Elizabeth Bergner's sun to shine.[4] This, before everything was replaced by the glory of the "Horst Wessel Lied" and Nazi idol worship: by people like Gustav Fröhlich, the pure racist, who left his Jewish wife and daughter. Our Hebrew newspapers were wrong: they wrote that "his wife is all this great actor's happiness, because he regards family with the same importance as professional life!" That was before Germany was illuminated by the sun of National Socialism.[5]

A few chapters of my book have been published in the daily newspaper, with slight but important changes.[6] I still believed at the time that our nationalism would withstand the gorilla's onslaught. Changes have occurred both in Europe and in Israel, and I have changed as well. It's much better to deal with gorillas—at least they don't have concentration camps and uniforms.

A Jew I know is astonished at my description of Wilson: "In your opinion, is he also not without guilt?" I read that Lloyd George doesn't hold him in such high regard anymore.[7] On the contrary: he speaks about him with suspicion. I don't believe in heaping praise on a country as rich, powerful, and "big-hearted" as the United States.

What good has come from the United States?

Has lynching stopped?

Northwestern Europe, although not included in my reports, is in the same situation as Central Europe. Self-evidently, America is also included in this chaos: it is, after all, built with the cultural building blocks of European civilization.

Let us not open our mouths to the devil: he doesn't need our help.

Hungary is in need of a new Zola: after all, wasn't he French?[8] Do you believe in the degeneration of the French nation? I don't believe that Hungary can descend into barbarism: I know it too well.

In any event, no worse than our own situation at the moment, which, to say the least, leaves a great deal to be desired.

I am prepared for an auto-da-fé in our "patriotic" state.

Better that this book comes out before then: another book for the bonfire.

Devotees of Avigdor Hameiri have long wished his books to be published together. We wish to fulfil this wish, but must rely on his readers to support our efforts. We know that it will be no easy task, yet we feel that it is our duty to overcome all obstacles. Readers—especially the young—need access to Hameiri's books, as they can provide an essential education during the period of insanity in which we live. It is also a service to the author to collect his scattered writings, the fruit of thirty years of unequalled labor. We are confident of success, even during these difficult days.

Va'ad Hayovel

Chapter 1

Drama

The crew order those escorting passengers on board to disembark as quickly as possible.

A young woman stands at the top of the gangplank, embracing the husband and love of her youth, whispering:

"My Avraham, you know that without you, life would have no meaning for me, here or anywhere else in this wide world. But now Europe is calling you. What will I do without you, Avraham? Europe is calling.—I'll die without you if you don't return. You're an independent male—and Europe is calling you; but I'm just a helpless female, who must remain behind."

"Stupid girl! Two things guarantee my return: you, and the homeland."

"But you're a male. It's so much easier for you than I, a woman alone."

"The homeland and you, the only woman for me."

A Jew—one of the latecomers—impetuously separates the two.

"Homeland, shmomeland—he grumbles stupidly, as if having participated in the pair's intimate conversation, angrily tossing his possessions onto the deck.[1]

"What a dear, wonderful homeland this is! Homeland? Hmpf!—It's a human zoo! Homeland? Pfui!" He mumbles fiddling with his things, finally disappearing with them into one of the lower cabins.

The ship begins to move—everyone is on deck to watch it depart. The ship is full. Dozens of people stand, eyes glued to the disappearing shore. In the beginning conversation is animated, but it gradually becomes fitful and, after a while, dies down altogether.

2 | Voyage into Savage Europe

Silence is broken only by the creaking of lifeboats on deck and rolling of the sea, which the prow of the ship proudly bisects into two channels of flowing water.

In the midst of this pregnant silence—a hum of voices: at first soft, and then ever louder. The sound augments and sweetens the beauty of the still, small voice of silence:[2]

"Our hope is not yet lost."[3]

As if out of the ether, "Hatikvah" emerges spontaneously from individual throats.

Suddenly the impetuous Jew appears on deck from his cabin lair.

Ostrich-like, he takes his head out of the ground.

He looks at the other passengers with scornful astonishment.

He shrugs his shoulders.

Face dripping with distaste, he introduces a discordant note into the harmony:

"What kind of song is this?—All this business of 'Hatikvah'! Sentimental claptrap! Pfui!"

This grating dissonance, which cuts like a razor, angers everyone.

No one asks the man why he has thrown acid into their gentle, sentimental souls. But, after an hour has passed, a broad-shouldered Jewish pioneer comes up to him.[4] He asks drily:

"Where are you descending to?"[5]

"Descending?"—The man is surprised—"why descending?"

"Yes, that's what I'm asking. Don't you know that one "ascends" when immigrating to the Land of Israel, and "descends" when leaving Israel for other countries?"

The Jew looks at him for a moment:

"I have already descended to the land of Israel"—he points with his head to the shore, which has by now almost completely disappeared. "It's impossible to descend any lower, after the Land of Israel." He concludes with contempt, even hate.

A second pioneer, leaner than the first and skinny-faced, remarks shrewdly:—"You obviously have a natural-born sense of humor. You have shown us that one can go up and down at the same time!"

"That is a difficult statement that needs a Rambam to expound it," the Jew says, half-confusedly.[6]

The pioneer replies: "You descended from the Land of Israel when you ascended the ship, don't you know? What kind of descent was that, to slap a curse in the middle of 'Hatikvah'? You are apparently unmusical, sir."

The usual argument begins—erupts is more accurate– about political, economic, and societal issues in the Land of Israel—the economy and the various parties: revisionists, universalists, anarchists, socialists, workers, even fascists and Hitlerites. Also, the country's rich contributions to world culture and science. All the while, the "descending" Jew remains ensconced on his Olympian height, above any discussion of political party. He curses and excoriates the Land of Israel with bell, book, candle, and fathomless bitterness. Luckily for the Land of Israel, the heavens intervene, cutting the argument off in mid-quarrel. The ship's yawing makes everyone more concerned about not falling than political arguments. During this interval, the shore—to which everyone's eyes have been glued—slowly disappears from sight. Gradually, a shipboard play develops: a sentimental drama, dramatis personae of three, with the remaining passengers faithful spectators.

The hero of the piece is the impetuous Jew, whose task it is to pour scorn and ridicule on Palestine.

The second character, the broad-shouldered pioneer, heroically defends his homeland's troubles, promissory notes, and implementation of its extended, intrusive bureaucracy.

The skinny-faced youth is the drama's comedian, who prevents the complicated situation from turning into tragedy. He is helped by the natural elements: the tossing of the sea, and everyone's often-comical attempts to avoid falling over.

In a very short time, the drama changes into pure farce. The hero starts to stare at the rapidly disappearing shoreline—the more "filthy Palestine" disappears into the distance, the more his terrible judgment of it changes, first to apology, then compassion, and finally to defense. The change is aided by biblical quotes Firstly, the classic complaint:

"You have brought us out into this desert to starve this entire assembly to death."[7]

Upon his saying this, a storm breaks out, emphasizing the words of the skinny-faced young man:

"Give us something as sweet as honey! Give us honey!"[8]

When the city begins to disappear into the mist, the angry Jew is reduced to words of submission:

"Why do you complain to me?"—"Look! Look! Soon they will stone me!"[9]

The argument concentrates on the skinny-faced man's words:

"No one is quarreling with you, sir. We just wanted to test 'if the Lord is amongst us or not'"[10]

When the city disappears from the horizon completely, the impetuous Jew's face is lit up with a happy-sad smile, which does him credit:

"It makes no difference. We are now at the creation question: 'whether a country can be born in a day or a nation in a moment?!'[11] Is that not so? I have lost more than 10,000 lira in that country! That's a lot of money, correct? Now I am going to 'try to make a living elsewhere,'[12] as it is said: 'Go down there and buy some (provisions) for us, so that we may live and not die.'[13] I still have some possessions 'there,'—I know what to do now—once bitten, twice shy, after all.—God will help me, so that I may fulfil what is written: 'You will know that it was the Lord when He gives you meat to eat in the evening and all the bread you want in the morning.'"[14]

The Jew seasons the events of his past life, and his future hopes, with Biblical passages of consolation, gradually quietens down, and falls silent. Eyes fixed on the now-empty horizon, his mind conjures up the city, country, his previous life.

The pregnant silence returns, given voice by the rhythm of creaking lifeboats and the sound of the waves. The still, small voice of the impetuous Jew is heard, as if talking to himself:

"Nevertheless—nevertheless—should I discount my promissory notes?—But where should I go? Where should I go? Who is waiting for me there?—One can't even pray there in peace anymore; you stand and pray—and meanwhile the church bells toll the passing time away into your head—Bim, Bam!"

He finishes by saying to himself:

"One hour in our Tel Aviv is better than an entire lifetime in Warsaw."

The voice of the skinny-faced youth is heard in the land:

"'They looked toward the desert, and there was the glory of the Lord appearing in the cloud.'"[15]

He says this seriously, with a straight face.

The skinny-faced man has the kind of face that makes one laugh even when he himself weeps: everyone is amused, despite the seriousness of the situation.

After a few minutes, the impetuous Jew hands out cigarettes to the passengers: there are plenty to go round, and he is very generous. He goes from man to man, offering:

"Please take some! Made in Israel! Help yourself!"

A sceptic mocks him:

"In any case it is forbidden to bring them into Europe, so it's better to hand them out here, and smoke them on board. Not so?"

The Jew—hand outstretched in the act of giving the man a cigarette—suddenly withdraws his hand disgustedly.—He looks at the young man with angry, slit eyes, raises his hand and angrily throws the box into the sea. One word is hurled from his mouth:

"Pig!"

The man apologizes—the Jew takes a new box out of his pocket and offers them again generously.

He looks for new guests to distribute his cigarettes.

He suddenly sees that the man now accepting his cigarette is the same with whom he had tactlessly interfered while embracing his young wife before the ship sailed. The man takes the proffered cigarette, The Jew lights it up for him, bends over and whispers warningly in his ear:

"Europe is calling."

They both smile.

The devil knows how he managed in so short a time to understand what the pair were talking about before they parted.

Chapter 2

A Scattering of Exiles

The sun sets with a bloodred glow.

Hardly anyone on board notices, because almost everyone is where they were before—facing east, towards the city dissolving into the horizon.

Little by little the hitherto closed lives of dozens of strangers open up and melt into one other. They pair up: in twos, smaller and then larger groups; conversations develop, and different faces and character types gradually appear, as if some long-gone stage director has given them voice and character. They fulfil their roles beautifully. Let me introduce them to you:

The impetuous Jew, who curses and excoriates Palestine out of a feeling of innermost love for the Land of Israel, at the same time missing and praising the Diaspora, which deeply disgusts him.

A young man with Samson-like shoulders has suffered from malaria no less than thirty-six times during the four years he has lived in the country.—Now he is travelling to help his two younger brothers immigrate to Palestine.[1]

The skinny-faced young man, who doesn't stop joking, has had, for the past five years, a maximum work quota of two days per week.—He is a hard worker, and enthusiastic proponent of shared planning, which he justifies as follows: "Why should my comrade Mohammed and I not starve together? Isn't it his land as well as mine?!"

Two truck driver Jerusalem brothers originally from the Hungarian *kolel*.[2] They have taken upon themselves the "task" of protecting—during the recent riots in the Old City—the sacred Hungarian "Awakening Magyar" zealots (Hungarian Jews who hate Zionism and believe in waiting for the coming of the Messiah to establish the Jewish State).[3] Each one is strong enough to carry an ox, and both sing continuously, belting out Zionist songs from the past forty to fifty years.

A silent young man, known by half the people on the ship as one of the "nonpioneers," whom nobody can get to speak, or move his lips even in a half-smile.

A Jerusalem *rebbetzin* travelling with her two young daughters, who speaks fluent, Modern Hebrew interspersed with pieces from the Torah and *Midrash*.[4] Her two charming daughters—"like mother like daughter"—speak a purer Hebrew than even their mother. She is taking them out of their homeland "to disgust them with the iniquities of Europe," so that they can the more appreciate their life in the Land of Israel, despite all its hardships.

A beautiful young maiden, born in Israel, who is finally travelling to "marvelous Europe," which she regards as the most important thing in the world, from her perch in the Old City.

A dignified old man travelling for surgery in Vienna, "city of perfect medicine," who is seized with horror when he thinks that he may die and be buried, God Forbid, amongst non-Jews. "How could I lie there in peace, surrounded by those who hate me with all their soul? What about the danger of grave desecration by hooligans, whose hatred of late centers on waging war on Jewish cemeteries?—Brrr!"

A respected, modest woman who prays, keep kosher, lives modestly, and doesn't even consider the possibility that lack of money or "emergencies" could prevent meticulous adherence to the dietary laws, or scrupulous performance of all other religious practices. She only allows exceptions for pioneers. "If a pioneer doesn't meticulously adhere to all 613 commandments—our institutions are guilty, not the pioneers themselves." She is travelling to Europe as an emissary from one of the foundations—when her mission is complete, she will collect wedding ring allowances for pioneers who wish to marry according to strict Jewish law.

An instructor travelling to the Diaspora to organize the *Shomer Hatzair*, and "awaken the appetite of the youth to go hungry in a kibbutz."[5] Why should he starve alone?

A young Zionist-Orthodox rabbi, carrying on his person exact statistics of how many synagogues, rabbis, ritual slaughterers, houses of learning, ritual circumcisers and purgers, Torah scrolls, ritual immersion baths, and *glatt* kosher butchers there are in the Land of Israel. A man carrying essential information, necessary for the life of every Jew!

Opposite is an elder from the *Agudah* rabbinate, sent to convince European Jews that "the commandment of colonizing the Land of Israel is possible without Zionists, and that the rabbinate is violently opposed to postponing the coming of the Messiah by forcing the issue with Zionism.[6] 'Without the Messiah, a Jewish State is an abomination!'"

A handsome youth, who immigrated to Israel eleven years ago when he was about sixteen, and in the interim has grown strong and upright as a cedar tree, and is now travelling to Germany to become a film star.[7] He is as handsome as matinee idol John Gilbert, and his primary goal is to star in a movie about the pioneers in the Land of Israel.[8]

Teachers, bureaucrats and writers travelling straight to Moscow, carrying in their pockets lists of counterrevolutionary members of the bourgeoisie and Zionist imperialists, "to hand them over for the coming day of judgment." Despite this, they adamantly refuse to leave their homes in Israel. On the contrary: "I will return by this time next year, because I believe with perfect faith that world redemption will come out of Zion."

The man who said goodbye to his lonely wife walks around glumly, and only the impetuous Jew can draw out the reason for his despondency: he has left his wife childless, "without first having established progeny in the homeland." He will get off at the first stop in Brindisi, and return back home at the earliest possible opportunity. His decision to leave was a mistake.

A Presbyterian minister from the Scottish Mission travelling overseas to proselytize amongst the Zionist Diaspora "in the name of redemption of Zion that will come through Our Lord and Savior Jesus Christ, when He reappears, under the wings of the Divine presence, in the Land of Israel."

One of the orphans of Safed, whose parents fell victim to their "neighbors," is travelling to Europe to bring back his relatives.[9]

An elderly woman, on her way to visit her new grandson with a beautiful gift in her suitcase: "a little bag of pure dust from the Land of Israel," taken from her future grave plot, which she has purchased on the Mount of Olives.

A boy of about seven from a collective farmstead whose members ceaselessly rail against "the abomination of living abroad" ("abroad" signifying a ship, sea, even the heavens over "foreign" lands).[10]

A Jew with Napoleonic vigor, going to "gather 1,000 signatures for the Western Wall." In other words: Diaspora Jews who are willing to pay one lira each for *kaddish* to be recited for 120 years after their death. He will receive a "writ" from the Jerusalem Chief Rabbinate, that *yahrzeit* will observed once a year, with *kaddish* recited at the Wall "until the coming of the Messiah, amen."[11] He hasn't spoken with the chief rabbi about it yet, but is convinced that the great and pious sage, long may he live, would not refuse this great idea, "which would bring in more than 1,000 lira for *Keren Hayesod*!"[12] A truly noble and pious man, in the best sense of the words!

A clean-shaven Jew, who compels all passengers to join him in daily *minyan*, and respond loudly.[13] He himself stands before the ark and prays regularly with an amazingly pure Sephardic accent.[14] He is a wealthy man, travelling to the Diaspora to fulfil his most important duty in life: "To be called up to read *maftir* in beautiful, pure Sephardic Hebrew."[15] He was born in Galicia and has a grocery store in Jerusalem, Mea She'arim.[16]

The singing brothers entertain us with their classic Zionist songs until the midnight hour. The ship floats in the pitch-black night under protection of God's stars, which faithfully accompany and watch over us.

The ship becomes silent again, and the assembled passengers start to slowly scatter, each one to his or her cabin, or elsewhere.

Someone sits next to me and whispers, as if to himself:

"Precious drops from the cup of consolation," which scatter and fall into the Mediterranean Sea, like a scattering of exiles.[17]

"We have a total of 250,000 such drops—our cup is small"[18]

"Only its contents are extremely potent,"—I hear in the darkness behind me. "They contain powerful spirits."

The voice of the skinny-faced youth is again heard in the land.

Chapter 3

A Telegram on Credit

The name of our ship is *Adria*. It's wonderfully clean and organized, off-white in color and not particularly big, with more speed than one might assume from its size.

The crew are polite, well-mannered and very friendly.

A Jewish ship with a polite crew? Is that even possible?

Polite Jewish sailors?! Unheard of!

The ship's captain is the only Jew in all the shipping companies. His wife is also interesting: she comes from the family of Rachel Morporgo, the gentle Hebrew poetess.[1] She had previously entreated the great, munificent Moses Montefiore to accompany him to the Holy Land as a domestic.[2] But Montefiore's wife refused permission for a poetess of Israel to travel to the Land of Israel—her life's dream. I suddenly remember—my friend the poetess Rachel (Bluwstein) told me that, a few years ago, her request for support from Zionist charities to travel to Israel, as a tutor for Mrs. Montefiore's children, had also been rejected.[3] (When she told me that, she knew nothing about Rachel Morporgo and the grand Mrs. Montefiore)

Against stupidity, even the gods fight in vain.

The ship has its own Torah scroll and, on Sabbaths and festivals, the captain makes the ship's reading room available for use as a prayer room.

The captain is well informed about the goings-on in the land of Israel—he is a true Zionist.

We arrive at the Corinth Canal—during the Bronze Age, this city provided copper for building the bronze gate leading to the inner temple.—One of the crew predicts a storm during the next day or two.

His prediction comes true. Although the storm is not very heavy, we are tossed around, fall, and pick ourselves up—attacks of seasickness appear and many sea-green faces can be seen leaning over the rails.

The *kevutzah* lad can overcome everything except sea-sickness.[4] While vomiting—he grumbles with eyes full of tears and bitter anger:

"Look how disgusting it is abroad!"

I look at the storm around me and search for the Land of Pamphylia.[5] This is the location where a storm descended upon Herod the Great on his journey to Rome to enlist his friend Mark Anthony and noble Augustus Caesar in the fight against Antigonus the Hasmonean.[6]

The tossing and turning makes most of us sick.

"Lord of the Universe! What do you want from us?! None of us are going to Rome to strengthen the Roman Empire—Even Jabotinsky doesn't enlist Mussolini's help against his brother Chaim Weizmann!"[7]

Brindisi—"Brindusium." The site where Herod docked with his great trireme, a mighty ship with three tiers of oarsmen, built for him on the island of Rhodes.

The ship is at anchor. The freezing night air nips and stings.

A mother wakes her small child and brings him up onto the deck:

"Do you feel the cold, my sweet child? This is real winter's cold!"—The child—well wrapped up by the mother so as not to catch cold—exclaims:

"This isn't cold! It was much colder in Jerusalem!"

His face contorts with the weeping of a small boy whose sleep has been interrupted.

"There's no snow! You promised me snow! Where's the snow?"

"Tomorrow, dearest, tomorrow it will snow!"

But the boy doesn't believe her:

"It isn't true! There won't be snow tomorrow either!—Here too, they make snow out of cotton wool: and that 'snow' is warm!"

The mother explains: "I showed him a display of 'snow' at Christmas in one of the Christian pharmacies in Jerusalem, and now he's demanding the real thing."

Groups of Italian frontier policemen and soldiers—part of Mussolini's gendarmerie –walk around on the seashore. They wear their hats Napoleon-style, as if each was a mini-dictator.

I visited Brindisi several times before the war, but this time something is missing. What could it be? Ah yes, there is no more garbage or mud in the streets. The beaches of Italy were, formerly, world-renowned for their filth. Now, their cleanliness is exemplary.

An Italian who speaks good German explains it to me:

"The Duce has said in one of his speeches: 'I want to see the sidewalks so clean that food can be eaten from them with appetite, as if on finest china.' Woe to anyone who tries to throw paper or cigarette butts onto the street!—Trouble awaits!"

I tell him the joke about the young Russian who is walking with his girlfriend in the streets of Moscow on New Year's Day. He says to her in a benevolent and gentle tone:

"Spit, Marusya! I'll pay the fine!"

The Italian tries in vain to understand and smile at the joke. What is the meaning of "spit?" Why must she spit?

Apparently there is no hope for reciprocal understanding between Moscow and Rome.

I feel a sudden flash of sympathy for dictatorships. Perhaps it might be worthwhile to attempt a reorientation in Israel from the Moscow to Rome axis, if only to properly clean the streets of our dear Tel Aviv at least once?!

My sympathy is not popular with other passengers, and a violent argument erupts about Fascism, Bolshevism, England, Weizmann, Jabotinsky, the workers, the bourgeoisie, pioneers, Arabs, outside assistance, Petah-Tikvah, Ein Harod, the different newspapers, the country itself, the plague, and God knows what else.[8] Only heavenly forces on high and in the sea below end the argument without bloodshed. The ship starts to rock and argument gives way to finding a firm footing and ensuring that everyone is not tossed overboard, providing an outlet valve for all the pent-up energy.

Morning dawns.

A tense calm prevails after yesterday's violent arguments. The God of political parties has erected a partition between the different extremist groups. The singing brothers succeed in driving away political devils, and calm returns to the assembly.

Now, every time someone tries to start an argument, he is attacked from all sides:

"Quiet! Don't compete with the sea! If you want *tashlich* (the name given by the skinny-faced man to seasickness), put your finger in your throat!"[9]

The only one who has not gotten seasick so far is the honored lady who keeps strict *kashrut*.

"You people who eat *trefa* food are responsible for the ship's rolling.[10] You must vomit out the forbidden food that is making others suffer. Look at me: I am almost old," the "almost" naturally sticks in her craw, "and I have never yet become s-e-a s-i-c—"

She has scarcely time to finish, before she too is leaning over the rail, heaving and green-faced.

The broad-shouldered young man comes up to her and says restrainedly:

"Not all nonkosher food that enters the stomach causes sea-sickness—otherwise all the oceans of the world would not be large enough to contain the vomit!"

Trieste![11]

Trieste—formerly a symbol for the world's filthiest coastal cities—is unrecognizable. Franz Ferdinand, heir to the Habsburg throne, once said about it:

"It seems that there is not enough water in the Mediterranean to wash its streets clean."

This, from a royal despot with iron discipline, heir to the throne of one of the greatest dynasties in Europe.

Before the war, it was usually impossible to sit in the open areas of Trieste coffeehouses, summer or winter, because the wind blew in a cloud of papers and miscellaneous filth. Sometimes these even blew into the windows of the fourth-floor dining room.

Now, the sidewalk looks like a polished mirror. How did this come about?

Apparently, there was no need for seawater to clean up this beautiful city naturally, only rivers of blood from the Isonzo Front.[12]

This cleanliness is also felt in the city's personnel. The police's courtesy has to be seen to be believed—even the porters are polite and honest!

I have the feeling that something is missing here again. What is it this time? I remember: it's the hordes of beggar children who used to surround me, wailing: "*Soldi* (money), signor, *soldi!*"

There is no memory of the panic, or jingles about "centrism," so prevalent before the war, although the city remains just as poor as it was then (perhaps even poorer).

If only I could put a little of the policemen's courtesy into my pocket, and send it to the police in my beloved Land of Israel!

"For a little honesty, I would even be prepared to become a thief!"

More (Austrian) German is spoken here than was the case before the war. Similarly, the people of Israel and their language have been compared to olive trees, both, as if to anger the existing authorities.[13] This language usage is exemplified by the fact that any nation living under a foreign government addresses its dogs in the language of that government, which now is Italian. Most chauvinistic Magyars still address their dogs in German.

Doves flying around the main street apparently only need German, in order to be understood.

I remember one explanatory example: in Tel Aviv, dogs are spoken to by their owners in English—but our "doves" don't necessarily require Hebrew.

When I see, after an interval of seventeen years, the Hungarian flag with its crown, and the sign on the door of the consulate, an uncomfortable feeling comes over me, and my heart convulses with the tragedy of poor, mutilated postwar Hungary.[14]

Are we Hungarians truly still foreigners and proselytes in our new Hebrew Zionist world? How long will it take before it's allowed to insult a Hungarian to his face, without worrying about his loyalty to the ancien regime?[15]

In the same way as it is still forbidden to make derogatory remarks about the "generous-natured Russian muzhik" in front of a Russian-born Jew.

I'm pleased that my daughter is not Hungarian-born.

The cold reception by the consular staff disturbs my compassionate reveries about poor Hungary.

"Jerusalem?"—the secretary asks. Despite the six languages which gush from her lips like an overflowing stream, she still retains the warm, pretty Turano-Mongolic features of her ancestors.[16]

"Yes. Jerusalem."

"A real Hebrew writer? In the language of the Old Testament?"

"Yes, in the language of the Old Testament."
"But how is it that you speak such fluent Hungarian?"
"I was born, educated, and grew up in Hungary, and served as a Hungarian officer during the war."
Apparently she is not pleased to hear this. It isn't pleasant to be indebted to someone whom one doesn't much like. During the revolutionary riots in Hungary after the war, the bravest Jewish officers were hated the most.[17]
"Why are you travelling to Hungary?"
"I haven't been there for seventeen years."
"You'll be disappointed. Budapest has changed."
"I've heard that it's even more beautiful than ever."
She appears confused.
"Yes. It has become more beautiful. But not—not—for—"
"Not for Jews," I help her.
This clears up her apparent confusion.
"Yes, sir. But—it really isn't so bad. As usual, people exaggerate. How are things in Palestine?
"In Palestine, we are very fond of Christian Hungarian pioneers: there really are a few, even if you may not think so."
"Real Magyars?"
"Absolutely—not Jews at all. Two were wounded in a recent Arab attack."
She looks at me with amazement
"How were they wounded?"
"While protecting us from the Arabs."
She looks at me with surprise, thinks for a moment, and breathes a sigh of relief.
"Oh, how interesting! That is very good to hear."
She laughs sweetly and charmingly.
"OK, so very good: that means that we are quits, correct?"
"Certainly, miss, our accounts have been balanced."
I stand outside, thinking of our recent exchange. Seventeen years ago, I was also in an overseas Hungarian consulate. The conversation went as follows:
"How long abroad?"

"Almost a year."

"A whole year? Aren't you ashamed, not to have seen your beloved homeland for a year?" She says this with a kind and friendly reproach.

"I think that the homeland could do without me for a year."

"That is absolutely untrue, sir. Our homeland needs all its citizens."

Then—and now.

Then: "the homeland." Now: a balance sheet of riots, pogroms and bloody settling of accounts.

I go into a post office, to send a telegram.

I write the telegram out and want to pay—but don't have any small change. I am momentarily confused—the clerk taking the telegram has no change either. I want to leave, but she stops me.

"No problem, sir," she says, taking the telegram from me—"Go and have lunch: you can get small change there, and pay me then."

I finally bring the money to her at 3:00 p.m.

"The telegram has surely already been processed"—she says to me.

An hour later, I hear from a female acquaintance travelling with me that she too has sent a telegram here "on credit."

I find myself making constant subconscious comparisons with our own beloved Tel Aviv. What can we learn from the European system to improve ours at home? Before my post office visit I hadn't learnt much: at most—clean streets. But now? I'm green with envy: "A telegram on credit?" Good Lord! Will we ever be privileged to see something like this in our own postal system—a community in which an employee has such trust that she sends a telegram off first, and gets paid later?

Mussolini couldn't achieve this on his own—not even 1,000 Mussolini's. It has to come directly from the people.

I find out that there are about sixty schools in Trieste. But not one of the hundreds of teachers is interested in politics.—They are high priests of education, and would not even think of moving from their high-educational perch, for any reason at all.

On the other hand, it would demean the noble politicians to get involved with everyday matters such as politeness and trust. That is not their domain.

I think how great an educator our elegant gentleman Dr. Mossensohn could be—were he not a politician![18]

Chapter 4

The Dawn of Europe

The train speeds on—toward Vienna.

In my previous life I travelled from Trieste to Vienna by train many times. During my initial trips, I used to stand at the window drinking in the wonders that passed by, starting at Miramare, with its eternal summer, and ending with Semmering, with its cheerful winter's song.[1] During subsequent journeys, I used to stretch out on the sofa, fall sleep, and awaken in Vienna. This was convenient, especially during night trips.

Fate decreed this to be a night journey. It has been seventeen years since I have been in Europe—cradle of humanity. My heart beats to see glorious Europe anew, after the torments of war, imprisonment, and my own disappointed, private hope for redemption. I want to recite *shehecheyanu*[2] to the accompaniment of the clacking wheels that sing out ever-new sweet songs of greeting, wafting their warm welcome to visitors through the wind.[3]

I forget for a moment that things have changed, since then. Oh, how they have changed!

I haven't even managed to get comfortable in my cramped quarters when a group of officials, armed to the teeth, barge in, demanding to see our papers.

I promise them that everything is in order. They laugh with devilish glee:

"That's a good one! 'Everything is in order!' Ha Ha!"

"Any Bolshevik could say that!"—their leader says to me. I hand my papers over with a feeling of humiliation: what has caused them to doubt my good faith?[4]

He takes my papers, pockets them, and leaves.

I look at him for a minute—and pull myself together.

Hardly have I done this—when a second armed group appears: these are real armed bandits.

"Open your bags!"

"I am a writer, and do not deal in goods—legal or illegal."—I show them my ticket.

Another hearty laugh:

"Anyone can be a 'writer!'"

This time they are correct: I remember our writers during the riots of 1929: in the Land of Israel, every second person is a writer.

But still, I try:

"I am a Hebrew writer—in the language of the Old Testament—from Jerusalem."

One of the officials examines my ticket. The expression on his face says: "That is another matter."

Oh well, I know that this "other matter" might not work. A Hebrew writer can do exactly as he likes.

He returns my ticket to me, and, like someone satisfying his curiosity, continues:

"Open! Open! I haven't got time to stand around and wait!"

The orderly process of opening bags begins. Orderly? It's disorganized chaos. The luggage louts tear the luggage apart, sweep up the contents with both hands, raise up, throw around, scrabble like hunting hounds, toss about, move, sniff.—

One of my party looks on, waiting his turn to have his bag opened, a broad smile of vengeance on his face:

"Well, I'll let you take a sniff—I forgot to sprinkle my socks with sweet-smelling finest incense!"[5]

He's right: they don't scrabble much in his bag.

Finally, after the bag and suitcase "pogroms" are finished, the order comes:

"Pack up and close!"

The luggage louts leave.

Packing proves a little more difficult than unpacking.

Half an hour later, the train supervisor appears.

"Tickets, please!"

I've just started to fall asleep when he wakes me up: I give him my ticket with barely repressed anger. But this time, my anger is unjustified: even seventeen years ago, ticket examination was routine, so in this regard at least nothing has changed.

He examines my ticket and I again try to get some sleep.

Hopeless—the first group reappears like a bad dream. They return my papers to me.

"Now, at last, will I be able to get some sleep?"

"Yes, of course. Everything is in order."

They leave.

A violent hand shoves me awake. It's the second group again.

Good God, what now?!

"All bags must be weighed!"

Couldn't this have been done before the "parcel pogroms?"

One of the bag bandits explains to me in a friendly way:

"No, that's impossible. Because if forbidden goods are found, we confiscate them, and their weight must be subtracted from the original total, so you don't have to pay extra."

What a delightful law: I don't have to pay for transportation of confiscated goods!

In fact, no forbidden goods can be found. However, many packages and bags exceed legal weight. Fines follow, with complaints, arguments, quarrels, almost ejection from the train. Even those who want to pay cannot because they only have foreign currency, which is not legal tender on the train. So, an additional nuisance is added (as if we don't have enough!).—Even money has now lost its international value, and obstinately depends on "national culture!"

With great difficulty and mutual assistance between the wretched passengers, united by shared inconvenience, we finally get rid of the "customs officials." One of the passengers stretches luxuriously, lies down and says happily:

"Please only wake me if the Messiah comes to let us all into the Kingdom of Heaven."

After a few minutes, however, it is not the Kingdom of Heaven that awakens us, but the Kingdom of Yugoslavia.[6]

We look at one another: bad things are about to happen.

They do.

In Yugoslavia, the same procedure, the same inconveniences, in short the same hell is repeated—only the clothes of the officials are different. Papers are examined and then collected, followed by baggage examination, ticket inspection, baggage weighing, and finally our papers are returned.

This all continues from the moment we arrive in Yugoslavia, all the way to the Austrian border.

It's a good thing that we are travelling at night: there is nothing to see or enjoy out of the window.

We arrive in Austria

Will we undergo the same Dante-esque inferno here as well?

The answer is yes—but this time with Viennese delicacy. Things are handled differently here: there are no luggage louts, only ordinary human beings. They don't rummage around in, mess up, grab, throw, or sniff the contents of our bags. Everything is done as if incidentally, with "please" and "by your leave," in order to politely fulfil the law.

They don't even want to wake up one of the sleeping passengers:

Der schnarcht so süss! (He snores so sweetly), the Austrian customs official says. Our word that the snorer's suitcase doesn't contain any contraband suffices.

Has Austria truly retained its old, comfortable, calm and cheerful nature, and way of doing things?

Here it is not the baggage boors who don't let us sleep, but dawn, which breaks with blinding whiteness.

"Snow!"—One of our lads from Israel bursts out—his happiness to see snow for the first time knows no bounds.

The train stops at one of the small stations, and we get off to buy various necessities. Almost instantly, our pockets become bureaux de change—each one of us becomes an international moneychanger: Grushim from the Land of Israel, Italian liras, Serbian dinars, Austrian gröschen, hellers, centimes . . . the man who knows his way about this confusion is very fortunate indeed. I travelled around these countries and their neighbors for about fifteen years before the war and never once had to change money: everywhere I went, I simply paid with the money I had.

And now—how, God forbid, can the Serbian dinar give up its exalted position in the currency world?—It's a matter of national pride!

It strikes me that savages can be bought with all manner of trinkets, colored glass, shining stones. All these serve as international currency. Each country has its own particular national trinket: Hottentots like teeth; Niam-Niam, red glass; Bushmen, shiny tin; Balinese, shells.[7] These objects are most valuable to them (or else, they know them to be so for the buyer)—and each requires payment in its national trinket (whose total value is not higher, and sometimes even lower, than that of his neighbor) before anything is sold.

Police guard each border, including Austria. Men who, for generations, have been educated traditionally, both secularly and in their hearts and souls, stand next to one another. But now they stand and stare at one another, and everyone who passes through, with cautious silence, with restrained, dumb hate, which could at any moment turn ugly at the slightest action or misplaced word.

Here, instead of urban Tungus, Papuans, Igbos, Balinese, and Bushmen, living in their native "wigwams," as described by Bernard Shaw, we have armed bandits on borders and in trains, walking around, and sniffing out the enemy.[8]

Behold the face of the new, national Europe!

Who said anything about the sunset of Europe?

I see the exact opposite—the continent is starting afresh, from its primitive beginnings.

We are approaching Vienna.

Chapter 5

The Viennese Smile

Devil knows what I did with my train ticket! I look for it nervously: the Austrian ticket inspector is waiting.

"No problem," he says in his musical Viennese drawl, "I'll come back later, OK?"—And he leaves.

To me, the name "Vienna" is a synonym for classical brightness, hundreds of books and operettas, uncounted anecdotes and, concentrated in one place, the wisdom of the world and all its stupidity. Old Vienna—praised by the whole world: Vienna, city of perpetual joy, waltzes, operettas, smiles, and fun.

A visitor comes to see the swirl of ballroom dancing in the open areas of the city—even in the morning, to hear its citizens speaking German in the lilting dialect of Strauss in the open market—which market?

Oh yes, the flower market.[1] What other market in Vienna can compare with it?!

Those who read the Baedeker travel guide get the impression of a city in which everyone talks with a smile on their face, the policeman accompanies the prisoner to jail with sprightly, *Fledermaus*-like operetta steps, and calls him *Herr Gefangener* (Mr. Prisoner).

The whole world talks about, and believes, this. But I have never heard the most important quality of this city discussed or commented on, perhaps because it is taken for granted: its essential nature and quality of *courtesy*, not found anywhere else on earth.

Is it possible to summarize all aspects of this quality with one short word, "courtesy?" I don't think so: because it is more than just that. If I could describe Vienna in one word—it would be *"trust."*—Trust in one's fellow man, trust in his humanity, rectitude, and essential child-like simplicity.

The Viennese put the entire stupid, evil world to shame—a world in which everyone suspects, and is suspected of, fraud, lies, pursuit of profit, and deception for a piece of moldy bread.

Yes, this is Vienna: city of trust.

Last night I passed through all nine infernal Dante-esque levels of paper examination, unpacking, and luggage fines from both Italian and Yugoslav loutish authorities—suddenly the Austrian train supervisor appears, and says simply: "No problem: I'll come later, OK?"

By contrast:

The Jewish mailman in Tel Aviv brings me a letter from my sister abroad: the postage is insufficient and I have to add twelve mils.[2] I look for coins in my pockets but don't have any. As if "by accident," he leaves, taking the letter with him, saying simply:

"When you have the money, you'll get the letter."

Then he disappears.

That memory is still a sore point with me. By contrast, the Austrian train conductor arrives a second time: when I still can't find my ticket, he smiles and says in *Wienerisch*:[3]

"You'll find it eventually." He doesn't stand grimly waiting for me to find it, doesn't warn or caution me fiercely, doesn't even register me in the book of fines or kick me off the train and take me to the station superintendent or the police.

All he says is:

"*Nu*, you'll find it eventually," in exactly the same musical drawl as the Austrian postal official in Trieste when I didn't have enough small change for the telegram, which she simply sent off on credit. The same accent and mentality that apparently haven't changed despite all the convulsions of war or even new postwar borders.

Perhaps the Viennese attitude to life and people is related to their easygoing dialect.

Might it be possible to adapt this dialect to Tel Aviv? I am sure that Bialik the poet would agree, but I'm not sure about Avronin the strict grammarian.[4] We would have to promise Avronin diplomatically to weigh the merit of every tiny grammatical detail although we know that this would never work with the Viennese drawl.

My first impression of the city is not at all threatening. At first, I thought that it was just an isolated feeling, and that surely the war and its accompanying upheaval must have brought death and desolation to Vienna as well. I have heard rumors of German carpetbaggers and the inflammatory effect of Bolshevism. With all these troubles, why should Vienna retain its sense of trust, its genuine smiles, and humanity?

Travelling from the station through the city, getting in and out of taxis, entering my hotel and arranging everything with the hotel staff—I am immediately struck by the miracle: Vienna has *not* "suffered" from the war and its sacrifices—not one bit. I remember what my grandfather once said to me:

"The most beautiful Austrian song is the song from the operetta *Vienna remains Vienna*:

> Summer comes and summer goes
> And then winter returns
> With its biting winds,—
> Kings come, kings go,
> There is a time for everything,—
> But Vienna—is always Vienna!
> Even in the midst of raging storms and earthquakes,
> Vienna will stand forever!"[5]

How true. This very evening I am going to see and hear Hansi Niese, after an interval of seventeen years![6] I have been walking through the noisy streets of Vienna for the past two hours. Despite everything, I feel a sense of disappointment, compassion, and mourning.

The city is just as beautiful as before. The eye and ear drink in the multicolored hum of technology, which intoxicates the senses like finest wine.

So what darkens all of this for me?

Viennese women are exactly as they were before. Their charm does not just lie in their beauty, fabled "chic," or Germanic vigor. Viennese women are simply and wonderfully—childlike and sweet.

Their sweetness lies in their ingenuousness, but their simplicity is anything but stupidity. A child is not stupid—he is naïve, and this naïveté gives a child exceptional wisdom and sharpness of wit. As Wordsworth says, a human being is nearest to God when he is a child.[7] Viennese woman make the streets shine and smile with childlike optimism, compared to the mocking laughs from Moscow, Rome, London, and the League of Nations (which preaches disarmament but practices the exact opposite).

But despite all this, something is darkening my horizon in this beautiful city. What can it be?

It takes several days walking around here, before I understand what it is:

the sun!

It's not Vienna, but I myself, who have changed. Seventeen years ago, I simply came from one European city to another—from Budapest to Vienna; but now I come to Vienna from the Land of Israel: from a land of sunshine to a city of shade. During an entire week here I have not seen the sun even once—seven whole days without the sun's splendor.

My friend Tartakover is surprised to hear my complaint.[8]

"Just the opposite: winter this year is dry; there have been no clouds in the sky for at least two months."

I look—he's right.

Not only that—there is no sign of snow in the city.

Yes, the sun is visible somewhere in the sky, together with blinding winter snow in places like Semmering and on the outskirts of Grinzing.[9] But in the city itself—I have to walk around through many winding streets for an entire hour to find a little light.

There isn't a cloud in the sky—but instead of grey or white clouds, the city is submerged in a grey fog—a mournful mixture of smoke and fumes.[10]

The entire city resembles a basement cellar. During the day you see the sky through narrow streets and tall buildings, and at night not a single star comes to the rescue. Where are Vega, Arcturus "the guardian," and Algol "the demon" glittering in the night sky?[11]

By 5:00 p.m. it's already dark, and at 7:00 a.m. I have to get dressed by electric light.

I look upwards: what kind of God dwells in such a murky sky?

The prophets were surely not born under such a sky.

Maybe there are no prophets here, but look deeper, my friends. The following are extracts from my diary of those days:

— The restaurant owner personally visits each and every customer, asking whether they have any complaints or special requests.

— The owner of the luxury hotel in which I visit one of my acquaintances helps me with my coat when I get up to leave.
— During the intermission, the movie theater owner passes through the hall asking if the audience likes the show, and if anyone has any comments, noting them all down in his book.
— The trolley car conductor doesn't have any change, and allows me to travel with the coins that I have. I ask one of my fellow tram passengers where I should get off. He answers: "at the fifth station from here." We pass several stations and I prepare to get off, but eight passengers say to me simultaneously: "Excuse me, sir, not yet: please get off at the following station."
I see that the group of eight includes two officers. These men have looked after me the whole time, ensuring that I get off at the right station!
— I ask a policeman standing in the square for street directions.— He looks in his booklet with detailed city diagrams, and tells me exactly what I need to know.
    While I am preparing to leave, an old woman says to me: "Please, sir, come with me: I am walking in that direction."
— The proprietress of the pension where I am staying treats me to breakfast in bed including a banana, and adds smilingly: "To remind you of your homeland." (I have been staying with her for about two weeks, and have only spoken to her once before: when I rented the room)
— The film breaks down in the movie theater—immediately the owner appears, explains the reason for the interruption to everyone, and asks their pardon for it.
— A rich woman of my acquaintance wishes to go somewhere, but her own car is currently being used, so she wants to travel by taxi. I go to the taxi rank: she asks me to call a specific taxi number, but it isn't available, so we get into another. Suddenly the taxi with her requested number appears. We apologize to the driver of the first taxi, get into the second, and drive off. When we get out and she pays, I hear her telling the driver: "I've owed you this money for a week. Thank you."
— I go for a drive in an acquaintance's car—it's driven not by their chauffeur but by the owner's wife or son. Why?—"Because the

chauffeur is a person too, and he doesn't drive us for pleasure, day or night." So, to compensate, she takes the chauffeur, his wife, and children out for a drive in her husband's car, and not only on Sunday: on weekdays as well.
— I buy a tramway ticket, travel one stop, and ask the conductor where I should get off. "Get off here, and change to another tramline sir: this is not the right one for you!"—He takes the ticket, gives it to another passenger, and gives me my money back.
— In the kosher restaurant Winia nobody pays on Sabbath—everyone eats on credit. I ask the restaurant owner:
"What happens if a new customer comes in on the Sabbath?"
"We always have new customers" he answers—"what's new about that? Everyone pays their bills after Sabbath ends, not one person owes us any money, nor ever has."
— Young girls show the people to their seats at the great circus. I ask one of them:
"Has anyone ever sat in a seat that didn't belong to him?"
"How can that be?"—One girl answers me in amazement—"how can someone sit in a place that isn't his?"
— I cross the road to take a second tram and ask the conductor which is the right one. He gets off his own tram, takes me where I need to go, and explains everything to me in detail, making sure that I don't get lost. Then he unhurriedly gets onto his own tram again. The passengers wait calmly until he returns: no grumbling, no surprise, just the most normal thing in the world.
— A policeman notes down the name of a driver for some minor misdemeanor—they both smile and laugh, as if telling one another an amusing story.—

I make these notes not to draw the conclusion that in Vienna there are no cheats, liars, and bad people, no bitterness, transgressions, court hearings, arguments, or anger, like in the rest of the world. I note only my own personal experiences, as living proof that things like this do occur in Vienna, even though they may well be isolated occurrences.

I make these notes, because in Tel Aviv things like this happen as well. However, in Vienna, I do not see them in the country of prophetic morality and idealism, but in a country where thousands of swastikas wave in the streets and houses.[12]

I remember my grandfather's bitter expression, said in a moment of holy anger:

"Only a nation of villains like Ahab, Jezebel, and Jeroboam the son of Nebat would have felt constrained to expel Elijah, Isaiah, Jeremiah, and Ezekiel from their midst!"[13]

However, he quickly sweetened his bitter opinion, in his profound way:

"On the other hand, only a holy nation is able to protest so tenaciously and eternally against their own transgressions through prophets like Elijah, Isaiah, Jeremiah, and Ezekiel!"

The presence of prophets testifies to a nation as full of sin as a pomegranate is with seeds—but also with an elevated sense of remorse.

No matter what, I am deeply envious of this city of Vienna. I pray:

"Lord of the Universe, I am prepared to do without future prophecy, if only we could live in a Tel Aviv like this!"

Perhaps morality without prophets is better than prophets without morality!

Perhaps a simple childlike smile—with a hint of lightheadedness—is better than an anger-filled prophet with a touch of National Socialist morality?—

"Vienna remains Vienna."

But not in everything.

Chapter 6

The Eye and the Ear

"Vienna remains Vienna."
 But not in everything.
 Her lightness, goodness, joie de vivre, politeness, and joyous naïvité remain.
 Nevertheless, something has happened which has changed both Vienna's face and her cultural essence. I have had enough time during the past few days to visit theaters great and small, and take a good look at her literature, more than I managed to do during my ten years in Israel. Gradually, the huge difference between the current character of this city—and I suspect all other European cities around it—from that of seventeen years ago has become apparent. It's an interesting phenomenon which requires more study, and confronts us with one essential fact. If one reads the literature, or studies plays presented in various theaters, it is obvious that everything desirable for great creation is available: good taste and depth, organization, technique, rhythm, dynamics, and sweeping productions that excite the heart and soul. More than anything else, there is talent, talent, ever more talent. Only one thing is missing: *content*. Compared to the rich prewar Viennese culture that yielded thousands of biographies, which—problematic as they were—still broadened and deepened our horizons—all so-called contemporary "culture" lacks content—a *real* theme or subject. The great talent that, before the war, grappled with the deepest problems of the human experience, now deals with trivialities and episodes of secondary importance. There is nothing uplifting that makes reader or audience plumb the depths—that *tells a real story* about the work or action; this despite being surrounded by every technical, musical, and other external facility. There is no *fabula*.[1]

Everything is available to decorate, deepen, and elevate the *fabula*; but the *fabula*—the creation *itself*—is lacking. In summary: there is civilization without culture, narrative talent with nothing to say. There was a time when attributes essential to artistic creation were integral to the work itself (book or play), whose purpose was to shed light on and penetrate the soul of the issue, and be absorbed and engulfed in it. The nub of the matter, homo sapiens, was put under the visual and auditory microscope. By contrast, today all that is important is to superficially satisfy eye and ear, and not delve any deeper.

In other words: the accompanying sweet music, spectacular décor, aesthetic splendor of beautiful people, glittering gold and silver and fancy costumes, everything that flatters and pleases the senses—all these were once not the rulers, but the servants and grace notes, of true art. True artists like Eleanora Duse managed without all of them, and some artistes were even talented enough to do without feminine beauty.[2] But now, physical attributes rule the content: indeed they *are* the content. What we have now is culture attuned only to the eye and ear: jazz and physical beauty exemplified in that instrument of instruments—the erotic female body.

There is enormous talent and insight available in all forms of art, but its sole aim and purpose now is—itself. *Talent simply for the sake of talent.* More precisely and honestly—talent for the purpose of intoxicating and dulling the senses.[3]

We now arrive at the moving picture, the apotheosis of pleasure, which provides maximum sensual, but minimum mental, gratification.[4] The [silent] movie, whose main (one might say only) purpose is the sight of two beautiful people entwined, kissing for an entire quarter of an hour until it becomes grotesque and pornographic (instead of what it really should be: erotic). All this lubricated by the merry jester that takes the place of wine to uplift the senses—strong drink.

It takes me a good long while until I find what is missing, and why. There is no content, no theme, no subject, no *fabula*—because:

There is no *ideal*.

All this glorious complexity—but no ideal!

In former times, an ideal had two faces: society and tragic love. Today, both are cast out like carcasses on the road. Social idealism has committed suicide through its own internal "civil war." National idealism has become blurred by socialism, and socialism, in its turn, has fallen victim to the New Nationalism. What writer today would dare create anything in the name of socialist idealism? Instead, what appears today is the nightmare of fascism, preaching in the name of national idealism.

The beautiful ideal of tragic love has been trampled underfoot by the bloody experiences of the recent war, with its ubiquitous fear of sudden, unexpected death. The saying of the day—"eat, drink and be merry, for tomorrow we die"—is not shouted ostentatiously from the mountaintops but, for all that, controls how people live. This haste in all things, which naturally follows any bloody war or great plague, has killed all the romanticism in love and replaced it with a new phenomenon. The Germans call it *die neue Sachlichkeit* (the New Objectivity). This, is, in reality, nothing but the coarse tune sung to a woman of sometimes dubious morals: "Straight to bed, my dear!" Before the war, the benches lining the wide Vienna boulevards were filled with couples, who "wasted" uncounted days and nights, until they dared entwine in a passionate kiss. These entwined souls were a faithful reflection of Heinrich Heine's *Lyrisches Intermezzo*: love was brought to its climax by—oh, most powerful of verses—"two lips coming together."[5]

Today, things are much simpler:

A man sees an attractive woman walking alone in the street. He goes up to her:

"Good day, miss."

"Good day."

"May I?"

"Certainly."

"With or without coffee?"

Commentary is only necessary for the feeble-minded. The meaning is: "Coffee first, or straight to bed?"

The more precise might add:

"With or without the theater (movie house)?"

That is the *neue Sachlichkeit* in action.

I meet a young writer who is still trying to write love poetry with some semblance of sensitivity. I ask him:

"With the fresh face of an innocent child, are you also a disciple of the *neue Sachlichkeit*?"

"What should I be?"—he answers simply—"I wasn't educated with Marlitt's sentimental style!"[6]

What about natural romanticism? Surely not that depicted in the novels of Marlitt (or Verbitskaya, for Russians), but from the type of novel we see today. How is love possible without romanticism?[7]

"Why without romanticism?" the sensitive young poet asks surprised.—"Romanticism comes later."—

"What about poetry?"

"I don't write poems simply to stalk my beloved. On the contrary, I write them to strengthen, even crown the romantic aspect of existing love. That should be the law for all poetry."

"Bravo! What a new idea! I didn't think of that at all!"

A new idea? I doubt it. Just the opposite: it's a very old idea indeed, which we have forgotten over the centuries. Those who first came up with this idea were primitive savages. It's well known that a male bushman who wants a woman goes up to her, saying:

"Black or white?" (meaning: a black or white "enemy" skull; instead of black or white coffee). Some anthropoid maidens may choose black, white, or neither for the time being; only after the first kiss do their romantic cranial rhapsodies and primitive love paeans begin.

I myself am inclined to give more credence to the anthropoid lover's "song" over that of the young poet. The "cranial rhapsodies" hint at a kind of sacrifice more than just a song of poetic promises: it is more dangerous, and the value of a sacrifice is commensurate with its danger.

Chapter 7

The Prisoner

I found them unintentionally—but have unknowingly been searching for them all along. Something found by accident is often the result of a long, subconscious search.

The Jewish youth of Vienna.

It has been difficult, during my first few hectic days in Vienna, to turn heart and mind to more serious matters. The wonders of technology, the new twelve tone chromatic music, Mimi Shorp, Max Reinhardt's plays performed by Paula Wessely.[1] The man who can turn from all this richness and search the icy wastes to examine Viennese Jewish youth is capable of discovering the philosopher's stone.

But a real Jew neither slumbers nor sleeps.[2] Someone regurgitated that neglected classic "The Jewish Pig" at me a day or two ago, while I was taking a quiet walk in the Hofburg Palace (the devil knows how he found out that I was a Jew, and a pig to boot!?). As a response, I immediately set out to visit the grave of Benjamin Ze'ev Herzl.[3]

I knew the Jewish youth of Vienna before the war very well: typical Jewish assimilationists, whose desire to blend in at any cost was exceeded only by their Hungarian brethren. That same Viennese Jewish youth who were privileged like no other, in that Theodor Herzl lived amongst them, but who ignored him and treated him as if he didn't exist: Herzl, whose dream of a Jewish State continues after his death.

That same thoughtless Viennese Jewish youth known and beloved by all.

However, a couple of things have changed during the past seventeen years.

Have they influenced the Children of Israel in the glorious city of Vienna?

I go out looking.

I find—Oh, what I find!

I find a Jewish Labor Federation, Hebrew club, Zionist Federation, *Keren Kayemet* (Jewish National Fund) office, young men and women speaking Hebrew, organizing Hebrew gatherings, arguing and debating, giving and listening to lectures in Hebrew. I even find a Hebrew newspaper—created with great effort—but a newspaper, nevertheless, which is published and distributed.[4]

I find real Hebrew schools, with principals who speak fluent Hebrew, using beautiful modern Sephardic pronunciation

All this is true. However, it's not Vienna's Jewish youth who have changed or improved. All these recent changes have occurred through the influence of Galicia. Those same Galician Jews who, even now, express and retain amity, honor, and respect for His Majesty Kaiser Joseph and meticulously teach Hebrew culture in his capital city. Excellency Pilsudski shouldn't dare turn his nose up at those Galician Jews now under his rule.[5] Politics and culture are two completely separate things. "The Old Gentleman" was never a political issue in Galicia, was he? Who can deny that Franz Joseph knew the entire Old Testament by heart in its original Hebrew? In Galicia, every young child as well as his favorite teddy bear was aware of it. I suggest that Excellency Pilsudski grow splendid golden whiskers like Franz Joseph, to help him become Jew-friendly—something so necessary to the vigorous development of his country.[6] In and outside the Land of Israel, for example, we are well acquainted with the significance of Herzl's beard. . . .

Surely the whole world knows that Franz Joseph's whiskers facilitated friendly relations between the snobbish Viennese Jews and our Galician brethren, who now smuggle the new Jewish culture into the city via Poland.[7]

If it really is true that there are currently about 4,000 Hebrew speakers in Vienna—I doubt that these include even ten indigenous Viennese Jews.

So what is really happening to the Jewish youth of Vienna? Are they really carrying on as if nothing had happened before? Have they really simply ignored the world conflagration, the Bolshevik Revolution and civil war, the Balfour Declaration, the pioneer immigration to the Land of Israel, and the rise of Adolf Hitler?[8]

This question occupies me on my way back from the cemetery to my pension. On my return, the proprietress tells me that a charming young girl (*ein nettes Mädel*) has been waiting for me for about fifteen minutes.

She is a young dark-haired girl of about nineteen, with thick, spiky hair, dressed in a pioneer's blouse and sandals without socks. She has all the simplicity of a typical sabra—so much so that I address her in Hebrew. She smiles and tells me that she neither speaks nor understands a word of Hebrew. Her aunt, who travelled on the same ship as I did, has told her that I am currently in Vienna, and she wants to discuss "various things" with me.

He name is Hilda.

Her parents are extremely wealthy: her father—a builder—owns eight homes in Vienna.

Her mother is a prototypical rich Jewish European matron, spending her spare time and energy doing charitable and benevolent work. She is a strong, handsome woman with energy to spare, who spends most of her time assisting the sick and unfortunate. However, she doesn't do this by cadging from others.

By contrast, the money comes from her own pocket, and she takes a personal interest in everything. She spends all day running, organizing and overseeing everything, because she worries that all must be done correctly, and refuses to delegate. She dresses like a queen, but wealth doesn't spoil her good taste.

Voilà Hilda's mother!

Hilda is her only child.

Hilda is a nineteen-year-old university student.

Hilda already has a child.

Hilda is already divorced from her young husband, who suffers from an incurable disease.

Hilda's parents live prosperously and treat her with great generosity. All the treasures of Vienna are open to her: the latest fashions in store windows, jewelry, all the beauty of the twentieth century, regardless of price, beckons—and yet she walks around in the cheap, worn blouse of a pioneer, who has lived in Israel for a decade or more.

She wants to speak to me about "various things."—But nothing that she has said so far makes sense.

She is astonishingly intelligent, wise beyond her years, and uncomfortably beautiful.

One thing that she says is clear—despite her rich and cultured life in Vienna, she says tearfully that she yearns for "something different." What does this mean? She has no idea.

"How can it be possible just to live like this?"

I begin to examine the overtones of what she has said, beginning with a detailed but careful conversation about Zionism. Her penetrating knowledge of the Zionist idea and the Land of Israel is a great surprise. She knows practically everything on the subject.

This seems to approximate what she is looking for, but not exactly.

Is she a character out of a story by Berdyczewski?[9]

No—she is too healthy for that.

"Why did you marry so young? Was it out of love?"

"Not exactly. There was another motive."

Further examination determines that this "motive" was an effort to "redirect her life" at the age of seventeen.

Quite naturally, the beautiful child born of her love union didn't help at all.

"The child will become as lost as I am, in this disgusting place."

"Why don't you immigrate to Israel?"

She looks at me with sad eyes, wise beyond her years, and smiles mockingly:

"You know what is happening there. All the news from there reaches us, though not through official channels. I hope that you don't have the same stale ideas, because it isn't worth it. I'm looking for something else from you, because I cannot find a place for myself here."

"I can't suggest anything else but the *kevutza*.[10]

She looks at me with the same smile, compresses her lips, and nods her head. It takes a few moments before she says to me:

"You talk about a *kevutza* as if there were only one type of communal settlement in Israel. I cannot be torn between two ideals such as these, both of which not only allow, but even encourage, mutual hatred. We cannot allow war between our youth: it's disgusting to be young and hate at the same time. Good Lord! Is there any other example of a divided youth in an occupied country?

"'Hate' is a luxury a nation can only afford when conditions improve. If Jews need something to hate—let it be the Hitlerites, not one another."[11]

Dinnertime.

We get up—the girl stands up straight, young, hale, and hearty:

"Oh, sir, if only a *Jewish* dictator would arise from our midst!— Someone like Moses our teacher—preaching the renewed commandment: 'You shall love your brother as yourself!'"[12]

We leave the room. Suddenly, she bursts out:

"If 'free *love*' reigns supreme in the *kevutza*, why not also *like* one another?"

We sit down for dinner.

The Austrian maidservant Anini—a well-rounded, jolly woman of about thirty—serves the food, with a kindly smile for everyone. She has worked here for many years and is treated as family. She is like a sister to the proprietress, and a young mother to the children. Each domestic servant is treated in the same way. The Bolshevik Revolution in Russia, Red Budapest, and their aftermaths, have not arrived here, at least not yet.

I enquire how things were during the revolution in Vienna that deposed the monarchy and split up the former empire. They all say the same thing, each one in their own way:

"No one can be forced into madness."

"We agree. If the Communists come, where is it written that we will necessarily become like them? We are not simple thieves."

"They have naturally already 'confiscated' everything they could. What happens now if the charity of the rich is taken away as well!?"

"Even my son or husband wouldn't give me what I get here,"—the old (female) caretaker says.

"Behold our '*kevutza*,'" the young girl says, mouth stuffed with stewed fruit.

After dinner the girl disappears into her lair.

After a while I go in and join her there. She is sitting studying.

Her parents have arranged a special study for her in a wing of the large house—a little palace with facilities that I could only dream of.

"Look, sir, how we have given her the room of a princess," the mother says to me.—"But, despite all, she says she is suffering and imprisoned, although she could fly away and disappear at any moment."

I talk to her again:

"If this is the case, why are you studying?"

"Who knows where fate will take me?—More than anything, I'd like to become part of one of the equatorial African tribes. There at least I can be sure that there is no intertribal hatred—at least not hatred caused by ideals.—And there I won't be in a country of free elections and [free] love."

When we part, I silently shake her hand.

She looks at me for a few minutes and bursts out:

"What don't you understand? I want to work, work and love, love! I want to love and not to hate! I spit on all the world's ideals, if they are not founded on universal Love, Love with a capital 'L'!! A glorious, loving dictator must come and redeem me from my prison cell!"

Sitting in the trolley car, I can still see her beautiful, limpid, loving eyes.

I carry with me a new program for our youth in Israel—Love.

Does wonderful, naïve Hilda realize that there is another kind of hatred, different from the one which flows from instinctual, primitive nature? A hate that comes as a direct result of war over the Eternal Ideal—a reciprocal hatred between optimistic intellectuals who believe in humanity and a future better than the past—and those pessimists with failed instincts, who simply adapt to existing conditions, and only believe in man's baser "nature"?

What dictator could differentiate between the two kinds of hatreds, and determine the razor-thin red line between objective intellectual hatred that is time-oriented and central to the war for good; and the natural, subjective, hatred present but concealed in all men, not as a means to an end, but as *an end in itself*. Is this primitive hatred? Does idealism necessitate hate?

Is it possible to fight for a good and noble cause without hate?

Yes—a father's war against his son's immorality.

But how can one raise every partisan political fighter to the level of father?

Chapter 8

Our Two Faces

I begin to understand that the "imprisoned young girl" is not a "character," but a "personality type," in the language of aesthetics. A personality with a strong, exceptional character—but for all that, just a personality. I come to understand that Hilda's impatience, together with her constant searching, revulsion for her surroundings, attraction to primitive African tribes and their traditions—is the personality of a public daydreamer. I gradually see that the Jewish soul—especially that of the youth—has two faces. One face looks toward a Europe that is wild, full of life, dancing in the latest fashions, whose motto is: "Eat, drink, and be merry for tomorrow we die."

"Tomorrow there will be a new world war, so we might as well enjoy the present."

The second face looks out into the unknown, towards a tiny escape valve through which to flee from the lunatic depths in which it finds itself. The image of Jerusalem sometimes appears in this dream of refuge.

To avoid misunderstandings: I am not saying that Jewish youth is simply divided between Zionists and assimilationists. I haven't had enough time to properly get to know Vienna's Zionist youth: those I do know are all from Eastern Europe: an ingathering of exiles from ghettos in Russia, Galicia, Romania, and Bessarabia.[1]

I find a family so large that it almost reaches the level of a good-sized tribe, living—at least for the sake of appearances—in the middle of European Vienna. The people are honest and truthful in sickness and in joy, but live their spiritual lives in the Land of Israel. These scions of an ancient tribe live in a constant state of waking nightmare, in which the dreamer tries with all his strength to loosen and burst out of the invisible chains that immobilize his entire body in one place.

They imagine their lives, trance-like, in the righteous, beautiful, well-developed, moral and aesthetic Land of Israel, whose secular name—Palestine—those living in the impure continent of Europe are not even fit to pronounce.

These are not the kind of Jews who create the problems. These spiritual citizens of the Land of Israel are the kind of citizens needed in the Diaspora, in the same way that Germany, Italy, France, and England are in need of their scattered settlements in Africa, America, even in the Land of Israel.

These Jews are "acceptable," thank God.

The problem lies in the "two-facedness," which puts assimilated Jewish youth in continuous, almost electric, tension between two worlds. Half of these souls wallow in celebrations of their current condition, the other constantly yearns to sprout wings and flee for their lives to a better place, perhaps the Land of Israel.[2]

Hilda is a distillation of the second personality of this confused Jewish youth looking for direction. Most of the time I spoke with her, her entire being resolutely turned outward to some unknown better place— like a bird imprisoned in a narrow, asphyxiating cage yearning to fly free.

"Dictatorship! That's the answer!"

Whenever assimilation comes up in conversation, whenever I emphasize that what Herzl knew resides in the depths of every assimilated Jew's soul—a fiery enthusiastic Jew rises from the mist, all eyes and ears to hear news from the Promised Land.[3] These subjects appear to be more important to them than anything else in the world. Every little detail "from there" is of interest. Please give us all—even the tiniest — details: don't be stingy with the information! We are hungry and thirsty for news!

I go for a walk with a totally assimilated Jew, who asks me repeatedly: "Do you have that there as well?"

I sit at a cabaret with a family who know nothing about Tallit and Tefillin.

"Does Hebrew—the holy language—also have rhyming couplets?"

My friend Dr. Sam Wolf, a past pioneer, invites me to the house of one of his rich assimilated friends. He warns me on the way:

"Please, my friend, don't speak a word about the Land of Israel in that house. They are the kind of people who aren't interested in it." I promise not to talk about Mars, the Dalai Lama, the Opel motor car, or the Western Wall. But the beauteous, dolled-up hostess frustrates Dr. Wolf's request: hardly have I arrived at the door and withdrawn my lips from her delicate hand, when she says with a beaming face:

"I am very pleased indeed to meet you! Tonight we will hear from your own lips all the latest news from Palestine!"

A scant half an hour later, all the beplumed, bejeweled guests sit openmouthed, greedily swallowing every word about Tel Aviv, settlements like Rishon Lezion, Nahalal, the Rutenberg project, Rav Kook, Esther Raab, Hannah Rovina, Bartonov, even simple things like children calling each other names in Hebrew.[4]

Please don't blame me for any of this!

Not only do they hang on my every word, but they express worry, cast doubts, and fear that we might, God forbid, not succeed in establishing a Jewish state.

Forgetting that I promised my friend on the way not to propagandize for the Land of Israel, I burst out:

"Ladies and gentlemen—this depends on you!"

"Why? What can we do?"

"Very simple: if you support our funds and foundations—we shall succeed."

"What funds?"

This entire, elegantly attired bunch of snobs hasn't the faintest idea of things like *Keren Hayesod* or the Jewish National Fund.[5]

"Who of you, ladies and gentlemen, are willing to invest? I have certainly not come here this evening to make Zionist propaganda—but I see that all of you are filled with interest in what is going on in the Land of Israel. Perhaps you might be willing to invest a few coins? Look at Lord Melchett or Viceroy Lord Reading, for example, and what they have done already."[6]

Eyes narrow, frowns appear.

"What a business!"

One of them, a *Geheimrat*, smiles very seriously:[7]

"The Kingdom of Judah—is this possible?"

"Honored guests, don't you read the newspapers?"

"Yes, but who takes notice of the Zionists? Their constant arguments, conflicts, and splitting into different parties turn people off. We don't deal in politics."

A young woman, dressed in the very latest fashions, smoking a cigarette through a holder a quarter of a meter long, licking the tasty rouge from her delicate lips—stretches herself languidly and says, half mockingly, half seriously:

"Soon they will arrange a party for the Homecoming Queen of the House of Judah—but without the Charleston. Have you any Jewish dances yet? That would be great!"

I return home at 3:30 a.m.; ringing in my ears I still hear the young girl's words:

"Dictatorship!"

But what dictator is she talking about? Is Herzl's spirit still dreaming his ducal dream of a state military, work battalions, state monopoly, House of Lords, workers' pensions, and people's rule based upon the example of the Rothschild family?

Let us carefully dissect dictatorship into its component parts: insignificant descendants of dictators crawling around in a political swamp, which cannot be drained even by the stoutest of pioneers.

Chapter 9

With the Almighty's Help

Vienna has its own Jewish aristocracy: the Orthodox, to whom, as early as seventeen years ago, even the name Herzl was an abomination.[1] Whenever they heard his name mentioned, they cursed loudly and spat. This rabble, beloved by Jerusalem-on-high living comfortably in their Austro-Hungarian diasporic haven, did not recognize the word "compromise," the very embodiment of the Biblical "stiff-necked people."[2] After piously donning tallit and tefillin every morning, they marched straight to the stock exchanges and, instead of "politics," preferred the holy Christmas tree in their grandchildren's home to that abomination of abominations, the Jewish National Fund box.[3]

Have they changed in any way?

Has the postwar tumult penetrated the marble palaces of the Leopoldstadt with their ornate *mezuzot*?[4]

It takes only one day to realize: absolutely nothing has changed.

Just as before: the Orthodox need a community *minyan* to pray.[5] But the world Jewish community of sixteen million souls, with their hardships, ideas, desires, and concepts of God, are as strange to them as if ordinary Jews lived on the moon

Some elderly grandfathers still do not visit sons or daughters on Christmas, because "it makes them feel bad" seeing their progeny gathered around the Christmas tree.

On the other hand, the Orthodox rabble still visit spas—where their physician prescribes a diet with as much meat as they like—during the "three meatless weeks" between the seventeenth of Tammuz and the Ninth of Av.[6]

The rich Jew with a long, well-kept beard and thickly curled moustache—entitled to be called *moreinu* (our teacher)—still runs after *shikses* in summer resorts and spas.[7] God forbid not after prohibited married Jewish women[8] ("you are called men, but the idolaters are not called men").[9]

They still practice the old "chancellery" politics (a worldly office for Orthodox Jewry), concentrating all wishes and desires in one great ideal: that the local "Diaspora head" be ennobled to duke. This, even though the monarchy was abolished in 1918.

They still hand down decrees from on high, thundering against Jewish settlements in the Land of Israel, Russian (Jewish) heretics, and Zionists in general (may God protect us from these).

Some of them still leave a "black square" (half a square cubit without whitewash or paint) inside their palatial doorposts, to fulfil the commandment f mourning the destruction of the Temple.

They still make absolutely sure that an etrog must not come. God Forbid, from the Land of Israel, but rather from Corfu the Pure.[10]

Just as before.

Nevertheless, something new has been added.

A new type of Hasid has appeared amongst their grandchildren:[11] these are men of the Moscow *yevseks*, who speak openly about Communist redemption of the world and, together with their elders, curse and nullify the redemption of Israel.[12]

The Orthodox rabble are careful to select bathhouses in which no Zionist can be found because the *Keren Hayesod* box may, God forbid, be lying in ambush for them there.[13] If they are requested (there or anywhere else) to donate a few coins, they find all sorts of compromises and excuses in their beloved arguments which take the form of "Biblical" hairsplitting, which is, in reality, hairsplitting about the bulls and bears of the stock market.

Chancellery politics has added something new: an attempt by the government to forbid Jewish National Fund boxes because they pose the danger of "national impoverishment."

These anti-Zionists prove their point of view by fraudulent citations from previous Zionist Congresses against religion and the Messiah.

The most pious amongst them travel to the Holy Land once in their lives, to bring home the "latest evidence" and "awful proofs" that Zionist labor is destroying the Torah and committing sacrilege.

They exercise the greatest time and effort to prevent illegal smuggling of etrogs from Israel, which are—quite naturally—"ritually disqualified."

The center of this sacred cult is, of course, still Budapest the Glorious.

The kosher, modest Orthodox women, descendants of our matriarch Sarah and all the other righteous Jewish women in Heaven, devotedly praying the *techina* from the *Tze'nah u-Re'nah*, also have something to say on these issues.[14]

I am sitting in the kosher restaurant Winia opposite a typical Orthodox man and wife. The husband is a rich, "silken" Talmud student who performs the mitzvot of hand washing and grace after meals with meticulous care.[15] Sitting next to him is the wife of his youth, a flaxen-blond daughter of Israel with hair like Mimi Shorp.[16] I look at her and am surprised at her extravagant blond hair. She sports a cat's-tail hairdo, bobbed according to the latest style.

How can this be? An Orthodox woman, with her own hair, without a wig or some sort of head covering?

I pose my wordless question to the waiter:

"Sir, that really is a wig?"—He answers: "What? God forbid that it should be her own hair!"

A new sensation: wigs fashioned like a cat's-tail hairdo!

I find out that this daughter of Israel was born with dark complexion and hair—but why should she not wear a blond wig?

I also find out that some of the Orthodox men dye their beards blond.

Who has ever heard of such a thing? What an idea!

Be a (Jewish) brunette in your tent but a (non-Jewish) blond when you go out![17]

I suggest another "business proposition": to make pork *cholent*—what an excellent idea![18]

An enthusiastic Hasid from the school of Rabbi Sonnenfeld, who curses Rav Kook with bell, book, and candle, is particularly meticulous about the laws pertaining to the three weeks between the seventeenth of Tammuz and the Ninth of Av.[19] He never, God forbid, puts on a clean, ironed shirt during this period. So what does he do, so as not to appear a "dirty Jew" in the health spas that he frequents? He buys a dozen shirts before the seventeenth of Tammuz, puts them on and takes them off one after the other during a period of five minutes, and so makes them "kosher" for wearing during the three weeks between the two fasts. After all, a "used" shirt is permitted.

What an inspired idea!

I am shown a love letter from one of the pious yeshiva students—a leader amongst Hasidim fighting bitterly against Zionism, written to his modest and righteous bride "from a highborn family, the holy, pure tree of our teacher." A very interesting letter. The reader must excuse me for not having the literary or aesthetic ability to properly translate this pornographic epistle that even the French periodical *Le Rire* would hesitate to force upon its servile readers.[20] The letter is written in purest Hebrew, and the writer uses his comprehensive knowledge of all the love expressions from the Song of Songs and Ezekiel—but with filthy ambiguity that would revolt even Immanuel the Roman.[21] This so-called ambiguity is, in fact, plain for everyone to see and can have but one meaning.

The letter also uses styles taken from the Zohar.[22] Of course, it has the same elegant intent that even the lowest cabaret artist wouldn't dare use in front of his intimate audience.

Naturally, the letter begins: "With the assistance of the Almighty blessed be He."

The letter is handed to me by the writer's brother—an enthusiastic Zionist, who suffers all the torments of hell from his self-righteous family.

I ask if I could meet the author of this noble, high-minded epistle as soon as possible.

That same day, I have the honor of becoming acquainted both with him and his modest bride-to-be. Naturally, the silken yeshiva student pounces on me at once, arguing vigorously against that filthiest of ideas—Zionism. He asks pardon from his bride, pulls me aside, and whispers his earth-shattering objection against Zionism to me:

"Do you deny that male and female pioneers work together in the fields, and that the females wear shorts above the knee, flaunting their legs at men?"

He excuses himself to his bride for this question. God forbid that she should hear such impurities from his lips!

I feel myself on the horns of a dilemma, but gird up my loins and say to him:

"Yes, I don't deny it. But, if you like, I'll send you a 'love letter' from Israel from one of those same 'immoral pioneers' to one of his female *kevutza* comrades.[23] Although he isn't as learned as yourself, and doesn't use such noble Biblical and Zohar citations, he still knows something about love, but he wouldn't show such a letter to his bride, because it wouldn't interest her—perhaps he might show it to his mother."

The astonished yeshiva student looks at me with cow's eyes, stammers something, and slinks away.

I decide not to send him the letter from the pioneer in Israel. I am worried that perhaps it would not begin "With the assistance of the Almighty blessed be He."

That is Orthodoxy for you!

I cannot make peace with the fact that this portion of my Jewish brethren—who are too pious even to utter the Name of God, are still living in the Middle Ages.[24] All their piety is reduced to scorn of the present tragedy taking place in the Land of Israel, and the idea of settling the country.[25] They use all kinds of Biblical and other citations (many misquoted), to justify the necessity of destroying this contaminated idea before it spreads uncontrollably. I lament this fact to one of my old acquaintances—a learned Jew, in whose house the Jewish, National Fund box sits demurely next to the box of Rabbi Meir Baal HaNes.[26] He takes me to one of the small privately run synagogues typical of Central Europe. About twelve faithful Jews are reciting the morning service with Sephardic pronunciation at about 10:00 a.m.

My friend introduces me to the synagogues "proprietor":

"This Jew only prays with a *minyan* of Jews who wholeheartedly support Zionism."

A Jewish National Fund box stands next to the Holy Ark.

Thanks be to the Almighty's help.

Chapter 10

The Dust of Criticism

Before I leave Vienna, I am invited to a huge ball, attended by about 10,000 people. All the halls of the Palais Beethoven are filled to overflowing.[1] I have a crazy feeling, shared by other guests from Israel, of seeing everything through the lens of something either good to bring to Israel, or to studiously avoid. I am put in mind of our own societal Purim parties, no less elaborate than this one in content and spirit. But how can I learn about the current celebration without stirring up criticism like dust from a dirty floor? Is this the only way in which nosy members of our own society react?

Is such action justified?

I pose this question to one of the ushers. He explains:

"Not everything depends on the quality of the floor: the guests themselves also play an important part, because they must take care not to track dust in from the outside—"

I note this all down:

"I suspect that a significant part of criticism by the respected Israel public of our institutions and officials depends not on institutions and officials themselves, but on those doing the criticizing."

I take my coat from the attendant, and leave the ball; the chilly wind makes me sneeze. I suddenly hear behind me:

"Bless you!"

The voice of the coat check lady is heard in the land.

Heavens, how long has it been since someone has been so polite as to say this to me?

I note this down as well; the woman asks jokingly, as if asking for something insignificant:

"Is the Herr really noting down that I said 'Bless You' after he sneezed?"
"Yes, that is correct."
She bursts out laughing.
"Where do you come from? Asia perhaps?"
She carries on laughing.
I remain silent and don't reveal my secret to her—yes, I do come from Asia.²
I recognize the conductor of the trolley car to the railway station. He is one of the young Hungarian pioneers who left Israel two years ago!
"What? You here? A trolley car conductor? Weren't you happy in Israel? Didn't you want to practice your trade there?"
"Yes," he answers, "but what will a man do, to scrape together enough money to return to Israel? I need more money, to survive there."
"Why do you want to return?"
"Why? Because it disgusts me here, it really does. I tell you: do whatever work you need to do, even the most humble and despised, so as not to need Europe's help."³
"Is life good here?"
"This life?—this life makes me even loathe the next life.⁴ The only thing that has been worthwhile seeing and hearing here, was the enormous German workers' choir that performed in Vienna two years ago on its fiftieth anniversary. Imagine: a choir of 100,000 men and women!"
"A hundred thousand? Really?"
"Yes. The choir was conducted by its director Franz Keildorf.⁵ Its discipline had to be seen and heard to be believed. A hundred thousand people, standing and singing as one."
"What about their pianissimo?"
"Their pianissimo was one of the most powerful moments of the entire performance: the sound was ethereal, as if floating on air. It is the only thing worth transferring from here to Israel—it would be a personal privilege for me to do so. As for the rest—please excuse me!"
I suddenly hear someone speaking fluent Hebrew:
"I would be happy if there were 100,000 Jews in Israel who simply shut up and said nothing!"
"What?!"

"I was in Israel three years ago," says the angry Jew, "as part of a delegation about to make an important purchase of great national value. Suddenly the newspaper trumpeted the deal around as a great national victory—our opposition leaders came, and ruined the deal. Everyone, including the Arab merchants, pulled their hair out with rage."[6]

After a short silence he continues:

"We don't need songs or singers there at the moment, we simply need people to shut up! A silent choir!"

He gets off the tram without even saying "good day."

Chapter 11

Sicarii[1]

I have been in Vienna for two weeks, awaiting a permit from the Hungarian consulate to visit my homeland—where I was born and grew up. Since I returned to the front in 1915—after recovering from war wounds, to defend the homeland from its many powerful enemies—I have followed developments there with great interest. When I enter the legation in Vienna, I wipe away all past issues, complications, and problems, and greet the first consular official I meet by offering my hand in genuine peace and friendship, a sincere and hearty Jewish *shalom aleichem.*

My hand remains suspended in the air. The official looks at me as if I am a complete idiot—why in heaven's name is he being so friendly? It makes no sense at all!

A cold shower is unpleasant during winter. I lower my voice together with my temperature, which has dropped dramatically at this cold reception. I calmly hand in all necessary papers. But when he asks me when I was last in Hungary, I cannot restrain myself, and burst out self-righteously, with an old-fashioned feeling of patriotism:

"In 1915, when I recovered from my wounds and returned to the front!"

"Wounds—front!" I say to myself: "These words will teach you some manners, you stupid pencil pusher!"

Another error—neither "wounds" nor "front" make any impression whatsoever, and both remain suspended in the air like my hand. However, a few moments later, after he has handed my papers to one of his assistants, I hear a dulcet female voice:

"Béla Kun was also wounded in the war, not so?"[2]

She laughs bitterly.

I understand, and try to calm the waters:

"I know nothing about politics. The minute I could, I escaped from Russian captivity to Israel."

Hardly have I finished speaking when I understand that I have cooked my goose: the word "Russia" is poison. Anyone who has even been in Russia, "land of the plague," is suspect and someone to fear. They are terrified of Russia.

Nothing helps: not even the fact that the Hungarian Academy has distinguished me for my translation of *The Tragedy of Man*.[3]

It takes several days before the cultural attaché informs me that "The homeland awaits you. Please come." This has only been achieved with intervention by the minister of culture and enlightenment, and the venerable president of the Hungarian Academy.

Despite what happened, I cannot rush to judgment. After all, there really was a problem with my paperwork: my own birthplace got mixed up with my brother's residence as "destination."

Thanks be to God: the problem was not in myself, but in my stars.

But the paper pushing official takes me severely to task for it.

On the way to Hungary, my thoughts are crowded with all kinds of questions, problems, and issues. Herzl solved these with the strength of his great vision alone, without the "benefit" of congresses, advisors, committees, elections, and petty party hatreds.[4]

How will citizens of the Land of Israel be received when they visit the countries of their birth?

An unbounded sense of honor and respect arises deep in my heart and soul—I, citizen of a Jewish state, am approaching the country of my birth. I overflow with thanks and appreciation for this cradle of my youth, where I was educated, misbehaved, grew up, and experienced my first feelings of young manhood; the country that gave me its fruit, flowers, and blue sky; the country that suckled me, and upon whose field of honor I spilled my blood. I am full of thanks and love, but also forgiveness for the sufferings it caused me in its hour of travail and collapse. I forgive it, because now I fully understand how it suffered—"one is not liable for what he says when in pain."[5] There is no need to say anything when a country is so steeped in suffering.

I feel all this as a son of the Jewish state, as a coequal member of the human race. Not as a guest who stays in his friend's house and eats from his table out of charity, but rather as a guest visiting his friend to express his thanks and pay him back for past kindnesses. I now have it in my power to compensate him many times over, in two main ways. Firstly, to create a feeling of international unity and understanding, and secondly to extend the glory of constructive mutual respect before the whole world.

This is the beginning of a new period in the history of the Jewish people and also—

"Passport, please!"

Ah, yes. It slipped my mind. I start to rummage among my papers. Then I remember: good Lord, I completely forgot to fill out all the necessary exit forms for Austria! I still haven't adjusted to this new world of passports, visas, and myriad paperwork necessary for travel from one European country to another. I boarded the train just as I did seventeen years ago: apparently I haven't changed at all since then. I forgot that Europe has gotten wise in the interim and doesn't allow anyone to enter, or leave, the hallowed halls of its individual countries without the necessary paperwork. Europe is not a city without walls, as it looks like from an airplane.[6] How can one need special permission to leave a country? We don't need permission to exit from this world, do we?

The official government representative awakens me from my daydreaming, and requests my passport, which is not in order because I did not request an exit permit.

The official examines the passport carefully, scrutinizes me, and finally asks:

"Are you running away from Vienna?"

How should I answer him?

"No, sir. Vienna is a city that one leaves with great difficulty: who runs away from such a beautiful city? One runs *to* Vienna, not away from it."

"That's true. But why are your papers not in order?"

Again, what can I say?

"What can I tell you, sir? I have never told a lie in my life and am certainly not about to do so now. The truth is, that I simply forgot, or didn't even know that such a thing was necessary. This is the first time in seventeen years that I've travelled in Europe by train, and during this period I haven't lived anywhere on the continent. Do you believe me?"

"Yes, I believe you. How can I not believe a man who speaks the truth? But—according to the law I must fine you and return you to Vienna."

"What a waste of time—they are waiting for me in Budapest because I must give a talk this evening on the influence of European upon Hebrew literature."

He examines my papers again:

"A writer—a Hebrew writer—from Palestine."

"Yes, and someone in my position could have easily have cancelled this tax."

"He looks at me again, returns my papers, and says:

"Well, all right. No problem: it seems as if you really don't know the regulations here. Please pay twenty heller: it isn't a tax, just the price of a stamp, and travel on in peace. That's the way to do things!"

I pay the stamp price (almost nothing), he wishes me luck for my lecture, and departs.

After he has left, a passenger whispers to me:

"Please be careful, sir. Only a Viennese would behave like this—at other borders you could get into serious trouble."

When we cross the Austro-Hungarian border, two young men carrying skis enter the coach: apparently returning from Semmering.[7] They are speaking Hungarian, and I see from their insignias that they are members of the Awakening Magyar movement. I'm not particularly pleased to see them, but it's still nice to meet Hungarians again, on the way to the homeland. I am very curious to hear their open, straightforwardly antisemitic speech; seventeen years ago, this would have been impossible, especially from the aristocracy. I can see from their faces and appearances that that they are members of the upper classes. By chance I am wearing clothes—received yesterday as a gift—with the insignia of the Vienna Jewish Federation on my jacket lapel, with its address in Hebrew on a blue-and-white background. At first, they notice this and say nothing. It appears that, as members of the upper classes, they have not received an "ordinary" education, and are not about to insult me openly. One youth is about twenty-five, the other no older than twenty. They are obviously students.

After about thirty minutes, one of them puts down the Hungarian newspaper he has been reading; I ask whether I might read it after him. Both are surprised that I speak Hungarian, and with great, almost obsequious, politeness, he hands me the newspaper.

"If you please. Are you a Magyar, sir?"

"No, I am a Jew."

Slight confusion, followed by a polite smile:

"Please accept our sincerest apologies, you are correct—we have become accustomed to speak in this way for a while now."

I am very surprised. After having seen my Jewish insignia, how could they have so far forgotten themselves as to call me a Magyar? Apparently, custom has made it so. But they are both young and it is more than ten years since this usage has ceased.

"I don't understand," I say. "You are of the younger generation, and have not been educated like those before you."

"Apparently this is a question of legacy," he says smilingly. "Inherited custom cannot be removed by education, even for as long as ten years."

He adds:

"But I assume that you don't object to this?"

"Oh, but I do. I stopped believing that I was a Magyar twenty years ago."

"Yes, this is how I understood it as well. You don't object, honored sir, to my admission that I do not regard you as a Magyar?"

"I have no objection. In fact, exactly the opposite: I regard your sincerity as a virtue. But that doesn't mean that I agree with what your insignia and mentality stand for. This is not what I fought for during three years at the front, and for which I then suffered all the torments of hell in captivity; I was a faithful citizen of Hungary, no less than you."

"This was a mistake on all our parts. A national error should be permitted, should it not?" He says this with praiseworthy openness.

"You, not we, made the mistake. I stood by the truth of my Jewish nature, long before the war; and nevertheless, I went to the front even before I was conscripted."

"Why did you do that?"

I decide to surprise them with an entirely new Jewish style of speaking—that of a Jew who eventually agrees to be ostracized—but precisely because he agrees, draws the final logical conclusions, not considered by those who are doing the ostracizing. I speak to them in their own style, but in Hebrew "code," as a citizen of the New Jewish Kingdom.[8]

"Why did I do so? According to the will of my lord and master," I say simply.

"A king's command does not oblige one to volunteer; secondly, the idea of a king was a mistake—he didn't rule over all of us."[9]

"I am not talking about Franz Joseph, but about Theodor Herzl."

Confused silence. The younger man says:

"Pardon me, do you mean Dr. Herzl, the founder of the Zionist movement?"

"Yes."

Another silence. The older man says:

"With all due respect, it is I who asks your pardon, sir."

"No need: Franz Joseph was the earthly king of my homeland as well.[10] But Herzl was my spiritual king, who commanded us not to leave the land of our birth before the war. Even if our new Jewish homeland already existed, he would not have accepted us as citizens of the new country once war had broken out. Herzl also commanded us not to lie to ourselves, Magyars, or any other nation. We should be loyal citizens and not masquerade as someone else."

"So why do you oppose our insignia?"

"Because it's responsible for pogroms and the desecration of Jewish cemeteries."

They react to this as if a viper has bitten them.

"Please excuse me, honored sir, but I hope that you don't mean this as an insult."

"Certainly not. If you think that I have insulted you I am quite prepared to ask for your gracious pardon."

"Sir, you err: our symbol is not one of hate and persecution, but rather the difficult fight to establish our homeland. During this struggle, no inappropriate or uncivilized methods have entered into consideration."

"What about the pogroms of ten years ago?"[11]

"We are as responsible for despicable acts during our war as you are for the cruelty of your own Jewish army during the wars of liberation against the Philistines and Romans. The main issue is that, during our struggle for national existence, we have realized that, even if Jews are not against us, they are also not for us—that's all."

"You are free to think so; however, allow me to warn you against the logic that classifies Jews as either Hungarian citizens, or potential citizens of a future State of Israel. You have already negated the first possibility. Nevertheless, I still want to support your war by injecting some healthy common sense into your way of thinking. In this struggle, you need sympathy and support from all civilized nations outside your country. Is that not so?"

"Certainly. That is what we are trying to achieve."

"If that is the case, I would advise you to look at the Jewish people like any other nation—a nation of about sixteen million souls, whose influence in the world is no less than its bad luck and tragic destiny. In summary, I would advise you to love or hate the Jews with the same logic used for any other nation. Not from a traditional instinct of hate, but from intelligent, patriotic calculation. A subjective feeling of hate for any nation—because of education or any other reason—at a time when the needs of the homeland require the opposite—is not patriotism, but just the opposite: it's treason. Am I right? It's impossible to know how we, the Jewish people, with our host of learned men, authors, and financiers, could assist your homeland, unless you give us a chance."

Silence. The older young man smokes a cigarette, saying, as if to himself:

"That is a new and interesting question."

The younger adds:

"I didn't think of this at all."

"No? But you really should."

Long silence while they reflect on my advice; the more they think about it, the better it looks. The older says:

"Yes, that's certainly true: I'll speak about this tomorrow at our society meeting. I think that there will be many questions, which we have not considered previously and might change our opinion."

I let slip: "For example, the question of *numerus clausus*."[12]

"*Numerus clausus?*—What is your opinion about this, sir?"

"I've already told you.—The same way as with all issues related to the homeland: don't be subjective. Weigh the question in the balance: will it be in your country's interests or not?"

"Hungarian Jewry are not solidly Zionist, sir: in other words, they don't feel themselves to be part of international Jewry. Therefore, I very much doubt whether your leaders would wish to defend it and fight their own war for equal rights among us. What does Hungarian Jewry—detached as it is from the body politic—care about our war?"

"Wrong again. Hungarian Jewry has been blinded by emancipation. But we are organized, and see the tragedy of the Hungarian people as our own."

"So?"

"Draw up a credit and debit sheet for your Jewish antagonism—that is the way you should act in all things related to us."

"Does that mean that we cannot even say something against you?"

"Certainly not. Because of our tragic history, we are able to understand the trouble and suffering of all other nations. Not all anti-Jewish campaigns are regarded by us as antisemitic. Antisemitism is, first and foremost, pure stupidity, which can harm the hater no less than the hated—sometimes more so."

"So what is your standard in this issue, honored sir? Do you even have one?

"There is one. In order to understand one another, we first of all require those who hate us to remove lies, false, unclean weapons, and useless physical violence aimed at the unarmed among us—no more senseless blood libels and pogroms. We know the strengths and weaknesses of our brothers all too well—these are the sources of the Zionist movement, and our aspiration for an old-new homeland.

Silence again.

I think about the issue of work exclusion by Jews (*numerus clausus*) and the poem "Sikarikin" (Zealots) by Uri Zvi Greenberg (and its association with the Awakening Magyar movement). In Hungary, there is an entire genre of Catholic art (paintings and woodcuts) and literature that heaps praise on—and makes heroes of—old and new leaders of pogroms and riots, and supports radical action as much as, if not more than, Uri Zvi Greenberg. Radical action is sometimes needed in defense of the homeland, no matter which side uses it.[13]

The train approaches Budapest. The older of the two youths gets up and shakes my hand with exceptional respect and friendship:

"It has been a real pleasure to meet you, sir: to finally meet a Jew who has a homeland and speaks in the name of his 'lord and master.' When you talk, as a Jew, about your 'homeland' it changes our way of thinking pleasantly and completely. Sir—we are not robbers and desecrators of cemeteries. We are a tragic people, whose enemies have caused our downfall. We are filled with thanks for all who come to help us arise from the ashes.[14] You are right, sir, we have to be coldly and calculatingly logical for the benefit of our homeland. We will try to follow your valued advice."

After we part, I do a mental accounting of what has just happened:

I have come to teach, and become the student. During a debate on the interests of tragic Hungary, I have found out why our struggle in Israel is failing: we are not fighting logically, but with emotion and foolish passion. Our emotions and feminine sensitivity, together with our history, are our downfall!

"Behold the Zealot!"[15]

Perhaps it's necessary to differentiate between zealots who are just simple robbers, and those who are patriotic, heroic hooligans in the mold of Eleazar ben Yair, hero of Masada.[16] There is no purely righteous way to defend the homeland when it is threatened.

Chapter 12

Journey to Ruin

As soon as I enter, the first question to myself is: "Is this really Budapest?" The city is unrecognizable."[1] I am amazed: it is even more beautiful and accomplished than when I last saw it. Can this really be the capital of the same Hungary that emerged from the war politically and economically ruined? It's almost unrecognizable in its splendid new apparel.

I, who was educated and grew up in Budapest, have become aware, during my time overseas, of how beloved this city is of overseas visitors and tourists. There is something about Budapest that arouses a special type of love. I have always known how beautiful this city is, but—as someone who grew up here—am not qualified to comment, because of bias—this must be left to others, to whom the city is a new and uniquely wonderful experience.

The beauty of this "Queen of the Danube" has been enhanced by all sorts of recent developments and discoveries. The shop window exhibitions, spectacular electrical screens extending as far as the eye can see; elegant buses that put the old trolley cars to shame, the same as trolley cars—in their time—did to the stagecoaches of the eighteenth century; Rolls Royces that mock our Israeli camel cars; automatic telephones; radios which fill every public and private place, even coffeehouses; public radio on Hungarian trains, through which, for a few coins, one may enjoy oratorios and symphony concerts from the Academy of Music or be bored by horticultural lectures on harmful aphids.

Coffeehouses provide splendid orchestras, with princely service and prices to match. Outside, from the fifth floor of the palatial building, a huge electric billboard proclaims the wonders of a certain kind of luxury talcum powder in a thousand singing colors. The splendor of the hotels is decades ahead of its time, with every kind of automatic dispenser, in addition to a plethora of servants and waiters speaking a secretive type of Hungarian and conjuring up everything possible for a guest's delight. Even your foot is not permitted to touch the floor without the interposition of a Smyrna carpet or luxurious Egyptian cotton.

And the women! We are lucky that the latest fashion dictates that they wear the bare minimum. But what fashion takes away in quantity, is more than made up for by the quality of the fabric: crepe de chine, silk, velvet and crepe romain. Additionally, "empty" nudity can always be covered with Catholic modesty by jewelry and adornments (there is a Catholic school in Budapest that teaches this art).

"What is the latest fashion in jewelry?"—I ask.

"The latest fashion is red rubies. There is a war on between the fashion designer Jean Patou and the two jewelry kings Mauboussin and Cartier, who, between the two of them, have the largest supply of rubies in the world: their combined worth is astronomical.[2] A year ago they put on an exhibition of emeralds, but this year it will be rubies. A snow-white background adds to the beauty and value of the stones. The whiteness is dictated by fashion and can be silk, or bare bosom but, in general, the wider the expanse of natural whiteness the better."

At one of our recent parties, I saw a very modest woman wearing a string of nine huge rubies that covered her neck (read bare bosom) from top to bottom in the fashion of Louis XIV: you can just imagine their size. In each one of the nine stones, a diamond solitaire sparkled.

The different types of rings and ropes of jewelry in necklaces, belts, and shoes, encrusted with precious stones, predominantly rubies, dazzle the eye. The color of the rubies comprises all shades of the spectrum, from scarlet red and blood red to the ruby red color of finest Tokay.

"To crown it all, a certain countess arrived dressed in a diamond necklace, each of whose stones was larger than the largest ruby we had ever seen! Imagine that!"

Apart from precious stones, there is also all manner of multicolored glass: plain and with every kind of decoration.

Watches, bracelets, nose rings, earrings—all the women's finery excoriated by Isaiah.[3]

Garden parties in every conceivable open place.

Celebrations in every hall.[4]

Every celebration has its beauty pageants and contests for the most beautiful jewelry, best-mixed cocktails, woman's legs, figure, graceful swan-like neck, straightest back, most honeyed smile, cherry lips, and sinuous loins.

Cocktails and jazz, one next to the other. The first: a mixture of drinks, spices, and seasonings, all served up in one glass; the second: a mixture of all sorts of instruments, playing together. Booty from cannibals and savages, who successfully steal drinks, mixing beer, wine, cognac, and gasoline together, and drinking it, calling it a cocktail.

But it could be much worse. Jazz still lacks one particular instrument: the enemy's femur banging on his skull. For the cocktail, we don't yet dilute the mix with the enemy's blood.

But the piper—in the form of the postwar disarmament committee—demands payment for all this frivolous nonsense. Riches, pleasure, and delights reign day and night—and there is another side to the story.[5]

Go outside early in the morning, dear reader, into the frozen street, made even colder by a cruel, biting winter wind. Look, and your eyes will pop out of their sockets: along the entire length of the street, men, women, and children are hurrying to work, shuffling in feet wrapped with rags bound by rope, cords, and iron wire; sometimes, instead of rags, they use newspaper and, if they are lucky, sturdy wrapping paper.

Their clothes are so tattered and full of holes that the women conform to the latest fashion of décolletage.

Two weak, damp eyes take the place of precious stones—not weak from too many cocktails or damp from atropine drops.

Behold a world celebrating, eating, and drinking as if it were the last day.

I read in the newspapers:

"Tonight there will be a masked ball with prizes for originality."

Next to it:

"In Vekerela (the Budapest workers' district), a worker has killed two starving families: his own wife and six children, as well as his neighbor's family (his neighbor asked him to put them out of their misery). The poor man then hanged himself."

My old and dear friend, the author Ludwig Nagy, says to me with his usual sardonic humor: "We are not walking to ruin like other nations:

we are travelling there in style—journeying to a ruinous nowhere with expensive Rolls Royces and Studebakers."[6]

These public celebrations have two main causes. Firstly, the situation that follows despair. Proud Hungary, which for 1,000 years had ruled over an area of 350,000 kilometers squared, has now been shrunk to 90,000 kilometers squared. Its most precious territories have been ripped from its bosom: the cornfields, gold mines, forests, and "black gold" (coal). Hungarians, who have become minorities in these lost areas, miss the feeling of being in charge and feel despondent, as if they have been diminished, now that they are being ruled by nations over which they themselves had ruled for the previous 1,000 years. In such disastrous conditions, people—especially Magyars—are prepared to relinquish control and give the horse free rein, so to speak. The German will grasp his quill and carry on his pettifogging bookkeeping until the last minute. The Hungarian says: "Have I gone bankrupt? Never mind, come let's have a drink!"

It's so good to sit, sing, drink, weep, and break glasses over our miserable lives to the sound of a gypsy band! It beats thinking how miserable we are!

On every Budapest door and gate—great and small—you'll find a little tin plate with the words: "We will never relinquish 'Greater Hungary,'" together with a map. This is, apparently, mainly for outside consumption, and is meant as political, not economic, stubbornness. This, in contrast to the Germans, who put all their pride and effort into protecting their new stable currency, eliciting a mixture of fear and envy, even among those who hate it.[7]

That is the first cause of this witches' Sabbath of celebration. Bankruptcy cancels financial considerations: "Eat, drink, and be merry for tomorrow we die!"

Secondly: "Bolshevism is the cause of everything!"

The Hungarian Soviet Republic only lasted for 133 days; but this short period was enough to whet appetites for unlimited hooligan rule. The war is still being fought, albeit with unequal weapons, especially Communist-inspired prisoner hunger strikes.

Lord Rothermere adds fuel to the fire with his statements about the "knightly nation" and "nation of noblemen":—"patience, brothers, we recognize your virtues and will not allow you to fall. We will not rest until the fifty-six counties lost to the common enemy have been restored to you. Stand guard on your borders, and don't allow the Bolsheviks to break through into Europe!"[8]

Hungary, that nation of naïve knights, believes every word he says.

They believe that Lord Rothermere and the defeated nation of Hungary have common enemies.

They believe, because they want to believe, in living for the moment, garden parties, cocktails, jazz, gold, and diamonds—let death and the devil take the hindmost! It is forbidden, even for a moment, to show the true face of actual weakness, distress, and poverty.

Radio Budapest is one of the largest and most advanced stations in the world. It broadcasts classical, gypsy, or light and joyful music, science, literature—but not one single sigh of pain.

Men wear top hats, as if life was one long celebration, the most splendid among them with fingers and wrists bespangled with rings and fine bracelets. Hungary is part of the European community! As far as nobility is concerned, it's in fact the head of the family!

The name of the high earthly priestess, Barbara Gould, is increasingly heard in the land.[9] Everywhere one looks around, in streets, in the center of advertisements, electric billboards, and newspapers, there it is, that blinding name:

BARBARA GOULD.

Nothing else is needed. Only complete idiots with no education at all don't know the name of this Great Lady.

Sadly, I am one of these uncultured boors, and my Hebrew reader will forgive me if I explain who Barbara Gould is. She is the European high priestess and messiah of beauty, taste, and discernment, whose every waking moment is devoted to supremacy in manicure, pedicure, cosmetics, tattooing, skin care, heady perfumes, hair styling, and erotic deportment. She travels throughout Europe spreading her doctrine of beauty and elegance, sheltering untold numbers of women and even men in her divine shade. One passage, even one word from her evangelium of beauty is regarded as the Law of Barbara from Sinai.

Her gospel is, however, not entirely innovative, but originates—at least partially—in places like Africa and Indian America. For example, hand care has long been a tradition amongst some segments of our Arabic population, with their hennaed hands. Paragraph five of the Laws of Hand Care dictates that nails be painted deep red. Women should walk sinuously, like Balinese, waists decorated by palm frond garlands, which twirl while they walk, and even more when they dance.

I suggest the addition of beauty spots, as sported by our beautiful Israeli farm maidens, and—for males—facial tattoos with beards, no sidelocks, and neatly shaved moustaches (to prevent forgetfulness), as worn by our Arab neighbors.[10] Hopefully, my suggestions will soon be accepted.

Another excellent custom, exemplified by Bushmen and Hottentots, is the democracy of (un)clothing and adornment between the sexes. We have a ways to go before we fully catch up with our African brethren's disregard for clothes, but are getting there: at present, it's on display in the rich woman in her décolletage, the poor worker in her bare feet.

But nobody dares suggest that the fun-loving aristocracy get out of their Rolls Royces:

"A journey to ruin must be made on foot if you please, ladies and gentlemen!" Even the tired, barefoot worker is staying put at the moment. He is consumed with his own troubles, drinks bile instead of cocktails, and instead of a jazz band his music is the wail of hungry babies. The worker will not change his condition under any circumstances: not only has he no strength, but there is another reason. The great masses in Europe are wrapped up in the metaphysics of patriotism. They are preoccupied with the enemy from without. The first signs of extreme nationalism have come from defeated Germany. The beast paperhanger is gradually conquering the peoples' hearts with conniving, hate-filled pseudo-kindness, ravings about the injustice of France and the Versailles decree, and the redemption and reestablishment of the homeland's degraded honor.

Hitler is rising in the polls.

The masses stream after him like a drunken, hypnotized mob.

"The master race" is choosing a leader that fits it like a glove.

Chapter 13

Blond is Beautiful[1]

The only hope for European renewal and value reassessment in the near future, in the face of current absurdities, is Rousseau's "state of nature."[2] This directive must be realized gradually and naturally, not by indiscriminate philosophic command—beginning in the country where it originated, France, official pioneer of progress—if it is not to remain a piece of barren journalistic philosophizing. It is well known that Paris leads Middle Europe in matters of culture, and that black jazz originated from the local inhabitants of French colonies. These dances have been imported from the forests and jungles of the furthest reaches of French Equatorial Africa, dressed up in tuxedos, and received with unbelievable enthusiasm—on the stages where great actresses like Rachelle and the divine Sarah Bernhardt once held sway.[3]

Follow them, and you will find black jazz, with dances from Java and other Indonesian isles. As is well known, this has reached its zenith with the dancing of the black Eve, Josephine Baker, who was only accepted in Berlin (after a cold initial reception) and other Middle European cities, after she later visited Paris, where she was raised to the status of national icon, beloved everywhere.[4] Her dance, knees knocking together and ankles seemingly distorted almost to breaking point, has received the name "Charleston" in cultured societal circles. The essence of this dance may be taken not so much as the dance itself, but her (un)clothing: bare-breasted, with a wreath of bananas around the loins (in other words fruit instead of the compulsory fig leaf). A certain European aristocrat gave Josephine Baker a sum of money for one of these "figs," with which 50,000 children of the unemployed could be properly clothed in fall and winter. The fruit enjoyed by this aristocrat was certainly not picked from the tree of knowledge. . . .

But we must be honest: something good is developing from all this Negro musical modernity—the new style of interesting black music, onto which the Frenchman Debussy has grafted music with his own, wonderful, new, unique sound.[5] This new Negro chorus is currently waging victorious war against all forms of conventional classical music. Instead of introducing European cultural values into their colonies, the victors are doing the exact opposite, introducing vigorous, new blood into European culture.

Let me make it perfectly clear: Europe, with its powerful military strength, is creating an export market for raw materials—but outside primitive forces are carving out a market on the continent with the strength of their "spiritual" convictions.

Neither Disraeli nor Bismarck thought, even for a minute, that such a thing could happen: the cultural conquest of Europe by African "savages" who have just recently been colonized by "civilized" Europe? Impossible![6]

How badly we need Max Nordau, prophet of paradoxes, to shed light on all this![7]

This cultural conquest has all the signs of any other form of conquest: controlled hate—related to fear of—all people of color. Hence the new maxim currently doing the rounds in Europe: "Gentlemen prefer blondes!" Bright, Caucasian, yellowish white hair *über alles*, not only for women but also for men! It would be worthwhile to collect statistical data on this subject. A blonde stage actress with no talent whatsoever is well received by any audience, solely because of her hair color. Modest, positive, "objective" criticism takes this attribute into consideration, going so far as to mention it by name: "Blonde Maria Galla demonstrated special talent." Stars of the silent screen like Vilma Bánky, Greta Garbo, Charlotte Susa, and many others owe a large part of their success to their luck in having been born blonde. If perchance one of these really has talent, the newspaper emphases—over and over again—variations on the theme of "the beautiful flaxen-haired Jeanette MacDonald."[8]

Of course, those blond stars (both male and female) of the silver screen, unfortunate enough to have been born Jewish, are especially lucky: a whole new work vista is open to them, because their hair color hides their dangerous origin. Newspaper reviews and advertising for these lucky few emphasize their blondness in big, gold capital letters, thereby attempting (usually successfully) to show their pure Aryan origin. During the to-ing and fro-ing about the possible Jewish parentage of Charlie Chaplin, some reporters assert, as if by the way, that "His flaxen hair is gradually turning white," "His flaxen hairstyle is not sufficiently banal," "His yellow-blond head of hair," etc. The obvious conclusion is that "there is no place for politics or race in the life of this great blond-haired artist who treats Jews with love and kindness despite the color of his hair.[9]

Doesn't everybody know that Clara Bow's hair is reddish blond? An entire book has been written about Brigitte Helm's blondness![10]

Who doesn't know about the book deifying blondes by Anita Loos, *Gentlemen Prefer Blondes?*, which has already sold two million copies in one year![11]

Woe betide those women unfortunate enough to be born both Jewish and dark-complexioned. Some of these unfortunate souls are even brave enough to mortify their souls by taking the veil, to atone for their shame!

When they asked the blonde Mae Murray why she had suddenly dyed her hair black, she answered, "I can do what I like with my hair: after all, everybody knows that I'm a pure Aryan!"[12]

The epitome of lack of talent and dumb blond beauty together, is the starlet Anita Pass.[13] Even if a visitor wished to commit suicide for her love on the stage, she would still stand there like a lump of wood.

I find myself in the country of the masked ball, otherwise known as assimilated Hungary, which takes first prize in this orgy of mimicry and masquerading. If Europe is really afraid of the hateful colored races that America has infiltrated into the continent Budapest's women react by saying: "I am Aryan." In other words, "I am Magyar." (Actually, "I am Magyar and Aryan")[14] The concept by Ahad Ha'am of "slavery in the midst of freedom" that comes to mind in this context is somewhat irritating because, for the first time, one sees how a highly creative, cultured man shamelessly spits in his own face, his own image.[15] Those same experts in the creative arts—writers, poets, stage directors, master interpreters—all know that they are Jews, well known by others to be Jewish, because the New Catholicism sees it as its God-given duty to stand guard on its [Christian] "racial purity." For this reason, Jewish writers and artists, whose religion is well known, ceaselessly try—to no avail, I might add—to cast and recast the image of the blond beast in everything they create. What hypocrisy! It's difficult to imagine a gentler, deeper, and more humane contemporary Hungarian poet than Ernő (Ernest) Szép—but even he describes, as if "by the way," his artistic experience with blondes.[16] According to modern literature, the stereotypical face of man the believer, dreamer, lover of truth and justice—must be someone who is flaxen blond and blue-eyed. The fact that the righteous, "most intense" heroine of every play is a blonde is a little suspicious. If the writer forgets the blond issue, it is certain that the regisseur will remember his duty.

The well-known Miss Hungary Erzsébet (Elizabeth) Simon, although unfortunate enough to be born Jewish, is, luckily, "almost" a blond. This "almost" has allowed her to win the "Miss Europe" contest in 1929, organized in Paris by Maurice de Waleffe (a fellow Jew).[17] "Miss Hungary had only one real competitor," de Waleffe said during a party after the crowning, "but she had dark hair." What luck! "Even Our Lord and Savior Jesus Christ was lucky enough to have blond hair," as depicted by master painters for hundreds of years. If this hadn't been so, who knows what would have happened!

The delightful truth about this business is that there are only two—no, one and a half—European nations who are blond by nature: Germans and Slavs.[18] Germans are blond and Slavs half-blond: the rest—May the Lord protect us—have black and brown hair. So why should the Magyar-Turan-Mongol establish rank blondness as ideal? Why is a blonde chosen as the ideal of Magyar beauty in Budapest?

The United States president's residence in Washington, DC, is called the "White House." The color of the Übermensch, the rulers of Europe,[19] the "crown of creation," is white. Not, God forbid, the reddish brown color of the despicable gypsies, who inhabit our country and whom we have not yet been able to destroy.[20] Let us not forget the brown and black skin colors of the cursed, despised, subhuman niggers, waste products of creation, who live outside the law in America, land of the Constitution and democratic Bill of Rights, and are barred from sitting next to whites on buses, trams, and in restaurants. What delightful social customs!

"Herr Professor, please excuse me, but only whites dine in this room."

I search in all the arts and sciences of modern, enlightened America for a single poet, philosopher, or scientist who has roared like a lion against that abomination of the twentieth century called by the well-known word "lynching."

Do you know the meaning of "lynching," honored reader?

A sickly, starstruck young girl yearns to be become a star of the silver screen. She is tall as a palm tree, flaxen blond, and overflowing with passion verging on hysteria. The problem is that she has no stage presence—nothing that would ingratiate her with a regisseur. She is currently looking for a trick that would give her a name that can be properly advertised—the only way out of her dilemma. She only needs one newspaper report—and contract offers would rain upon her like autumn leaves. What does she do?—She sits on a park bench until a black person sits next to her—after a moment or two, she engages him in pleasant, even flirtatious, conversation. She almost asks------. A few moments later, she starts to yell: "Help! Save me! A young maiden is in trouble! This filthy nigger is trying to rape me!" After a few more moments, the crowd hangs the black man on one of the park trees, in front of everybody—bystanders in the street, the shoemaker, tailor, worker and clerk, teacher, poet, and Nobel Peace laureate—everybody. And nobody lifts a finger to help him.

This is the meaning of "lynching" to whites.

A fair trial by fair-skinned people with blond hair.

But let us not be dogmatic, and stick to the truth. Lynch law is only permitted during normal, peacetime years. Not, God forbid, during the years of a social revolution. If a hungry, emaciated mob, banging on empty dishes, and fed up with cold, abuse, exploitation, slavery, and hunger, dares—God forbid—to hang someone without judge and jury—this is looked on as shameful barbarity, which endangers all concepts of culture and civilization. This is so even if the victim is a black man who is rich as Croesus and throws produce away in order to artificially inflate prices.

Hooray for international capitalism!

Chapter 14

The Costume Party

This new game of beauty pageants is more than a mere idle exercise. It's the new "intellectual" face of the twentieth century, created by war, on which the modern man of culture now spends ninety-nine percent of his time. Sport itself has long ceased to be sport for its own sake. Now, inexperienced people are interfering with matters about which they know nothing.[1] This concludes with a tragic sigh of, "Will this all never end?"[2] I am convinced that the next war will start with an argument over some sort of sport.[3]

What sport is better than the Miss World contest?

Imagine what a terrible tragedy would ensue if it became known that not only was Miss Hungary Jewish, but that—oh, day of national shame—she was also elected Miss Europe! To make matters worse, Miss Austria—Lisl Goldarbeiter—was elected Miss Universe in 1929! How is this possible? As if to rub salt into the wound, Lisl is of *Hungarian* Jewish extraction! Celebration has been turned in on itself into national tragedy! A Jewish girl from our beloved homeland wearing the Miss Universe crown—shame and disgrace!

The newspapers emphasize that not only her beauty won her the crown but also her gracious modesty and intelligence.

That cursed badge of intelligence—a Jewish trait through and through, which has brought us nothing but trouble.

A group of writers and artists sit together at a table in their local Budapest haunt, the Café Japan. I arrive, to meet with "the gypsies," a group of friends from my youth. They are in the midst of a vigorous debate on a thorny subject: does purity of pedigree alone make a young nineteen-year-old girl beautiful both within and without? Are these two gorgeous young women really a product of Hungary's complex history and culture, with its mixture of races and cultures? Are the enchanting, ingratiating smiles and words, and coquettish grace, of Miss Europe Erzsébet Simon and Miss Universe Lisl Goldarbeiter just as important as physical beauty? What plays the greater role?

At first, I don't realize what a commotion my entry onto the scene brings. I arrive with my childhood friend, the famous actor Ludwig Gellért.[4] With his Jewish temperament and mocking Jewish sense of humor, always disguised by ambiguous seriousness, he introduces me—even to those who already know me—with sweeping, dramatic pathos loud enough to be audible throughout the large coffee house and beyond—a real live Hebrew poet!

After he finishes his inimitable introduction, heavy silence reigns throughout the café. Everyone present is overwhelmed by the power of his theatrical rhetoric, which can be heard from several blocks away. He is loud enough to be a Berlin carnival barker.

At first I don't understand the reason for the dead silence—then I realize that I myself am the reason—a Hebrew writer!

Not only Jewish, but more than that—a *Hebrew* writer!

Not because this is something new for them: almost all present knew me twenty years ago as a young Hebrew writer and publisher in Hebrew and "Zionist" newspapers; also my affinity for that strange and incomprehensible thing, "Israeli Nationalism."

Knowing all this, they still treated me with affection. But since then, the world has rotated a little on its axis, and this "strange and incomprehensible thing" has leaped out of its skin overnight, to become an international political issue: the Balfour Declaration![5]

Something else—*horribile dictu*—has disturbed the even tenor of the country: Jewish pogroms, followed by open, unashamed economic embargos. The company in the café have been complicit in this for a while. The boycott bomb exploded in the form of an official government ban on Jewish talent in literature and the arts, causing the non-Jews in our merry throng to show their real face with bared fangs. Oscar Beregi, that actor of genius, who created the cult of Shakespeare in Hungary, and whom the National Theater in Budapest, with pressure from Max Reinhardt, returned home before the war started, is now living the life of a wandering mendicant outside his homeland.[6] Julius Hagdiusz, that talented Bohemian actor, that charming gentleman, who has so refined and deepened the culture of the New French School—has showed his true colors as a simple, coarse antisemite, railing against any form of Jewish talent.[7] These two examples suffice—no more are necessary.

It's not only Jews whose spirit is suffering from this new form of racism. Gypsies, who before the war were regarded as simple barbarians, not worth bothering with, have now become a front and center issue which, after seething for a while, has boiled over and crystallized into pure, savage hate, that can be seen, smelled, tasted, and touched in every walk of life.

Hungary being Hungary, the grisly Balfour Declaration hasn't penetrated the country, never mind made waves or had any audible or tangible effect. The entire world can turn upside down, Britain can crown the King of the Jews in Jerusalem, the Jewish delegation committee can hand an ultimatum to the Hungarian Ministers Counts Apponyi and Andrássy—all in vain.[8] "We Jews of Hungary scornfully reject any kind of outside interference, as it were, that comes to our aid. We are pure Magyars, who suffer together with the homeland and, even if the homeland itself beats us with iron rods, we will lovingly embrace and kiss the instruments of torture."

But despite all this, a spark still glows inside and outside that "holy of holies"—the pure Magyar soul.

The same spark that doesn't allow honor in the human spirit to be entirely extinguished, but glows and burns, in the direction of—that majestic hidden but living thing, called by Zionists the "Kingdom of Judah."

But there is no strength in the Jews of Hungary to raise their voices and yell!

Suddenly, that same friend of my youth reappears, bearing news from the Kingdom of Judah.

The idiot yells so loudly that the entire street can hear:

"The Hebrew national poet!!"

Silence.

The same Gellért, the most Jewish of Jews, whose pious father had a long beard and side locks, and whose modest mother took special care to light Shabbat candles, kept *kashrut* and all the other myriad Jewish laws incumbent upon a pious rabbinical wife. The man who, despite large-scale recognition of his extraordinary talent, still believes that he cannot achieve the greatness commensurate with his ability. He interrupts the silence, as if by the way, with a wicked smile directed upwards:

"Why the silence, ha-ha-ha-?" He starts to floridly declaim a well-known portion of "Israel" by Henri Bernstein.[9]

He saves the situation and the ice is broken. Our old friendships are strengthened and broadened by distance and the passage of time. Friends of my youth, among whom, twenty years ago, I took my first uncertain footsteps to the world of the mind and pen, surround me with warm friendliness and a myriad of questions, mainly about the Land of Israel and its culture.

After a few minutes, the Jews in the company split into two separate groups, as in a play.—Gellért plays the role of the "conscience of the king." The first group, after the official welcome and obligatory niceties, distance themselves, squinting at the Hebrew writer as if from afar, eyes filled with fear and antipathy—"who asked you to interfere and shake up our peaceful existence here?" After that, some begin to leave, avoiding me as much as possible.

Is it necessary to remark that not one of the above is a native-born Magyar?

The second group shows endless interest in everything happening in the Land of Israel. As the flow of questions develops and increases, the atmosphere "thaws out" more and more. The first question is half in jest but half deeply serious:

"Have you a serious candidate to be King of the Jews?"

The questioner immediately adds:

"I myself am not a fan of monarchy—but the Jews have yearned for a king for the last 2,000 years."

(He personally isn't in favor of this, but the Jews are.)

A second asks:

"How are the workers doing in Israel?"

"Exploited! Like everywhere else!" a third answers.

"What about class warfare? Oy, Oy, no one needs that. We have enough of it here!"

"What do you mean class warfare? Jew against Jew? Isn't it enough that the rest of the world is fighting each other? Must Jews do so too?"

"Fool! Wherever there is money, there is class warfare!"

"The country must be functioning according to the last word of scientific knowledge, honesty. and rectitude."

"Certainly. So that we can proudly present our national achievements to the rest of the world!"

"I am satisfied if Israel is like all other nations."

"What do you mean? Exactly like them! That's not the idea!"

"Surely the name 'Jerusalem' carries some responsibility with it? It's the cradle of religions, which are gradually becoming worthless. A new religion must originate in the City of David, and spread throughout the world."

"Yes. And the new religion's first commandment must be: 'And you shall love the Jew like any other people.'"[10]

"A new religion is unnecessary. The Jew must redeem himself before trying to redeem the entire world. A prisoner doesn't let other prisoners out of jail."

"So how should be redeem himself? With cannons?"

"I tell you again: *our* new state will be an example to the world!"

"How are writers treated there? They probably have no value at all. Show me a Jew who isn't a great and prolific author!"

"The world's greatest patrons of the arts are Jews, so how much more should it be so in the Land of Israel? After all, Jews are the People of the Book!

What a glorious pantheon of the world's greatest Jewish geniuses could be brought together there!"

"Moses, Rabbi Akiva, Jesus of Nazareth, Bar Kochba, Disraeli, Heine, Spinoza."

"Marx, Rachelle, Sarah Bernhardt."

"Maimonides, Moses Mendelssohn, Yehudah HaLevi."

"What about Rashi? I distinctly remember learning Rashi!"

"Which Hungarian would be part of this Jewish Pantheon?"

There are so many here that it is hardly possible to write them all down.[11]

"It's worth dying, just to be able to enter the Jewish Pantheon!"

"I suggest," Béla Salamon, well-loved director of the Budapest Satirical Theater says, "a pantheon for the worst Jew-haters[12] Why not a special museum for these monsters? What a collection that would be, my friends! Torquemada, Pefferkorn, Istóczy, John of Capistrano, Lueger, Plehve."—

"Goliath the Philistine."—

"Leave him alone: he got what was coming to him, although he didn't hate the Jews. He was an ordinary enemy, like all the other nations fighting against Israel."

"Titus, Caligula, Vespasian."—[13]

"Excuse me, I didn't mean enemies of the Land of Judah. The Greeks and Romans got their just desserts from the Jews in their time: which other nation caused them as much trouble as Israel? No, I mean the miserable wretches who abused the Jews at a time when they were defenseless. I would suggest a special menagerie, to properly display these 'heroes.'"

"Who would be Hungary's (non-Jewish) representative in this zoo?"

Silence. The subject is too "sensitive" to touch on.

A non-Jewish actress pipes up, breaking the silence:

"I'm interested in the issue of a king. The Jews have no dynasty. A king must be a man who commands respect in the eyes of the world: how much more so for a king of Judah!"

"Are such men lacking amongst the Jews? Take the Rothschild family!"

"No," the actress says, "Jews set no store by money in a king's anointment."

"But look at Lord Reading: he is the viceroy of His Majesty, the King of England. Soon he will be King of Judah!"[14]

This suggestion sets minds at ease.

"We've already had one king—Hungarian born," I say. "His name is Herzl."[15]

I don't anticipate the degree of reverence that this name—which has not entered into the conversation till now—arouses.

If these people were just a little better educated about Zionism, everyone would have stood up at the mention of Herzl's name and sung "Hatikvah."

My friend Gèllèrt breaks the respectful silence, announcing imperiously:

"Herzl the First!"

"What was his Hebrew name?"—someone asks.

"Benjamin."

"So," announces Géllért, "Benjamin the First: Benjamin Maximus Rex Judaeorum!" in a commanding voice that resounds throughout the coffeehouse, interrupting the peaceful clicking of billiard balls.

"Everyone should know"—his proclamation continues—"that a Jewish state is arising in the Jewish homeland! Soon the present comedy will end! Here (he points to me) you have a Hebrew poet, and here (to himself) a Hebrew artist! Both are 100 percent genuine Jews! Have you any idea what Judaism, Hebrew culture, and a Jew with international repute mean? We are an aristocratic people with a 4,000 year history. Instead of counts and barons, we have Moses our teacher, Moses ben Maimon, Yehudah HaLevi, and hundreds like them, any one of whom is worth more than all your counts and barons put together! I am a Jew!—Do you understand?—A Jew! Exactly as Shylock of Venice put it."[16]

His poignancy intensifies and he becomes passionate. Citations from the classics change over to the words of a tragic Jew—more than words, they are a public catharsis, full of Jewish consciousness, bitter declarations that have been choked and pent up for years without number. Very soon, the declaration takes the form of "I believe," and then a sharp, grating "I accuse."[17] Such candor has not been heard in Hungary for a very long time—certainly not in a bohemian coffeehouse.

"Crazy"—someone says—"crazy Gellért."

"It's you who is crazy!" Gellért exclaims, "especially the Jews among you! On the contrary: I am restrained! I've become sober! I've always known that I am a Jew! My father was a bearded *peyes*-Jew, who prayed every day with tallit and tefillin, and my mother was a pious woman—1,000 times more saintly than your "Saint Elizabeth!"[18]

Great and general consternation. Those of the second group who have remained, all the while looking askance at us, start dribbling away—several immerse themselves in card games and billiards, arguing loudly about the games (or so it seems).

There is a third class of people in the group—the non-Jews, who have gradually left their games and discussions to talk with us:

"He isn't mad at all—on the contrary, a lot of what he says is quite correct. First and foremost, he is an artist and it's forbidden to choke off an artist's inner conviction."

Géllért's tormented soul overflows:

"In vain do we try to close our eyes and ears to what is being done to world Jewry. In vain do your newspapers try to ignore Jewish congresses, the war for Jewish liberation, and movements towards the establishment of a Jewish state. In vain do you purposely delete the names and achievements of great Jews of our time from official lexicons. In vain do you ignore the greatest sensation of our age—the Balfour Declaration—in your learned tomes![19] Our friend the newspaper editor Géza Feleky publishes an obituary for Lord Balfour, without mentioning a single word on his life's crowning achievement.[20] This, despite Feleky being a Jew himself! Strange: those of you who are non-Jews understand us better than our "Magyar co-members of the Mosaic confession," who belong to the Magyar race in exactly the same way they belong to the religion of our forefathers! Lies, lies, everywhere lies! Herr Ober! A glass of wine, please! Tonight I want to get drunk! Drunk! Because I cannot bear all these lies if I am sober! We Hungarians are world leaders in fine Tokay and Bordeaux wines! We have wines comparable to Carmel and Rishon Letzion![21] There were Jews among the first conquerors of Hungary! Jesus of Nazareth was a Jew and Lajos Gellèrt (points to himself) is also a Jew. In the name and permission of His Majesty the great Benjamin the First, may his memory be blessed, I raise my glass to the life of the New Jewish State!—Lechaim!"[22]

He sits and says, half-joking, half in earnest:

"It's midnight—*La commedia è finita!*"

He is right. The non-Jews in the group understand him better than the Jews do, although some Jews were encouraged when the First Zionist Congress occurred.[23] Béla Salamon says to me:

"I have to pay you a visit in Israel soon."

"Yes," I say slyly—"anyone involved with the arts should visit the Middle East: Egypt, Luxor—"

"Luxor-Shmuksor," he interrupts me as if denying a lie. "I don't want to visit Luxor, only our own Land of Israel."

Despite all, the non-Jews amongst us have received all this very warmly, if purely objectively. Perhaps more correctly: because their understanding *is* objective.

One non-Jewish woman in the group sits frozen and silent the entire time, eyes and ears directed at crazy Gellèrt. It takes about an hour after his "scandalous" outburst, before she suddenly says to him:

"You, sir, have no business with the Jewish state. Let the Jews build whatever they want there– you remain a Hungarian artist. Do you understand?"

The speaker is Gellért's wife, a talented actress in her own right, a Hungarian Christian, who married him out of true "gipsy" love—and recites Hebrew songs *in Hebrew* at Zionist gatherings. Her Hebrew knowledge comes from the young Jewish poet Joseph Holder.[24] It's much more than a game with her—rather an effort to blur the religious borders between her husband and herself.

"He is a complete goy.[25] *I* know Hebrew, but he is a total ignoramus!"

Her attempt to blur the difference in their religions comes as a result of current Catholic tenets emphasizing the preservation of racial purity. Before that, nothing like this was necessary.

This lady, who participates in Hebrew gatherings, recites Hebrew poems and gives "lessons on Zionism" to her Jewish husband, has become alarmed at what her husband is saying during the debate. She says to me bitterly, almost venomously:

"Surely you yourself don't believe in this whole business! What are you telling us? You would happily remain here and not return, if not for your current situation! You have simply abandoned Hungarian literature, immigrated there, and become a great Hebrew writer. And now? The way things are, you wouldn't be crazy to return here! I can see that even if you don't say so!"

She has become alarmed by the changed way in which her husband stands by his Judaism:

"Look—I am a good Jewess, but my husband is a complete goy." That is nice to hear, but perhaps the opposite is true: that her husband is the good Jew, and she the goy. The trouble is, that to proclaim this openly is very unpleasant—because it's the truth.

A few days later, I read the words of Gellért as a kind of confession on my works for the stage. A Hungarian Jewish authoress has written a play on a Jewish subject and sent it to Gellért to look over, requesting that—as a Jew, whose heart is deeply touched by the tragedy of his people—he plays the main role. His reply is as follows:

"I'm not a proper Jew at all— only a Jew by virtue of religion; but my artist's soul remains that of artist, no more and no less. I have nothing to do with politics, and am therefore only moved by human tragedy—the tragedy of Russian Jewry doesn't move me one bit. I am much more moved by the tragedy of amputated, mutilated Hungary—I'll have no rest until they return the fifty-six provinces that they robbed from us."

Bang!

The Jewish artist sometimes has momentary lucid intervals of light and compromise—but now his wife comes and steals his limelight!

Interesting logic: first: "I have nothing to do with politics";—then, "I will have no rest until they return the fifty-six provinces that they robbed from us."

Also:—"I am only moved by human tragedy" but "not with the tragedy of Russian Jewry."

"Even If you grind a Hungarian Jew to powder in a mortar, you will not remove his mask."[26]

Chapter 15

A Hebrew Novel

The interest of Hungarian journalists in the nascent State of Israel is surprising. After all, they have no previous knowledge or education on the subject. The novelty of the concept of "a Jewish state" impresses them mightily: a feeling from afar, but which touches them closely. I enter the main Budapest police station to arrange proper documentation for my upcoming travel. When the chief of police sees my papers, he looks at me:
"The Holy Land? Jerusalem?"
"Yes," I reply in Hungarian.
He peers at my papers again.
"How come you speak Hungarian?"
"I was born in Hungary: Hungarian is my mother tongue."
"Ah, yes. But how did you get to Palestine?"
I summarize the issue of Zionism to him. He asks more questions and I answer.

While we are talking, a variety of policemen and detectives arrive, and join in the conversation, which interests them more and more.

By the time I notice the time, I have been talking about Israel for over half an hour: about Tel Aviv, living modern Hebrew, and many other things. I am surrounded by a group of guards, policemen, and detectives who—even during the liberal Tisza regime—would hardly have devoted a minute of their free time to the Jewish question.[1]

"Sir, you keep on saying 'homeland.' Do you really feel that Palestine is your homeland?"

He asks, and answers:

"So, in truth, Hungary is your previous homeland: that is very good to hear. But I would appreciate it if you didn't interpret my words in the usual way—that I simply want to get rid of the Jews. There certainly are such Jews—but you have brought up something new which I hadn't previously thought of. You have presented it in a new and very interesting light."

This is the legal position in the ministries.

And in the academy.

And everywhere else.

Everywhere except where there is a personal or blood connection with Jews or Jewry. For non-Jews, direct contact with the Land of Israel and the Jewish race presents a fascinating psychological problem which sometimes assumes pathologic proportions. But it isn't personal. For anyone with Jewish blood, however, especially those who try to repress it, this Jewish problem gives rise, according to Freud, to disabling repressed psychological complexes.[2] I have seen something like this in my friend the Hungarian writer Frigyes Karinthy.[3]

Frigyes Karinthy is well known—also in Hebrew book circles—as one of the foremost modern prose writers and playwrights of the new Hungarian literature; some of his writings have become famous and very popular with major international authorities. Karinthy belongs to the same group (but not school) as Edgar Allan Poe, H. G. Wells, Leonid Andreyev, Edward Bellamy, and others, who use utopia and the metaphysics of imagination as literary subjects.[4] Karinthy differs in being more a moral than a dogmatic utopian, who dreams of a higher system of morals and wisdom with which to rule the world.

But even such a talented writer, who stands today at the pinnacle of his achievements, is now narrowly focused on daily impressions of life, and vacuous everyday humor, lacking all literary value. This becomes even more astonishing when we take into consideration the fact that Karinthy is not a misogynistic pessimist who despairs of the world—two attributes that are likely to dry up creative juices in the midst of their fullness. What has happened to him?

I intend to raise this question with him when I we meet again after an interval of seventeen years, but a few minutes of conversation with him are enough to make me understand that things have changed.

Our meeting concerns me. Our childhood friendship has been strengthened, in the course of time, by a strong creative relationship. I have translated three volumes of his writings into Hebrew, most of which have been published in Hebrew newspapers. His letters to me are filled with professional and personal regard. I arrive at the party where I am to meet him with other friends, but he welcomes me—to say the least—very cautiously. At the same time that the remainder of the group pepper me with friendly questions about Hebrew literature and the building of a modern Jewish state, he sits there like the skull at a banquet.

I remember a passage from one of his letters to me:

"I know the meaning of the word 'Jerusalem'; I am developing different concepts about Judaism, which I want to make use of in my latest writings. We must stay in constant touch: a good book will result from our letters to each other."

That was then—but now he receives me as coldly as a block of ice.

What is going on? Is it just cowardice on his part?

It's important to know that Karinthy was the only Hungarian writer who, throughout the war—even during the bitterest fighting—wrote ceaselessly about its lies, tragedy, and stupidity. His book *Jesus or Barabbas*, which encapsulates his views, is one of the most important pieces of world pacifist literature.[5] If the author of his works belonged to a great and powerful nation, the fascists would lionize him: Karinthy is no coward.

There is one fear, however, that almost no one in the world can overcome: that is Jewish self-fear which sometimes develops into self-hate. Karinthy is not a Jew by birth sensu stricto, but is of Jewish lineage. His father converted to Christianity and his son was therefore born a Christian. I remember that, before the war, Karinthy often praised and justified his Jewish lineage. But now, after everything that has happened to Hungary, beginning with its defeat in the war, followed by the short-lived Soviet Republic and today's new Catholic dogma, a new Karinthy has appeared: the frightened Jew, whose fears of the environment, regime, and tyranny of his stupid colleagues' opinions, cannot be overcome even by the power of his own literary genius. Because Karinthy is a very moral, logical man, he realizes that this is not to his advantage, yet cannot bring himself back to his real destiny—writing purely for the sake of literature. These modern "concepts" agitate him and give him no rest to write pure literature—and his creative juices are choked off.

This leads to a wariness about our friendship that disturbs his soul—the soul of a man who is not of Christian lineage, despite his parents' conversion before his birth. The eternal question: who is a Jew? What does it mean to be Jewish?

This is also the reason for his overpowering desire and limitless curiosity about Hebrew literature and everything that is being done in the Land of Israel, so near yet so far—but *only on a one-to-one basis*. If we sit alone face-to-face and I relate all the news from Israel, Karinthy listens with rapt attention, posing innumerable questions. But when I talk about "that subject" in company, I am astonished by the mask drawn across the face of the entire creative "intelligentsia." I mention the self-censorship exercised by some of the people present, even those who really are famous and have something significant to say from their Olympian creative heights. Karinthy gets very upset, knocks on the table and says:

"To hell with it. Why all this pussyfooting around! To hell with it all! Let us speak plainly and sincerely!"

Karinthy has another "claim to fame." His wife is Jewish—few can compare with her in wisdom, enlightenment, intelligence, and inner tragedy. While she tells me how she is treated like an outcast by a society that prides itself in "racial purity," her husband sits listening in suffering silence—not because of his wife's suffering, but his own cowardice.

Karinthy says to me:

"How good it is to see a Jew from the Land of Israel, who has peeled off his outer Diaspora shell, and appears just like a member of any other nation! Without eternal Jewish suspicion, an exaggerated inferiority complex, and self-hate."

He adds:

"It would be worthwhile to visit you, to see how your children behave."

I think silently to myself: "Our education is generally not first class (many of our teachers are really politicians with many other responsibilities, and our children are quite wild). But our Hebrew children have one great advantage: the freedom to be Jewish, which has developed astonishingly quickly, within one generation"

I suddenly remember: "The nose surgery."

I said to Karinthy that he is rumored to have had nose surgery.

He laughs confusedly:

"What would it help me? I would have also needed surgery on my eyelids, lips, and maybe other parts of my body."

"Perhaps also on his psyche, much of which is genetic," says his wife. "But what kind of surgery would I need?"

"You, *gnädige Frau*? You are a typical example of Jewish womanhood, so beautiful that you could be elected Miss Jerusalem."

The woman replies to the compliment carefully:

"Really? So gentlemen do not necessarily prefer blondes? If that is the case, we really must take a trip to Israel!"

"I agree on condition that I can become "Mr. Jerusalem." (Karinthy is well known in Budapest for his ugliness) "I would be satisfied to accept the role of cupbearer in the Hebrew literature pantheon."

I am put in mind of critiques in the literary supplements of our own Hebrew newspapers and periodicals, such as *Moznaim* and *Doar Hayom*, or Yeivin's revisionist "aesthetics," discussions on putting forth S. Y. Agnon for the Nobel Prize in literature, and the poem "Sikarikin" by Uri Zvi Greenberg.[6]

I say nothing because, with all of Karinthy's shortcomings, he is my still my dear friend and I am not a cruel man: why destroy his Jewish illusion?

What a wonderful autobiographical novel Karinthy could write, with his own "Jewish concept."

Now *that* would be a Hebrew novel for the ages!

Chapter 16

Frozen in Time

I read on the front page of the newspapers:

> The Budapest City Council has announced a prize for any domestic servant who has worked more than fifty years for a single family. Three prizewinners are found, amongst them an eighty-two-year-old woman who has worked in one house for no less than fifty-seven years. The old lady receives, in addition to the cash reward, floral bouquets from citizens all over the city.

On the second page of the same newspaper, I read:

Hunger strike

> Communist political prisoners in Budapest and provincial towns began a hunger strike yesterday. It appears that this was all prearranged by shared command, and then communicated to all prisoners, no matter how distant from one another.

A "superior intellect," with a nasty, satirical sense of humor, has yoked these two articles together on two adjacent pages, in four different newspapers.

I leave others to argue about whether this is a coincidence or the fruit of some sort of "predestination" or "supervision from On High." This is surely a subject for Einstein, Bernard Shaw, or disciples of Martin Buber or Karl Liebknecht.[1] But I do not permit even so high and mighty a personage as the chancellor of the Hebrew University in Jerusalem to debate its symbolism.[2] The great and general fear of Bolshevism, and need for national calm, make it a symbol not only in Hungary, but all over Europe. The panicked cry: *Lenin ad portam*! (Lenin is at the gates!) cancels the logic even of the most intelligent, and, like all fear, gives rise to foolishness. I am not clear how the price for the servitude of a person who has worked in one house for over fifty years can serve as an antidote to the "Red Menace." At most, it is an imitation of yesterday's Moscow—by other means. Perhaps it would be better to announce a prize for factory owners and employers of every stripe, who over a period of fifty years, have increased workers' wages at so rapid a rate that it has permitted them to exchange their miserable footcloths for real shoes!

Or perhaps a prize for those who haven't attended a diamond-studded ball for an entire year!

Or a prize for males who haven't worn top hat, monocle, and arm bracelet for a whole year!

"The monocle"—Franz Molnar says—"is a visual aid through which one sees less, not more.[3] Through it, only half of life is visible: the other half, for all intents and purposes, doesn't exist. It's about as useful as an ostrich that buries its head in the sand, so as not to see the dangers in front of it."

Jews use eyeglasses, which magnify objects and make them seem nearer than they are. But their use doesn't alter Hungarian Jews' mortal fear of "Lenin's boys," rendering them incapable of even joking about it. Everyone who knows traditional Hungarian Jewish humor—"even a sharpened blade at the throat doesn't prevent one from joking"—knows this type of fear well. Jews change expression of this fear into: "What will the non-Jews say?"

This fear has even confused the great, talented author Baron Lajos (Ludwig) Hatvany—one of the most faithful disciples of rich landowners like Count Karolyi—well known from his trial for defaming the government when he returned from exile. That same Baron Hatvany, author and patron of modern Hungarian literature, led by the great poet Endre Ady. Before his exile, during the short-lived regime of the Social Democrats headed by Count Karolyi, he was fully prepared to follow his mentor, dividing his money and land holdings among the peasants and farmers.[4] But after Admiral Horthy took power, he and the president of the Republic escaped the country, and took up a life of wandering.[5] When Hatvany returned, without his president and under pain of death, he did so not out of betrayal of the Social Democratic republic—his soul is far too noble for that. No, his real reason was his "wretched" Jewishness, which anguished him even after conversion. Anyone can be accused of Bolshevism, except someone who is born with a Jewish soul. When Hatvany returned and was put on trial for treason, he was scarcely recognizable as the great and noble man of letters that he was before. He burst into tears when he publicly confessed this "sin."[6] Despite general scorn, he emerged unscathed, indeed with raised human worth: a wretched man with an upright, pure, and childlike soul. Scorn does not elevate the scorner—on the contrary, the superior human being does not scorn, but understands and loves the scorner.

One thing is clear: had Hatvany not been a Jew (by birth), fear of "what the non-Jews would say" would never have led to this outburst.

Jews of all classes and "races" are affected by this fear. It blinds even the intelligent and enlightened, and makes them do things whose cause is difficult to explain: foolishness, or an extreme effort to demonstrate their loyalty to the state; a kind of "Jewish" loyalty that makes them act more Catholic than the pope.[7] Member of the upper house of parliament Sándor Pál—whose recent visit to Israel has given him the Budapest nickname "the Israelite autodidact" does not appear in my list of "intelligent" Jews."[8]—A man who learned all about the Land Of Israel from inside a car. During a few short hours, he travelled the length and breadth of the Land of Israel, all the way from Rabbi Sonnenfeld to the Hungarian consulate in Jerusalem, no power on earth would bring him to, God forbid, even cast an eye on Tel Aviv.[9] Sándor Pál is the symbol for the core of "enlightened" (or Neologistic, to give their official name) Hungarian Jewry. He is not afraid to talk about Zionism—on the contrary, he enjoys a good discussion on this "piquant" subject. But only in his private office, his home, or in his role as "private citizen," as he emphasizes. It does no good for the *Keren Hayesod* envoy to repeatedly tell him that, as a "private citizen," what he says is of no interest.[10] A private citizen who is a Zionist-hater like Trotsky or a supporter of Zionism like Einstein, is of much more interest, because he has clear-cut opinions, which he is not afraid to share in public.[11] Like other "Magyars of the Mosaic faith," he doesn't even understand the implied insult. Apparently instinct for this has been atavistically blunted through the centuries. Pál's principal opposition to the "symbol" of Zionism is not Zionism itself, but the taint of "Bolshevism" inherent in it.

"Because, as a Jew, I find the idea of Zionism in its purest form to be most admirable." He begins to open his heart a little, and his interviewer hears, straight from the "Magyar's" lips, words of love about Israel full of secret confessions and genuine enthusiasm. But, right at the end, the diplomat in him wakes up again and, when he shakes hands with his interviewer at their parting, he says:

"I must warn you, sir, not to write any of this down or reveal it in public, because—because—I will strenuously deny it."

"Very good," his interviewer says, "I'll write this in your name as well."

"What will you write?"

"That you told me you would deny everything you said."

The diplomat is dumbfounded. He never thought of that! The only way he can extricate himself from this confusion is to cry, on entering his house:

"That's Bolshevism for you!"

This "Wise Man of Hungary," despite being a symbol, is not who I am talking about. His kind of diplomatic "wisdom" is, in reality, mere foolishness. But something strange has appeared, to add an extra dimension to this thorny issue: Jewry's crème de la crème—pious, orthodox sages of learning and tradition, who haven't changed their perspectives one iota since the time of Abraham, despite the present struggle. In fact, any changes that have taken place are retrogressive. This does not speak well of these learned men—a most unpleasant testament to the Jewish religion in its present form. These same meticulously observant, educated Jews—punctilious followers of all 613 commandments—who, seventeen years ago, found 1001 weighty biblical, Talmudic and rabbinical reasons to forbid practical Zionism—have now "expanded" their point of view on this issue. They have increased their anti-Zionist diatribe using the same proofs their opponents the Zionists bring, about settling the Land of Israel before the coming of the Messiah, against them. Their brilliant use of rabbinical and Talmudic exegesis to prove exactly the opposite of the Zionist interpretation from the same citations, is wondrous to behold.

One of their most learned and pious sages expounds it to me as follows: "The true interpretation of 'settling the Land of Israel' before the coming of the Messiah—may He come quickly—is that 'settlement of the mind' (in other words perfect and Heavenly repentance) must precede settlement of the country!"

He adds:

"Anyone who lives in the Land of Israel and speaks in the Holy Tongue is promised a place in the World to Come. The Zionists have distorted these words by Rabbi Akiva as well. The proper literal interpretation of 'speaking in the Holy Tongue' is 'to expound Torah.'[12] You desecrate the Holy Tongue by using it for profane purposes!"

What a brilliant literal interpretation!

It's a pity that this brilliant interpretation is in reality not worth the paper it's printed on. What interest this Pfefferkornian hairsplitting would provoke, if it were collected, for study by later generations![13]

Orthodox Jews sometimes arrange trips to the Holy Land: those who participate do not require a monocle because they only see what they wish to see. They travel, as it were, to their institutions at the Hungarian *kolel* in Jerusalem.[14] During the course of their travels, they see the most extraordinary things, invisible to everyone else. One rabbi sees "great and wondrous announcements signed by the hand of Rav Kook, in which the chief Zionist rabbi gives permission to play soccer on Sabbath."[15]

A second sees a Tel Aviv store sign: "Pork available—cheapest prices!"

His friend adds: "And with the *glatt* kosher stamp of the chief rabbinate.[16]

A third sees a cigarette with the label: "Sabbath incense."

A fourth hears the sound of the *shofar* on Sabbath eve, just before dusk, calling for stores to close and work to cease. He examines the *shofar* and sees that it is indeed a horn—not from a boar—even the Zionists wouldn't dare go that far—but from another impure animal prevalent in Israel. What's its name again?

I help him:

"A rhinoceros (*karnaf* in Hebrew)."

"Yes, Yes. Rhinoceros." He thanks me very much for my assistance.

I expand my knowledge of Israeli zoology. I didn't know that rhinoceroses were so prevalent in Israel. A *shofar* can even be made from its horn! That is something else that I didn't know!

I suggest that the zoology department at the University in Jerusalem carefully note this new and valuable material.

The fifth sees—what can I add?—Each man has seen these terrible things with his own eyes. There is only "one thing" that has escaped their eagle eyes in Tel Aviv: the many synagogues, different Talmud Torah schools, Rabbis Uziel and Aronson, who are able to solve rabbinical problems of multiple Rambams, which place Jewish legal obstructions in the way of Orthodox Hungarian Jewry and its rabbis.[17] It's unnecessary to add that they have neither seen nor heard of Rav Kook, who has more knowledge of Torah, wisdom, and Fear of the Lord in his little finger than their entire assembly and disciples together multiplied many times over.

Some of their chiefs are princes of the land. At the head of these monocled Jews, who look down their noses at the Land of Israel, World Jewry, and its manifold tragedies, is a man who requires our attention for a few moments: the banker Frankel.

Frankel is a particular kind of Orthodox Jew: externally, he looks like the president of the French Republic—dressed in an immaculately ironed and pressed tuxedo (perfectly complemented with polished shoes). He is a learned man, an exalted Torah scholar expert in the *Mishnah*[18] as well as all things secular. The study hall in his private home is adjacent to his dining room, and he only prays with a community. He is punctilious not only with the commandments incumbent on Diaspora dwellers, but also with customs related to the destruction of the Second Temple in 70 CE. He has warned his only daughter, a true "Princess of Israel," against the evils of singing. Despite her known talent with musical instruments, all music is banned in his house, in memory of the destruction of the Temple. It is unnecessary to cite the Talmudic exhortation that "the voice of a woman (singing) is a form of eroticism."[19] But, nevertheless, this "Princess" knows Hebrew (both old and modern) and her two children speak pure Sephardic Hebrew at home with their mother.

By the way: on the day of her wedding, her golden tresses—the epitome of blonde beauty—(the color only served to anger the pious) were mercilessly shorn off. What a pious, compassionate father!

This same righteous, charitable man, whose secular enlightenment is equaled only by his Jewish erudition, has recently done the following:

The Jewish National Fund office, in an attempt to broaden its fundraising abilities, applied to the government for a permit to double the number of donation boxes in Budapest, to a total of 10,000.[20] Out of fairness, the government referred the matter to the National Office for

Orthodox Jewry, whose president promptly advised them to remove the existing 5,000 boxes and close the office.

Full stop.

I am not responsible for this response from the Office for Orthodox Judaism—all I can confirm is that it was the fruit of Frankel's intellect. An important Orthodox member of the National Office explained to me that it is forbidden to "hemorrhage" money from the homeland abroad.

So the Land of Israel is simply reckoned as any other overseas country.

A world war, the destruction of world Jewry, revolutions, the collapse of monarchies; the League of Nations wants to solve the Jewish question; the Holy Land is being built anew; new dangers and catastrophes threaten the world; the effects of the mighty war are still felt; we are on the threshold of thousands of new calamities—and the Hungarian Orthodox Jewish community search for passages that rail against settlements in the Land of Israel, with their chief rabbi recommending clamping down on small coinage contributions for the redemption of the Jewish people.

Can such people change?

No: they are frozen in place and time.

I discuss this issue with one of the ministerial advisors in his office. He asks me about Jewish National Fund boxes in poor, impoverished Hungary. I agree with him that hard-pressed Hungary's scarce coinage must not "hemorrhage" overseas: for this same reason the flow of millions of coins to Rome through Peter's pence, and of coins to Jerusalem via Rabbi Meir Baal HaNes boxes (directed by the leader of the Orthodox community!) should appropriately cease as well.[21] He looks at me with surprise, then laughs, blinks his eyes, clasps my hand, and says:

"Here's an idea for you!—Let's quietly agree not to disturb each other. I the Catholic, Frankel the Orthodox, you the Zionist—in the name of this 'Holy Trinity,' let us close an eye to these dangerous contributions."

Chapter 17

The Baptists[1]

It gives me a deep, spiritual "Jewish" satisfaction to report that bona fide Hebrew authors are treated in Catholic Hungary as who they really are—citizens of a real country. The same applies in other countries and is something really new. The writer of these lines is, thankfully, not the first to have been received in such a manner. Tschernichovsky, who was not born or educated in Hungary, was also received a few years ago like a poet from a legitimate country.[2] Non-Jews are not inherently complex people: a Hebrew poet simply means a poet from a Hebrew, that is, Jewish, state. They are not aware of the bickering between different Jewish parties on the question of a "Jewish state" or "national homeland." The matter is clear: whatever Jews want from the land of their forefathers in the twentieth century is exactly what other peoples want from their own country: a true and relevant state of their own, with its own institutions. Their questions to me clarify the real meaning of a state. Every non-Jew (Hungarian and non-Hungarian alike) sincerely interested in establishment and development of a bona fide Jewish state poses questions concentrating on one or more of the following three principal issues:

"Is there a Jewish majority in the country yet?"

"What is your official national language? Is it Hebrew?"

"Yes, but what about the army? Is the army there solely British, or Jewish but under British supervision?"

I am asked these questions everywhere I go: the ministry, police, academy, coffeehouses. Everywhere, I meet non-Jews with a sincere interest, or merely curiosity about, a Jewish homeland.

I find the inability of their own reactionary elements to conceive even the possibility of a reactionary element in the nascent State of Israel fascinating: the thought doesn't occur to them.

When a Hebrew writer is welcomed into the company of non-Jews, his citizenship of a Jewish state gives him a unique feeling—far more important than any personal, subjective honor that he may receive. Because what is the value of personal victory or talent compared to the eventual victory of an ideal that, only a few short years ago, might have got you arrested or admitted to a lunatic asylum by the same company of learned men who now crown you with a victor's laurel?!

It is important to note that this welcome is only extended by non-Jews. This includes even the stupidest, who don't even know whether Palestine is included within the realm of antisemitism—in other words, whether they should "hate" Zionism itself or just the Jews around them, with their admittedly objectionable character traits.

In the midst of their hesitation, or even rank hatred: I still feel: "We have a homeland!"

With Jews, however, it is entirely another matter.

Obviously, what I have to say does not refer to the "old comrades" of Zionism, whom I call the Baptists, or "New Apostles."[3]

These apostles are "veterans" of the Zionist ideal who, in psychological terms, should be about 200 years old but obviously—in real terms—are still very much with us. They are the first Jews who felt the young Herzl's winds of change hovering over them.[4] They are the ones with whom we scrubbed floors at different Zionist societies—*Herzliah* (families); *Maccabiah* (students); *Yehudah* (clerks and officials); *Devorah* (young girls), *Ivriah* (school pupils). People who themselves did all the work—carrying the society's tables, chairs, and other furniture—when we moved to the sanctity of new quarters, in proud and silent procession in front of all passersby in the streets of teeming Budapest. People stared at us with wide-eyed amazement and one large question mark hung in the air: Who in the world are these people? Does the city have no porters? Their questions were answered simply and concisely:

"These are the 'New Apostles' of Herzl and the Zionist idea."

"Really? Why not? Don't they resemble Christ's apostles who went out to preach the gospel after the death of their leader?"

A group of serious-looking, bearded, and clean-shaven young men gather together in a gloomy outside apartment which, even during the day, requires electric lighting, to talk about Zion, and sing songs of prayer in the language of the Holy Scriptures. One of them ascends the platform to talk endlessly about Zion and redemption; afterwards they again break into sacred song and walk around, shaking Zionist collection boxes into which the faithful throw coins. These true believers exude a spirit of devotion, faith, and love found nowhere else in wanton Budapest.

Behold the New Apostles!

In other words, people whose private lives are normal and moderate: attorneys, engineers, physicians, bank officials, artisans, and simple workers—typical members of the community. They only differ in having "suspicious tendencies toward unhealthy religiosity." After work, they enter God's realm, to sing songs in the Holy language. There really are such people in the world: half of their lives are normal, but the other half lacks something vital, without which they cannot live.

Quite often, priggish Christian women stand inside the gate of the pitch-dark yard, peering sanctimoniously and listening in holy awe to our songs: "There Where the Cedars Grow"; "The Pledge"; "On the Road," "May You Have neither Dew nor Rain," and other songs of the troglodyte generation before the flood of Zionist diplomacy.[5] After we finish, they try to imitate the sounds:

"I-yar-ba—David-cha-ana."

The president closes the meeting in a commanding tone:

"Tomorrow, Dudya Vider will sweep out all the rooms and Jossi will rearrange the benches after he has finished."

We meet at night in the coffeehouse Ker to expound, hagadah-like, the Exodus from Europe.[6] A woman approaches us and asks, in awe and reverence, piously crossing herself:

"Might I be so bold as to dare ask if a person from the outside can witness your baptismal ceremony?[7] I am after all a good Christian who searches for the truth of Zion"

"Yes, for us apostles."

These veteran Zionist apostles, each a heroic personality in the great unwritten epic, whose name will surely be *The Exodus from Europe*, are alive and well today, living with their original zeal for the Zionist ideal. They live and work: but you will search for them in vain, even in the new "Zionist Lexicon." Several now live in the Land of Israel, but do not trumpet their existence and have changed their names. Let me introduce a few to you: Jossi the bench arranger and organizer of the New Jewish Youth, whose previous name was Oskar Fürst. He is now a director of language education in the youth village of Meir Shfeya and is now called Dr. Avraham the Prince. Then there is Hugo Shai—the early Zionist who fought for the Hebrew flag, statehood, and an orchestra with original Biblical instruments even before the Law came down to Herzl on Sinai. He supported research, described the instruments in detail with the aid of a German professor, and eventually had them constructed and brought back as a gift for Zionist religious schools in Jerusalem.[8] Other apostles have risen to great cultural prominence among diaspora Jews. Dudya Vider (the room sweeper)—for example—is now the national Hungarian language poet of Israel, newly named "Yohanan of Gush Halav."[9]

These great men regard everything that comes out of the Land of Israel as a symbol and guarantee of their "crazy optimism," which would have been fodder for mockery by every would-be journalist-for-a-day twenty years ago.

But after their diplomatic victory, you will look in vain for these apostles, because they don't search for recognition. The new generation—educated at the knees of the old—has schooled a young generation of new apostles. Some of can be found today in the land of Israel: Dr. Chaim Weissburg, who founded the first and only daily Zionist Diaspora newspaper in a foreign language, dreams of construction of the town of Tzur Shalom and international victories of Israeli sport.[10] Shlomo Pelai, a well-known Haifa attorney, is called "Mr. only Hebrew" because he hasn't spoken a word of any other language for many years.

The third generation, who drink in spiritual sustenance like mother's milk from today's Land of Israel, has split into two groups: in the first group are the "true believers," but the second are now "men of action." The first base their dream of redemption in the Land of Israel on the establishment of a Jewish state. The second group understands the concept of "the Land of Israel" in much more "practical" terms:

"A healthy state cannot tolerate free labor! Everything costs money!"

One of the mental midgets of Zionism tells me: "In a healthy state, no one works for free!"

"A healthy state!"

He has the chutzpah to use Herzl's words as proof of his point of view.

The first thing a Jew coming from Israel with citrons must do, is to have them sold by a group of enthusiastic youngsters, who, of course, get paid for their effort from the profit. No one would think of selling produce from the Land of Israel without paid middlemen!

Political considerations (without the Zionist party itself, of course!) also play a role when someone wishes to impart knowledge about Israel. A Hebrew writer comes from Israel to lecture on the homeland, the recent riots, Hebrew culture—none of this is possible before he first loudly announces his party affiliation.

"A healthy country!"

What a miracle!

Zionist youth have become accustomed, during the past few years, to hear only "practical" requests—demands for money in the land of their dreams. Not one of us original apostles demands more than generous souls can provide: enthusiasm for Hebrew culture, a war for ideas; nor do we dare create another outlet for their excess of zeal.[11] However, as a reward for creative strength, if they are lucky enough to meet His Holiness, the *shaliach* from Israel, they are doused with a cold shower.[12] "Your ideas are your own business—what we need from you, are endless supplies of *money* to save the *yishuv!*"[13] If the poor lads are even luckier, they are drenched once more—together with the "pure Zionist" past inherited from the original apostles—this time with cold scorn. The end result is destruction by the dictatorship of the *sochnut*, and complete lack of knowledge of Zionist history in the diaspora.[14]

The old *shaliach* in chief shares the yeshiva with the initiators of the Zionist movement. They discuss the money and fundraising, which will help us. Among them are the movement's "veterans," who have had to use all sorts of tricks and stratagems to make the first round of fundraising successful—a grave responsibility which they took (and still take) extremely seriously.

Suddenly His Holiness gets up and says:

"During my one week here, I have achieved more than all of you together, during the past twenty-five years!"

Deathly silence.

A moving picture of the wonderful—and sometimes not so wonderful—New Apostle Period passes before my eyes:

A mighty battle among the four kings in the valley of Siddim (sea of salt).[15] Kedorlaomer, King of Elam, stands for Neolog Jewry, which disregards its brothers scattered over the Diaspora.[16] Amraphel, King of Shinar represents the assimilated youth, who shake off their identity the day they embrace assimilation.[17] Arioch, King of Ellasar stands for Orthodox Jewry, which has turned away from the ways of the Lord.[18] Tidal, King of Goyim represents the non-Jewish university students of the St. Emmerich guild, who constantly assassinate our character and despise our struggle for national identity.[19]

Another image:

When the great Zionist orator Dr. Shmaryahu Levin arrives in Budapest, the city council only agrees to give him a hall in the old parliament building in which to speak after a prolonged struggle—victory![20] A second tactical propaganda victory: convince journalists to attend his historic lecture. Yet another victory: all newspapers send representatives—"We now see that the Zionist issue is much more serious than we thought until now and must address it in all seriousness and urgency."

Another image:

Dozens of students dressed in frock coats, even formal evening attire, clear snow in the Budapest streets day and night to make up the deficit for the annual Jewish National Fund budget.[21] The suit idea comes from the respected Dr. Demen, as a public demonstration to support Zionism.

Another image:

Publicity pamphlets are distributed in the corridor of the Orthodox synagogue—police are brought in, followed by an official police investigation, and a stormy meeting at the local *Maccabiah*.[22] Victory: the venerable Chief Rabbi Dr. Koppel Reich forces the synagogue managers to resign, saying to us; "you are always welcome in our synagogue during prayer. But no fundraising in the halls, please!"[23]

Another image:

An antisemitic argument within the university, directed solely against Zionist youth. Arguments—violence—duels—cautious victory.

Another image:

The first Jewish kindergarten—general laughter and mockery at such a thing—denunciation to the ministry. A permit is received: another victory! The head of the Neolog community, advisor to the king, is present at its first celebration. When a little girl comes up to him, Jewish National Fund box in hand, and asks in Hebrew for a contribution, he bursts into crocodile tears.

Another image:

A second denunciation—this time of the "Zionist Society"—to the government. An order comes down to close it. Much discussion by the country's leaders—another victory! Count Batthyány announces in parliament that he empathizes with the Zionist ideal. "Jewish youth has arisen to national resurrection and we, with our liberal national traditions, are obliged to support them in this worthy endeavor!"

Another image:

A *Maccabiah* anniversary celebration, attended by major figures from the Jewish assimilationist movement. Professors Shimon Bacher and Yehudah Blau.[24] Another victory: our greatest and most dangerous enemy, the assimilationist editor Savolczy, favors us with his presence; after a silence that can be cut with a knife, he suddenly stands, and admits emotionally: "I have dreamt of such a Jewish youth for thirty years!"

Another image:

Assimilated Hungarian Jews from Transylvania immigrate to Israel and found a settlement.[25]

Transylvanian Jews decide to build a town named Tzur Shalom in the Gulf of Acre.[26]

Another image:

Transylvanian Jews collect about 10,000 Palestinian pounds for the Jewish National Fund—despite empty pockets, tattered clothes, and miserable general conditions.

Images continue to roll by in my imaginary film: a new, truly Jewish generation has suddenly arisen out of a sea of assimilation and now rules in society, at home, in the street. It arranges, organizes, creates, learns the Hebrew language, and emigrates in groups to the land of their forefathers.

Back to reality: I hear His Holiness, the *sochnut shaliach* announce:

"During my week here, I have done more than all of you together during the past twenty-five years!"

Two days later, the *shaliach* is informed that, in order to collect the necessary funds, I—a writer, born and educated in Hungary—will have to deliver a series of public lectures both in Hungarian and Hebrew (for the youth). That is why I have come here, isn't it? The alternative is for someone else to raise funds by going from door to door.

The old man replies:

"But *I* am prepared to give the lectures!"

Another request:

"The Hebrew author must write articles in Hungarian newspapers to influence those with money, and their pen pals, not to fight against Zionism."

The old man repeats:

"But *I* am prepared to write articles as well!"

One person contributes 1,000 pengő (fifty Palestine pounds!) to the Jewish National Fund and announces: "I make this contribution in honor of the author, as a token of thanks for, and recognition of, his lecture."

The old man protests with the greatest vehemence:

"I object in the strongest possible terms. The donation is not in honor of the Hebrew author, but rather of the *sochnut*—represented by me!"

One of Budapest's great financial and societal moguls, owner of an electrical factory, organizes a party in his home to honor the Hebrew author, in the hope that it will raise a significant amount of money for the Jewish National Fund. The old *shaliach* initially refuses, but is later prevailed upon to come. I tell those present about the defense of Tel Aviv and Jerusalem against attack: there is a trembling silence and many are moved to tears. Suddenly the old man bestirs himself, claps his hands, and says:

"Again that barbarian tongue! Please, honored sirs, speak in a cultured language that I too can understand!" Silent amazement—strong whispered objections about the old man's cynicism. As if nothing has happened, he tells meaningless stories about meaningless subjects.

When he is introduced to a veteran Zionist, who wants to boast about his young lads already learning Hebrew, His Holiness responds:

"The language they speak—Hebrew or another barbarian tongue—is completely immaterial. The only important thing is their monthly contribution to the *sochnut*."

When I try to relate the heroic deeds and almost superhuman victories at Hulda, Motza, Be-er Tuvia, Tel Aviv, and Jerusalem during the recent attacks, the old man admonishes me in public.[27]

"Why do you tell such lies?"

I meet one of the original apostles, one of the first members of the Herzl and Nordau group.[28] He says, sighing:

"This doesn't help our struggle much. What we have built with the sweat of our brows, suffering, and forced bachelorhood for twenty-five years is swatted away in one night by this hypocrite, like a bothersome fly. Is it really possible to send us a character like this to collect money without taking one word of counsel with us beforehand?

"During the course of twenty-five years, these true apostles have achieved more than those who call themselves Zionists in any country in the world. Theirs is a true religion—of holy resurrection.

Twenty-five years—why is there no new generation of apostles, only this odious little man?"

A thoughtful, enlightened woman from Budapest replies:

"Selfish, self-satisfied 'missionaries' like him radiate no light for the youth—an *inner* light is essential for fundraising."

A high ministry official tells me that, upon obtaining an audience with the minister of religion and education, Rev. József Vass, the *shaliach* bowed low, blessed him, and kissed his ring. (Note: Vass was a priest, but not a cardinal).

That same Magyar official adds:

"That was a pity: it was superfluous and nauseated me."

How many years of zeal and enthusiasm for the Land of Israel has this "missionary" ruined?

How difficult it is to erect a foundation stone—but how simple to remove and discard it!

Chapter 18

Mosaic

A Righteous Convert

Born of a noble Magyar family, a locksmith by trade. Two loves stronger than death—his gorgeous Jewish wife and a pure Zionist love of Israel—have drawn him to Judaism.

He has a question and request for me:

"I have been a Jew for nearly twenty years. At home we keep strictly kosher. Before I married my beloved, I learned all the religious laws incumbent on a son of Israel, also to pray in Hebrew. I even learned the laws of ritual slaughter."

"Why did you do that?"

"I saw that all Orthodox rabbis and ritual slaughterers oppose the establishment of a Jewish state. I said to myself: these are not rabbis but Jew-haters, not ritual slaughterers but simple murderers, whose meat I refuse to eat.

"However, there is one thing that I cannot do myself—there is one commandment without which I cannot be a Jew—and to my sorrow I can't fulfil it alone. All the *mohels* I know are Jew-haters, and I will not hand this holiest of all commandments over to religious transgressors![1] I ask you very kindly—could you suggest an upright, kosher rabbi, who is also a Zionist?"

An Idiot's Curse

Orthodox rabbis have placed the Zionists in *cherem* (excommunication). This is not uncommon here: every rabbinical Chaim Shmerl-for-a-day decrees excommunication for Zionists in his own congregation.

Would the same apply to a cultured rabbi, a Herr Rabbiner Doktor, a man occupied with world science, a poet (albeit a plodding one)?

Sadly, the answer is yes: one of these "cultured rabbis," Rabbi Dr. Heves Kornél, *Av Beit Din* of the Szolnok Jewish community, has invoked a thunderous curse—in the form of a poetic ode—not only on those who are building up the Land of Israel, but on Zion itself.[2]

"A curse be on Zion, on all your ruins!"

Excommunication—by strict holy decree from the head on which tefillin are laid—the head of an idiot.

Is there another nation in the world from whose gravesite such a flower can bloom? No, because there is no other nation in our position—from the bottom of my heart, I wish that our haters' gods would grace them with a whore's fee for such a religious muse, so that they too can experience the stink of the Diaspora.

In the form of an ode.

A Pure Magyar

A secretary in an electrical factory, a young man of about twenty-five with dark, curly hair. He looks exactly like a Jew.

"To my great regret, I cannot be a Zionist," he tells me, "because I am a pure-bred Magyar."

"Where were you born?"

"Here in Hungary."

"And your father?"

"He was born in Galicia, in Tarnow."[3]

"And your mother?"

"She was born in Iași, Romania."

"Do you feel yourself a pure-bred Hungarian?"

"Of course."

I leave my business card—written in Hebrew—with him, to forward to his superiors. The young man takes a look at it, suddenly grabs a piece of paper from the table, and covers his head with it.

"Is it allowed to read this with my head uncovered?"

"Of course it is."

He looks at me, and puts the card down angrily.

"Is this how you want to build the Land of Israel? By desecrating the sacred language, using it as everyday speech there?"

Truly, a pure and decent Magyar!

Terrible!

I sit on the train, speaking to a local small-town rabbi. Of course, conversation revolves around the Land of Israel. I tell him of the many synagogues in Tel Aviv, the various Talmud Torah schools, and other things that replace mocking and resentment with love in the heart of every decent, God-fearing Jew.[4]

Suddenly this small-town rabbi, his soul inspired by Heavenly powers, says:

"Sir, that is all well and good, but you haven't told me that women in Tel Aviv use electricity instead of Sabbath candles!"

In truth, I didn't mention this—terrible!

Thank you, Herr Rabbiner, I will be sure to mention what you have said when I return to Tel Aviv. How could I have forgotten such an important matter?

Vengeance on the Goyim[5]

A discussion on the train about the eminent Hungarian writer Desider Szabó, who recently announced in the newspapers that he will leave his Hungarian homeland and become Romanian.[6] The Hungarian nation does not deserve him because it doesn't create conditions for its writers to ply their craft in peace and enlightenment. Such a nation doesn't deserve a writer of his caliber, and he will leave this miserable, ungrateful place.

The Hungarians taking part in the conversation greatly resent this crazy writer. How can a man leave his homeland? What does he mean by doing this? How can a man leave his blood, his very being?

I suddenly hear a voice from someone behind the benches, who hasn't taken part in the discussion so far:

"What he is doing is very good," the lonely stranger says calmly and emphatically. "One day you too will feel what it's like to be an apostate!"

War Stratagem

A woman half covered in a shawl sits in a corner. A pretty young woman with a good figure, who acts with dignity worthy of respect. Up till now, she has sat silently, speaking to no one.

She suddenly comes up to me, cigarette in hand, requesting a light.
I give it to her and she offers me a cigarette.
She says:
"May I sit here, please? I too want to say something."
All the men stand up politely.
"Of course! Please do!"
She sits down.
"Thank you. But please don't be so polite. I'm a whore, after all."
General consternation. One of us pipes up:
"If a woman says that about herself, then surely it isn't so bad."
The woman blows smoke in his face, and says mockingly, eyes like slits:
"Stop philosophizing. I didn't come here either to hear or speak nonsense. I have something to say to this man,"—she points at me—"but if you all hear it too, it won't do any harm."
She relates:
"Perhaps you know that a few years ago our holy Hungarian patriots, true Magyars all, founded a great patriotic club—named 'Adonis.'"
"I'm sorry, I don't know of it."
"So, let me tell you about it. The purpose of this splendid club was to seduce and then deflower (forcibly, if necessary) young Jewish maidens. All its members were magnificent young specimens, tall and strong as cedars."
"Who founded the club?"
"Who? Take a guess!—Its founder was a holy sister."
"She must be old!"
"The devil knows how old she is, but she is certainly a nun.

"The club opened, functioned as planned, and the young men had the time of their lives. They even had a 'fund' to pay for cars, expenses, champagne dinners, etc. Their enterprise succeeded in bringing disaster on scores of Jewish families."

"But what about the authorities? The police?"

"The police? Which Jewish father would dare bring his daughter's desecration into a public court? You ask me how I found out about all this? The answer is simple: one of its poor victims was so despondent that she became a member of our 'institution'—the local whorehouse. A daughter from a good family—her parents disowned her. She told me the whole wicked story. These gentlemen (she points to the Hungarians in the coach) recognized—and carried out—their patriotic duty with great zest: everybody knew about it."

Someone objects: "By my life, I've never heard anything about this!"

"Where have you been all this time? On the moon?? Don't you read the newspapers?!—But perhaps that's not so important. The main thing is: how this patriotic group was brought to an end"

"The police, no doubt."

"A pox on the police! All they know is how to persecute us 'official' prostitutes! It wasn't the police, sir, but I myself who destroyed this den of wild beasts. I dressed up like a modest, decent girl and allowed myself to be seduced.—Afterwards, I told the young man that I have many beautiful young friends, enough for all his comrades. He fell over himself at this amazing find. And I—I 'arranged' scores of wanton girls for them: I selected the most beautiful, dressed them up modestly and taught them how to behave politely but slyly. The matter was brought to a head when, under influence of female wiles, the group went out for dinner one evening—ex post facto, of course—in a fancy restaurant frequented by the nobility and other important people. I arranged that—without anyone knowing about the other—each would meet up there with his own individual 'Jewish victim.' After momentary surprise, all were overjoyed. The patriots started to whisper amongst themselves. After having taken counsel, one of them rose, raised his champagne glass, and proposed a short, mocking, vengeful toast announcing their great victory unashamedly to everyone there: 'Look! Dozens of girls have sacrificed themselves on the noble altar of patriotism!'

"A burst of terrible laughter echoed throughout the large hall and the group's leader instructed the gipsy band to break out in a celebratory tune! Joy and delight overflowed, and each man clinked glasses with his own young woman: '*Prost!*'

"Then, I rose, raised my glass, and said:

'I toast this entire despicable, swinish group in the name of all the prostitutes of Budapest, for their great victory in seducing dozens of official whores! *Prost*—also to the diseases with which we have infected you—Hurrah!'

"The whores burst out in great peals of laughter, the like of which had not been heard in Budapest before!

"We walked victoriously (aka fled for our lives) from the hall.

"That, sir, is how the respected Adonis club bit the dust. To tell the truth—the men paid quite dearly for all their patriotism—many of them are still recovering—"

Chapter 19

My Two Souls

I sit in a railway carriage leaving Hungary and a kind of accounting accumulates inside me: number by number, fact by fact, feeling by feeling, recognition by recognition. All these gradually melt together, in the form of one big question mark:

"Homeland?"

My thought process is complete as the train approaches the border station. The station is not particularly big, a small town which is really a village. But at the present time it serves as the Hungarian frontier, and the concept of "border" begins to stir up in me a complex set of emotions. This is the second time I have felt this way: the first was when I got off the ship in Haifa, upon immigration to Israel.

At that moment, I felt my unique position as a Jew is this wide world. Who else has such a feeling? Which nationality? I descend onto the soil of Asia, and feel: this is my homeland.[1] Now, for the second time, I approach the Hungarian border, and again I feel—homeland. But this time there is a fly in the ointment, something that insists on an immediate solution: "I have two mothers!"

Absurd—how can this be?

I search for analogy between these two concepts in terms of traditional motherhood: one is the birth mother, the other the stepmother? No, that's wrong.

One gives birth, the other raises the child? No.

One loses me but I find her again—and the other?

No, there is no analogy—absurd remains absurd.

There is yet another reason for this. My fondness for them, not my obligation, plays the principal role. Obligations may be divided, dissected, arranged. These belong with these, and those with those. But how can fondness be divided? This is the hidden nub of the absurdity: my fondness for the two of them differs greatly!

But I don't know the extent of the difference.

I would like to confer secretly about this with someone objective: perhaps he could clarify it. But where could I find such a person? He cannot be a Jew, because a Jew is either in my own situation or wouldn't understand me at all: what is my bond with that strange country in Asia? The person can clearly only be a non-Jew.

A non-Jew? Absurd! Which non-Jew in the world could even dimly begin to understand me?

None.

If so, my feeling is saddening, even tragic. Is this not the definition of a tragedy—complete and universal lack of understanding?

Perhaps this is the essence of the great Jewish tragedy—lack of a partner in understanding.

I remember:

When I was a boy, our coachman caught a young eagle chick, whose mother was slightly wounded and couldn't save her young. She tried—but couldn't manage. When the coachman carried the chick off, the mother flew in wide circles around the robber, accompanying him home. Even then she didn't dare fly down and attack him.

For days after that, the bereaved eagle flew in wide circles around our house, where she sensed her orphaned chick was.

Never once did she swoop down to attack and devour any pet bird in our house—she just wanted to save her chick. After a while, she stopped coming.

Later, when the chick had grown a little, started to spread its wings, and had tried to fly, the coachman picked it up and returned it to its mother's nest. The mother wasn't at home, so to speak, so he stood to the side with my grandfather and myself: we waited and observed.

I'll never forget what followed for the rest of my life—it made me weep bitter, childish tears, and I couldn't be comforted. The eagle returned, and the chick in the nest opened its beak to greet its mother. I was overjoyed and burst out: "look! It wants to kiss its mommy!" After a moment of alarm, the mother eagle looked at the chick, examined it carefully—and attacked it with raging fury, threw it outside onto the rocks with its talons, and attacked it again—if we hadn't frightened it away, it would have gutted the chick like a fish.

The terrible scene allowed me no rest or sleep for many days afterwards. How terrible: the mother looks for her son, the son wants to cling to his mother—but she doesn't recognize him and thinks him a stranger. Even worse—on the same day this happened, the eagle appeared again over our yard, circling around for many hours.

I cannot begin to describe the terrible pain that devoured my soul, because there was no hope at all of repairing the damage. Once, I took the chick out into the garden: the eagle hovered over (it must have felt something), descended for a minute, and—to my immense joy—observed the chick for a minute; but then it swooped into the air, flew wide circles over us, and disappeared, never to return.

When my father saw my terrible sadness, he said to me with a sigh full of hidden grief:

'This is the manifestation of our Divine Presence in the Land of Israel—we stretch our beaks out to it—but it doesn't recognize us anymore.[2] The land searches for us and we in our turn call out to her—all to no avail."

I remember something else:

I remember something that our revered teacher, the learned Orientalist and Hebrew scholar Professor Goldziher once said to us.[3]

"Most sections of Arab (including those who are Christians) and Bedouin society in the Land of Israel, are remnants that didn't go into exile after the Assyrian and Roman expulsions.[4] After that, the Prophet Muhammad came and converted them to Islam by the edge of the sword; many had already been converted to Christianity before the advent of Islam."

Some of our brothers are protesting and objecting to our return to Zion.

The same brothers who would like to murder us, if they had the chance.

What does *shechinah* (Divine presence) mean?

Amongst our brothers who did not go over to Muhammad and Christ, those who were exiled are now returning. Are there really those who, when the time is ripe, are prepared to murder each other to gain a little patch of ground one cubit square?

If we could catch two chicks from the same nest, distance the one from the other, and then bring them back to their original nest, they would probably pluck each other's feathers out, without recognizing each other at all.

What does "Divine presence" mean?

My thoughts are interrupted: we have crossed the border into Romania.

I descend from the train to get my entry permit into Romania stamped. Up till now, this has been done inside the train. I have already passed through five different borders—in all five, document inspections have taken place inside the train. Why must I get off now?

It quickly becomes clear: in Romania, things are done differently!

I hand in my papers, and the official says to me:

"Please go and buy the ticket for your onward journey; then come back and retrieve your papers."

I go to buy the ticket, but only have Hungarian money, which has to be exchanged. The clerk in the exchange booth "does me a favor" and exchanges my money, "even though it's forbidden." The Romanian money fills both my hands to overflowing. I am still an idiot when it comes to the new Hungarian postwar currency, let alone Romanian currency—the clerk counts it out and I try to as well, but I rapidly become confused. The train is whistling—I, and many others, rush back—many have not yet had time to buy tickets. I haven't had time to retrieve my papers: surely they will return them to us on the train, as has been the case at other border crossings? If not, why would they allow the train to move before the passengers all have their tickets and papers? There are many in my position.

I enter the train—chaos! I was supposed to collect my papers at the frontier office next to the station! What will happen now? One man yells: "Damn—how much change did I receive?" He is also no expert in Romanian currency. I show the coins that I have received to one of the passengers, and my world darkens—I have received less than 500 lei. What is 500 lei worth, damn it all? To hell with the 500 lei! I now have no papers!—What's going to happen? Why did they allow the train to leave before we had finished buying tickets? If the train is already moving, why are they still selling tickets, especially when passengers still need to pick up their papers? Why do they allow such chaos?

"Allow it?"—Someone on the side says calmly and shrewdly: "Allow it? They set it up this way on purpose!"

"But why?"

"Can't you see why? Count the number of passengers who have received the same change as you."

I wise up:

"Is that the reason? Do you mean to say that they do this on purpose?"

"Not only because of the money but also because of the passports."

"I don't understand."

"Money!" (He rubs his finger and thumb). "It is all about kickbacks!"

I get off at Satu Mare station to take a connection—a young man comes up, looks at me, and calls me by name;

"Yes," I reply.

"Sir, you are forbidden from getting off by the police."

"Because of my passport?"

"Yes. You have to go back again to get your papers. Travel without papers is forbidden!"

Now I understand what's going on.

Certain nations require special understanding: Romania is one of them. I only have to pay a 500 lei "entrance fee," so to speak, because the detective who arrested me is—by pure chance—a Jew (perhaps the only Jewish detective in Romania!). I explain to him that I cannot go back, because they are waiting for me in Klausenberg this evening to give a lecture.[5] The young man, who seems a decent sort and knows what's what, solves the problem. He puts in a call to the local Jewish community, who send their secretary, accompanied by another local woman, to the station—and everything is arranged. The frontier office sends my papers on the next train.

Someone who can't do this is simply returned to the border station—or maybe he isn't, if he can "arrange" matters satisfactorily. Romania is such a convenient country—everything can be arranged here—everything, that is, except a lack of change at the ticket booth.

Never have I experienced such a strange and disturbing feeling about being a Jew as now—journeying to Transylvania, now in the new Romania. I see the enormous distance between the two concepts of "homeland" and "politics." I have no hint of desire to get involved in politics, although I cannot escape it. But suddenly, a flash of insight:

Hungary has ruled this land of wonders for about 1,000 years—how many wars have been fought in this region, in how many causes? But now, only one war (not even between Hungary and Romania) has been enough to change the long historical status quo.[6] It would be like the Kursk region being torn from the breast of Russia. And, to rub salt into the wound, Romania has taken the region of the Székely Magyars captive![7] How does the Hungarian saying go? "Dear is the blood of the mighty Székely, the bold / Each drop of their blood is worth more than gold."

A Székely and his wife truly make a splendid-looking people: they have the imposing looks of Wallachian Romanians and the attributes of Mongolian Turans,[8] paired with a Latin influence.[9] From this mixture, you get today's Székely. This is the people whose crowning glory is that greatest of Hungarian poets Endre Ady.[10] The same burning eyes, the same nose—that most tragic of prophetic poets who predicted the devastating destruction of his homeland and the scattering of its wretched peoples, years before the war. Long before the war, Ady lamented the loss of Erdély (Transylvania) (homeland of the Szekely) by their war god Ha dúr:

> Ha-dúr will scatter his people like dust,
> Judgment of a furious God,
> As it was once written in a book,
> By Erdély's ancient, melancholy prophet,
> Searching for kinship with the Jews.[11]

The dreadful national prophecy of an angry prophet, which came true like his other prophecies that, in their time, were seen as the ravings of a lunatic.

Where did his prophecy come from? What induced this awful vision, several years before the war, at a time when the very ideas of war, and the scattering of the proud, secure Hungarian people, were ridiculous, one more than the other?

Why would the proud, ancient Magyar god Ha-dúr suddenly scatter his people, and how did Ady first see and hear the "ancient melancholy" of Erdély's (Transylvania's) prophet?

Even if their fates were similar, why should the Magyar people seek a shared destiny with that most reviled of peoples—the Jews?

I remember once when strong wine loosened Ady's tongue:

"Believe me, my friend, I am my people's Jeremiah—not only because I am sinking into the mud of the same Hungarian prison, but also (and maybe principally) because the terrible words 'I am the man who must bear witness" resonate ceaselessly in my heart.[12] If only I didn't have to announce them again!'"

In the end, he was denied his terrible victory. He died two months before the Social Democratic Republic fell and was replaced by the Hungarian Soviet Republic. A short time later, Ha-dúr scattered his people like the dust of the earth.[13]

I remember another of Ady's astonishing prophecies which, according to my notes, he uttered the morning of 1 May 1909:

"Our exile and your redemption will take place at exactly the same time, my friend: a strange confluence of circumstances indeed. Maybe this is a sign that we share a covenant with you."

In the meanwhile—may the spirit of angry Ha-dúr forgive me—Hungary's destruction won't be softened by any sign of redemption in the foreseeable future.

We arrive in beautiful Klausenburg. The Jews haven't yet received my telegram, so they are waiting at the station on the off chance that I might arrive.

What a rapid train: it arrives before the telegraph!

On the way into town, one of the members of the Jewish Union for Young Girls *Aviva* says with charming bashfulness:

"I know one of your poems by heart."

"Really? Which poem?"

"The little poem 'Two Souls.'"

She murmurs it, and it sounds like the gentle gurgling of a fresh spring of healing water bursting forth from the Transylvanian mountains:

> One sits on the hills of the East,
> Radiant peace reflected in her godly eyes;
> The second sits at the rivers of the West,
> And dreams her dream.
>
> When heaven wishes, if you lift up your eyes,
> You will see two shadows embracing on high,
> And know that the two souls above
> Belong to me.

I look at her suspiciously—is this a coincidence? That particular poem at this particular time?

She has put her finger on all my thoughts in the train—homeland—two homelands—two souls.

"Why are you looking at me like that?"—she asks suddenly.

"You are blindingly beautiful, my dear."

Chapter 20

The Living Scarecrow

"Damn you to hell, my dear friend, what have you been doing 'there' all this time? Seventeen years ago, we were sitting together in Café New York in Budapest, when you suddenly got up and said: 'Excuse me please, I must go out for a minute: I'll be back soon.' You left, but I am still waiting for you to return! What have you been doing 'there' for the past seventeen years?"

Thus, the welcome of one of the friends of my youth: a Hungarian writer who has done hard time in jail for the sin of writing a poem on 1 May 1919 in honor of the socialist revolution.

"My friend, no Hebrew writer has yet merited such 'payment,' for services rendered," he tells me, describing his suffering in jail. "One other man was granted such a 'lecture fee' for a talk he gave on the Mount of Olives in Palestine, but he turned traitor, changed his mind, and subsequently attained a high position.[1] I am not particularly proud of my current honored status, even though I too have gone up in the world. I live like a Hungarian count here.—And you? Have you become a Rothschild yet?"

"Rothschild stubbornly refuses to become a Hebrew writer, and I won't become a Rothschild.—But how did you become a Hungarian 'aristocrat?'"

"Very simple—I have no land to plough, so we are all in the same boat. The Romanian government has simply divided up the land amongst the people without any insight or forethought, so we all starve together."

"Has the Hungarian breadbasket been emptied?"

"What is the 'Hungarian bread-basket' but the region of Transylvania, richer in cereal crops, vegetables, and fruit than any other region in Central Europe?"

"Hell has emptied, not it. On the contrary, it is full to bursting. Travel through the length and breadth of our country, look at the fields and gardens, and know what a clown your God Above is—just like that old Habsburg idiot, who caught one of his servants stealthily licking at his *Kaiserschmarren*. What was his reaction? He 'showed him his ass,' unctuously ushered him to the beautifully laden table, closed the door, and said with royal courtesy: 'Now eat, my dear man, eat to your heart's content.'

Our granaries are full of grain, our gardens exude heavenly fragrance, but farmers are burning their produce. They have no room for it and it cannot be exported. Conquering without war is not sufficient: one must also know how to use the booty—and that doesn't happen here. Our storerooms are full of every type of produce—and we yearn for bread. But at least we share that privilege with the Hungarian aristocracy."

"What about the Jews?"

"The Jews? Brătianu—that cleverest of Wallachians—concentrates all his efforts and talents onto forcing Jews to leave the country.[2] This is a little difficult because Jews don't want to leave a country that forces them out. But the shrewd Wallachian Brătianu says: 'The cow was thin and entered through the narrow gate. Now it has become fat and must be made thinner again, so that it can leave the same way it came.' The cow is certainly becoming thinner, but the bosses are starting to protest: the cow cannot be milked anymore! Now, Romania has become richer with 250,000 more Jews; this is the fly in the ointment of the gift called Transylvania!"

"What gift?"

"Oh, my friend, you people in Asia don't seem to know anything! We have become wiser and know now that there is at least one Cleopatra in the twentieth century. Cleopatra vainly requested the land of Judah from Mark Anthony. But this new Cleopatra has received Transylvania with its 250,000 Jews."

"Which Cleopatra do you mean?"

"That most beautiful of queens who travelled to America and waged a successful campaign: 'I came, I fucked, I conquered!'"

"Who is this new American Mark Anthony?"

"*Nomina sunt odiosa* [names are odious]. A man who had it within his power to play the part of Anthony, to hand out countries as gifts. Romania's war for Transylvania took only one night of whoring."[3]

This conversation is in reality a "short primer" on the political and economic history of Transylvania—that most beautiful of all Central European regions—and its Jews, since the end of the first Word War.[4] A few days ago, I read the words of Miss Constance Drexel, a journalist for the *Chicago Tribune* and member of the Chicago Women's Suffrage Alliance, who accompanied the American delegation as the first American journalist to cover the Versailles Conference and birth of the League of Nations.[5] Everything decided in Paris was done in haste under the pressure of victory, in order to expunge all vestiges of the war as quickly as possible. This was the wrong way: all decisions, such as new borders, should be done carefully, subject to careful revision, and not taken as final unless absolutely necessary.

Under the pressure of victory—Cleopatra's pressure. Drexel did not hear that—even if she had, it would have been after the fact, in other words worthless and without obligation.

Unimaginable lack of talent has been necessary to cause the total economic destruction of Transylvania, this fair land of "Canaan" flowing with milk and honey.

I have travelled the length and breadth of this "land of seven fortress cities" for seven days.[6] A heavenly panorama of dense forests, brooks teeming with fish, majestically flowing rivers, and roaring rapids with waterfalls singing nature's hymn, with countless birds and yellow fields of grain filling the eye from horizon to horizon. Even the mountain districts are covered with grain and vineyards, forests, and fruit trees of every kind.

The grain fields of Transylvania have a special quality: every kind of cereal grows and the fields are surrounded by garlands of flowers. Crop cultivation here is a religious ritual.[7] Each farmer adorns the area around his fields with corn and garden flowers, in which, from mountain or plane, you can read the book of blessings inscribed by God and man. Each field resembles a page decorated with a bounty of colors in the holy chapters of ancient books, ornamented with spectacular, many-hued adornments, with boundless, childlike love.

Fields are weighed down by the golden blessings of corn, wheat, and barley, which has not been harvested for over a month.

"Life is waiting for harvest's song, but it has been struck dumb," a Székely Magyar says to me.[8] "Even our pigs are sick of wheat in their feed. We will have to burn God's blessing."

"Life is waiting for harvest's song." A Magyar calls wheat "life," just as Ukrainian uses one root for both concepts.[9] I remember the verse in Genesis: "And there was no man to work the ground."[10] Surely the aim of man is to till the soil and the object of the land is not to ruin mankind. The entire purpose of crops is, as my grandfather used to say, the song of harvest.

I am travelling by car with another Hungarian Jew on the Romanian side of the new Romanian-Hungarian border near the Maros (Mureş) River, talking about the bad economic conditions in neighboring Hungary.

"I am preparing the subject of a story for you," he says with a little smile, "in a short time, you will see something."

"Why not tell me now?"

"No, because then it would have no effect and I want you to be as furious as I was when I saw it for the first time a week ago."

We drive up a hill—when we go down again, he shows me:

"Do you see the scarecrow on the other side of the river, across the border?"

"Yes, I see it."

A scarecrow waving its arms around.

"Is this a modern electricity-driven scarecrow?" I ask.

"It's certainly modern, but doesn't run on electricity." We stand on the river bank, coming as close to it as possible.

"Hey there, young man! How are you doing?" my friend cries.

The scarecrow turns to us, still waving its hands.

"Thank you! I am doing very well indeed!"

"Well," my friend asks me, "what do you think of this modern invention? My friend, is this not a divine irony? On this side of the border, crops are so plentiful that they have to be burned in order to get rid of them; and over there, a few meters away, a man makes a living as a scarecrow!"

I can hardly believe my eyes.

While he continues, the scarecrow faithfully continues his work, waving his arms, sometimes calling out, to scare birds away.

"This symbol of Europe in the twentieth century should be photographed and sent to the League of Nations! Why should they be surprised by Bolshevik victories on all sides?"

I talk to the scarecrow:

"How much do you earn?"

"Meals and lodging. At first, just standing here, I only earned food. But now, waving my hands, I am also given lodging. I made a new discovery today: using my voice to scare away the birds—for that, I'll ask for money! A pox on them! No voice without money!"

"Why do you only stand in one place?"

"What? I should walk for money?! To hell with him! A scarecrow waving its hands is enough, Right?"

Quite right.

What kind of work do you really do?

"Excuse me, sir, I am a certified scarecrow! Please don't insult me!"

"My apologies, I didn't mean to insult you. But I don't think that you have a lot of work to do. All the fields on this side are full of crops."

"I see that you are not an expert in the politics of Central Europe. The Romanian birds come here and ours fly out of the country, to Romania."—He shows me with his raggedy scarecrow hands. "Birds don't recognize the new peace treaties or borders, and that is strictly forbidden here because it smells of peace!"

"Aha! What is your name? I shout with a voice that has already become hoarse.

"Your honor, I am a raggedy, dry treehouse, from the dynasty of Kufu the First of Egypt, descendant of a Romanov on one side and, on the other, Wilhelm the Last, of the species *homo scarecrowensis*!"

In truth, he is the first of an ancient ruling dynasty of rulers, who has finally found his place. The place doesn't honor the man—just the opposite. But I see that I cannot talk sensibly to him because his language is too allegorical. I cannot even get him to tell me his name, but he seems cultured and enlightened.

On the way back my friend explains to me: he is a man of advanced education, who has gone mad.

I remember the old proverb: "Children and fools speak the truth."

Today I have the great privilege of being detained for an hour by the Romanian police—"on suspicion of being a Bolshevik spy." While I am being questioned, I see the chief of police fiddling with a postcard and constantly looking at it. He shows it to me and poses learned questions:

"Do you recognize this postcard?"

"Yes, I wrote it."

"Who is this Reuben to whom it's addressed?"

"My young friend Reuben, Romanian-born, but who has lived in Tel Aviv for the past few years."

"Why do you write this to him?"

"He is my friend and I wanted to please him by showing that I know a little Romanian."

"Hm—yes."

He hands the postcard to me.

"Please read loudly, so that everyone can hear, what you have written."

I pick it up and read (in bad Romanian):

"Don't lean outside while the train is moving."—"Bureau of Post and Telegraphs."

He interrupts me.

"Please translate."

I do so.

"Now please read everything on the card and translate it immediately."

I continue in halting, bad Romanian, translating each phrase:—"Go fuck yourself." "Washroom with bathroom and tub: for men and women."—"Third-class waiting room."—"*Fumatul interzis* (smoking prohibited)[11]—um—um—um—I am sorry, but I've forgotten that one."

"What do you mean you don't remember?"

"I don't remember."

"So where did you find the expression?"

"Where I found the rest. I saw it written somewhere and copied it."

"Hm. Read further, please."

"I think that this means 'Romanian railroad track.'"

"You say you've forgotten the rest?"

"Yes. I'll try to learn more and remember what I have learned."

"Did you fight in the war?"

I get cold shivers. This is a bad business.—If I tell him that I was a Hungarian officer during the war, he might beat me up, or worse. I decide not to lie, although I know how serious and dangerous this is. What is the meaning of a lie in Romania anyway?

"Yes, I did."

To sidestep the question I know is coming, I add:

"As an officer."

"Officer—hm—good. So if you were really an officer, tell me truthfully on your honor: do you really not know the translation of these words?"

"On officer's honor, I have forgotten."

I am saved from the lion's den. He finds me innocent of suspicion.

"But why did you write down these words specifically?"

"I saw them in the different stations while travelling on the train—so I wrote them down. If I'd had enough spare time to read and study the poems of Octavian Goga, I would have sent my friend one of his poems."[12]

He smiles and holds his hand out to me:

"I'm curious to know what Reuben the artist will have to say about all this. Please send me his response: just a copy after you have received it."

I see at once that he doesn't know Reuben. Would Reuben reply to such a letter?! Especially one that doesn't include an order for one of his paintings? So I escape by the skin of my teeth from terrible suspicion and don't have to share the lot of my fellow Jews in this paradise of persecution!

Finally I find some use in my officer status! Because of this, they believe that I don't know any Romanian. How did they get hold of my postcard?

While travelling to the border, I see my friend the certified scarecrow from afar, waving his raggedy hands at the pacifist birds.

If only the commerce ministries of Romania and Hungary would learn something from the birds' international trade, Romania would not be stifled with too much produce and Hungary would have no need to continue their scarecrow dynasty.

Hungary hasn't had royalist tendencies for a while now.

Chapter 21

The Messiah's Entreaty

To ensure that I do not leave without a good feeling about the security of their Jews, the Romanian government grants me an official visit to one of its border villages. It is a dire vision.[1] The Jews of Sighet in Maramureş County welcome me in a spirit varying between depression and furious silence.[2] The farmers have burned down all the Jewish houses in the village of Borşa.

The entire area is in ferment. During hundreds of years of Hungarian rule, Jews here never knew the meaning of fear. They occupied important government positions—the Sighet chief of police was a Jew for many years. Now, all this has changed.

The Jews, including Zionist leaders, do not look well on a Jewish writer—especially from the Land of Israel—participating in an antigovernment "protest committee." They are probably right: in such "internal" matters outside interference may be dangerous. But I can't leave the area without seeing what is happening there with my own eyes.

A frightening image unfolds: hundreds of men, women, and children scattered in muddy streets, tattered, and torn, scorched by the sun, hungry, and exhausted. Many children sleep in the mud. Zionist leaders have called for urgent assistance in the form of food and clothing. They have urgently summoned several members of the government, led by the minister of Moldavia.[3]

The minister, his officials, and Jewish leaders stand together and look in silent pain and embarrassment at the dreadful scene. On top of the hill, in the Christian part of the village, a group of farmers—at their head a student named Danilo—and their priest stand together, talking and laughing loudly.

The student Danilo and the priest are disciples of the great and valorous Professor Cuza, who inflames a burning hatred of all Romanian Jews.[4]

At the bottom of the hill, silence of the grave—at the top, laughter.

The minister of Moldavia is deeply moved: he takes out his handkerchief and wipes away a tear.

At the top of the hill—bestial laughter.

I obtain an audience with the minister in the town. He welcomes me with a politeness that I did not expect in Romania.

"So I take it that you blame the government for this sorry state of affairs?"

"Yes, Mr. Minister. But please allow me to tell you something: we Jews would be a very stupid people if we had not learned at least one thing from the many pogroms we have suffered through the ages—where a government wishes it, there are no pogroms. There were pogroms during the reign of Tsar Nicholas II and his predecessors, but when the Bolsheviks took power they ceased."

"Sir, you don't know our nation of farmers."

"Excuse me Mr. Minister, but not one farmer has been added to the number present when this region was ruled by Hungary, and not one additional Jew has arrived here from somewhere else. These are the same farmers and the same Jews who have lived peaceably together, without pogroms, for generations. There is nothing else to say."

"Sir, I ask you to wait here a few days more before you make your final judgment."

When we parted he shook my hand and said with emphasis:

"Neither I, nor our young king, wants pogroms."

That is true. Romania's young king, who has caused, and will still cause, many problems for his people and country because of his slightly exaggerated love life, doesn't need more confusion in his country than there is already. This good and sympathetic royal prince has unsettled the people by the scandalous fact that a king's son also has a heart, with blood instead of holy oil coursing through his veins. It is unnecessary to add that he doesn't need more Jewish problems, because of his own affair with a woman commonly known to be Jewish. Only a Jewish woman could have arranged his successful "putsch" to ascend the throne surrounded by his opponents! Just two days ago he arrived by plane from abroad and yesterday every soldier in the army swore a solemn loyalty oath to him. At the hour of anointing, he kissed his wife publicly on the lips "in front of everybody." He won't kiss her again—a public kiss in front of the entire country is a dangerous thing![5] He would never kiss the beautiful Jewess Miss Lupescu in public: in this lies her hold over him![6]

Such a king is, by most accounts and also by monarchical tradition, not inclined to pogroms. However, by the same token if there is a perceived "need" for pogroms, he is not inclined to interfere. His Jewish mistress is much more important to him than Jews in general, and because of this his gendarmerie include bullyboys who incite anti-Jewish violence, because—the Lord preserve us—they've uncovered the dread secret that "the Jews crucified Christ."

In this same region, there is a village named Iod, in which it has been customary for the past several years that each Orthodox Ascension Thursday local farmers attack the village's Jews. In order to avoid harm, Jews leave their homes and hide in the nearby forest. When they return, they find their houses burned, smashed, and broken, plumes of fire arising to the heavens.

Something similar happened again, just before the burning of Borşa. The government sent in the gendarmerie from Klausenberg, but the senior officer took the part of the bullyboys.[7]

When the Jews asked him why he did this, he answered in holy anger: "You deserve everything coming to you! Only today I found out that you Jews crucified our Lord Jesus Christ! Do you dare deny this?!"

I suggest to my friend Dr. Avraham Fried (head of the Sighet Jewish community and one of the original apostles) that he should make an immediate appointment with the minister of Moldavia. He should ask him for heaven's sake to give an order that all Christian schools in Romania teach the children that the Jews crucified Christ! How could they not know this?

What irony—Klausenberg, capital of Transylvania, a city that for generations has given birth to some of the greatest Hungarian writers and artists. The city from which the gospel of Zion went forth to Budapest and the rest of Hungary.

A city in which things have now come to such a pass that the head of the gendarmerie doesn't even know the first thing about Christianity. "The Jews crucified Christ!"

During the days of mourning for the destruction of Borşa, the Jews of Transylvania consider a possible fundraising campaign for *Keren Hayesod*, to settle the victims of Borşa in the Land of Israel.[8] Anyone who knows Sighet recognizes how inconceivable such a question is. Sighet—only a few years ago site of the largest and most pious yeshiva in all Central Europe—center of boycotts and censures of Zionism and everything related to it, where Rabbi Teitelbaum held sway.[9] He used to say:

"I would rather be in hell with Haman the Wicked than share Paradise with 'that so-called doctor'"[10]

The sainted rabbi followed words with actions: it was forbidden for any of the young students studying with him to derive any enjoyment whatsoever from anyone suspected of the least trace of Zionism—even from a Jew as pious as himself, who punctiliously fulfilled every one (even the most minor) of the 613 laws of Orthodox Judaism. His boycott comrades, the other pious Hungarian rabbis, didn't forbid Zionist contributions. On the contrary: "even a pig has its uses."

It happened once that one of his pupils failed the test and committed a grave transgression: he continued to eat his daily bread at the table of a Jew who, in the meanwhile, had brought a Jewish National Fund box into the house. The young Hasid noticed the box while reciting grace after meals. He was seized with convulsions, fell off the chair, and vomited the meal out on the floor. After he recovered, his pious teacher decreed a three day fast.

That was long before the war. Now the head of the Sighet Jewish community is one of the new apostles, and the city's Jewish youth enthusiastically support the Land of Israel and the Hebrew language, which becomes more accepted with every passing day.

One of the members of *Hashomer Hatzair*[11] tells me that many years ago, when Dr. Avraham Fried was still a pupil at the Budapest Gymnasium and returned to his parents' home in Sighet with Zionist publications in his book bag, the pious Rabbi Teitelbaum called him and warned:

"Now see here, young man, while I am alive there will be no talk of Zionism here! Do you understand?"

Gymnasiast Fried replied:

"While you, honored rabbi are still alive? Very good: we are in no hurry." He then fled for his life.

Now, in holy Sighet, they are suggesting that Jews from Borşa are settled in Israel! What has the world come to?

The suggestion is not taken further. A few days ago, a letter is received from one of the Transylvanian families in the Valley of Jezreel, announcing that because of a combination of inaccessible mountains and arid land, they are forced to return to Transylvania.

The tone of this letter is no less frightening and terrible than the destruction in Borşa.

They take me to the house of a Jewish woman more than 100 years old in a tiny Transylvanian village. The hour that I spend with "Grandmother Hadas" teaches me more than all the issues of *Der Veker* combined.[12] She says of the current pogroms and immigration to the Land of Israel:

"Every evening at dusk, our Messiah appears to me, hands raised and spread over us, saying: 'Go, go, go! Emigrate to Israel! Don't stop, even for a moment!' Each time a new anti-Jewish decree appears or there are more pogroms in the Diaspora, He adds the words: 'With all your strength: emigrate with all your strength—do not stop!' Every time a calamity, God forbid, is about to occur in *the Land of Israel itself*, He adds the words: 'For God's sake, do it with all your strength and do not stop.' If, God forbid, someone returns despairingly from the Land of Israel, He appears in mourning garb, sits on the ground, and covers His face without saying a word. When this happens, I fast all that day."

After a long silence, she says:

"Just do not return!—Do not return! Do not block our Messiah's entreaty. God have mercy on me—I am old and have no more strength to fast!"

Chapter 22

My Birthplace's Agony

My birth mother is the Carpathian Valley, stretching lazily on both sides of the Latorica River, which, at least to my childish eyes, resembled the Jordan Valley. For a *cheder* pupil like myself, who dreamt daily that he saw regions of the Old Testament in everything around him: the Latorica really was the Jordan River, just as Munkács was Jerusalem; the clock tower, the Tower of David; nearby Palanok Castle, the Fortress of Zion; the old ruined *beit hamidrash*, the Western Wall; and one of the old beggars—to whom my grandfather always gave double—was Elijah the Prophet.[1]

The little village in which I was born, Ó-Dávidháza, resembled Lod.[2] Thus, I was born in Lod, and the *cheder* in which I studied was Nitzah's attic".[3] Rebs Leib, Yehudah Yizhak, Wolf, and Yaakov Leib the merchant all lived in Lod.

The village non Jews were Canaanites and Perizzites and the gypsies who visited from time to time, dressed in clothes with large copper buttons, were Caftorites, Avvites, Casluhites, Zamzummites.[4]

But now, when I return here from the real Land of Israel, these images dissolve into the mists of childhood fantasy. When I walk the streets of my hometown village, not only do I feel a great spirit of contentment, but more—I feel revenge for my past cruel fate. Look till you burst, friend—my dream has been fulfilled! I have come from the Land of Israel! At least one dream has been realized! Not only have I been there, but I actually live there!

An old farming woman recognizes me:

"As I live and breathe! It's Hadassah's son! Hadassah's son!"

She "takes" me under her care (that is to say, covers me with her apron, embraces me with great compassion, and spits three times):[5]

"Pfu! Pfu! Pfu! How you've grown!"
She looks at me again—and her old, rheumy eyes fill with tears.
"Oy, if only your mother could see you now!—Where do you come from, my boy, America? Oy, if only your mother could have seen you so wealthy!"

If only she knew—not "rich" at all, although she might think so—I remember the nasty red notes from the Tel Aviv income tax office sitting in state on my table for all to see.

I explain to her that I come from the Land of Israel.

"From Palestine? What are you telling me? From the Holy Land? Oy, if only your mother could know that you pray for her soul day and night at the Western Wall near the Temple site! If only she could know!"

"Day and night"—"near the Temple"—I remember the riots near the Temple Mount.

The old woman weeps.

A rich *Prezzite* now lives in the house where I was born.[6]

The house looks at me with its weak window eyes: they look tired and torn, as if painted with deep-blue makeup, laughing like an old whore, wanting to rejuvenate herself, but a little embarrassed by my presence.

The thick, prickly top of the wild pear tree in the garden, whose small sour fruit only ripen around Rosh Hashanah, waves to me.

"Oh—Oh—Oh—since you left me, there is no one to follow your grandfather's directive to pronounce the blessing on new fruit"[7]

Silence in our yard: our dog Hector doesn't run outside to greet me, growling reproachfully: "Where have you been all this time?!" Where is he now? If only I could find his bones—he had such a splendid tail!

I can't stop myself, and call out loudly: "Hector!!"

No answer; when I enter, a rude Canaanite puppy barks at me in the New Hivite language.[8] I answer him in Hebrew, which he doesn't understand. The puppy dominates the late King Hector's realm, sitting on the throne of Zaphnath-Paaneah, barking at me cheekily.[9] Hector would have made mincemeat of this impudent pup!

But Hector is no more. Vanity of vanities, all is vanity.[10] Thousands of years will pass before the eternity that is the great zero—and Hector will never be seen again. How sad eternity is.

I am about to burst into tears.

"You're a sentimental fool!—I hear the voice of the visiting Hebrew writer from faraway Tel Aviv.

"Sentimental? What are you talking about! Tell me, have you any idea what the word 'eternity'—which you use ad nauseam in your poetry—means? What wonderful eternal life has nourished us all—myself, grandfather, Hector, Yossi the parrot, Maria girl of my dreams, Peter, the family of storks living on top of our cowshed, and the wild pear tree—all of us together?! Now only two of us are left: the tree and myself. Old man pear tree is gradually losing his hair and becoming blind—he hardly recognizes me, but still hears my voice. And I—I? A few futile springs have passed.—I am not—I am not 'sentimental.' Where is Hector? Don't you hear that you have a visitor? Where are you, Hector?! Where are my other friends? You don't even allow me the compassionate untruth of an immortal soul after death! Wicked people? Where is Hector? Maria! Peter! Yossi! Yossi!!"

The house's new proprietor invites me into the house where I was born—suddenly I see the white shadow of my grandfather up on the hill, arms outstretched, Hector at his side. He commands me urgently in his strict but tender voice:

"Quick march! Go home to the Land of Israel, whence you came! Quick as you can, little boy!"

I entreat him dumbly: "Just one moment more, Grandpa!"

"No! Do not enter! Our house has no *mezuzah* on its doorpost! Quick march, little boy!"

I hurry out; the Perizzite can't understand why I refuse to come in.

How hard it is to leave the blind, old tree!

The Perizzite accompanies me through the village and shows me the houses and their new occupants:

Instead of "Nitzah's attic," there is a pigsty.

Enough!

I hurry away from the village—the church bell tolls behind me, as if mourning the death of someone important.

There is a single but telling past analogy between the Carpathian Valley and the Land of Israel—between the Dead Sea, lowest and most desolate place on earth, and the Carpathian Valley, poorest and bleakest inhabited spot on earth. Where else in the world do Jews eat corn roasted into cakes on a stove? Where else do the Jews prepare corn mush for

Sabbath instead of real bread? Where else does a Jewish mother prepare a pot of food (beans or potatoes) that must last her and her children an entire week?

Where else do they let out an "attic" for the Sabbath for one heller (a tenth of a Palestinian mil)?[11]

Instead of increasing and developing, possessions shrink in value from generation to generation. Take Mr. Benjamin Kaidanov, for example: he himself was a wealthy man; his sons not so rich, but still well to do. But his grandsons have come down in the world—they are now butchers.

Interesting things can be seen in Munkács today: silken *yeshiva* students walking aimlessly around the streets, tallit and tefillin bags under their arms, at the noonday hour; hale, healthy people walking around aimlessly, without work or purpose; in the *beit hamidrash*, half study out of pure custom, the rest play the "political" fool—they insult the *mitnagdim* and curse the Zionists with bell, book, and candle.[12] They are blind to the privilege of witnessing a holy, centuries-old prophetic dream coming to fruition before their eyes, and their imagined terrible Zionist activities exceed the fantasies of even an H. G. Wells.[13]

"Zionists play football and rear pigs in the courtyard of the Western Wall!"

"Zionists cover their horses with blue tallitot!"[14]

"Zionists travel in wagons on Yom Kippur, which falls on the Sabbath, eating camel meat with bare heads, loudly reciting grace after meals."

"Zionists shave off the beards of learned scholars in the streets, and sell the hair to Arabs to make winter clothes."

"Zionists teach their children to make snowmen that look like the wise men of Israel, so they can melt them with their urine."

"Zionist youths lie in wait for Rabbi Sonnenfeld and hurl abuses at him in the Jerusalem streets."[15]

"To blind the eyes of the righteous, Zionist *mizrachis* build houses of study, grow childrens' sidelocks, set them in front of the *Gemara*, and make profane and blasphemous conversation with them in front of the Living God."[16]

Where else in the world do those concerned with Israel's happiness and welfare have such visions?

The director of this heavenly orchestra is the saintly, pious, gaonic rabbi, Shaker of Mountains, Light of the Lord, Purest Heavenly Candle, our pure, devout teacher and rabbi of the entire diaspora Chaim Elazar Spira, may he merit a long and good life.[17]

The all-wise Rabbi Spira, head of the Munkács *beth din*, who excommunicates *Agudat Yisrael* with bell, book, and *shofar* blast because they dare to settle in the Holy Land and sing songs of Zion, may the All-Merciful protect us from such blasphemy.[18]

Who excommunicates all Zionists, singularly and collectively.

And that spawn of the devil, Colonel Wedgwood.[19]

And Lord Balfour, who forces the issue of a Jewish homeland and, by doing so, delays the coming of the Messiah.[20]

And the entire British government, which delays the redemption of the Jewish people.

And anyone who doesn't belong—at any time—to a party other than his own agrarian party.

The saintly, all-wise rabbi who had to pay a hefty fine for spitting on the coffin of one of the *mitnagdim* during his funeral. Who was the dead *mitnaged*? Unbelievable, but true: his childhood teacher, a great scholar, who had died at an advanced age. His former pupil spat on his coffin when it passed by in the street on its way to burial. What piety! What godliness!

The holy leader, his relatives, and followers post the following announcement:

> In the Name of the Lord:
>
> *Jews, have mercy!*
>
> For many years, our holy Rabbi Chaim Elazar Spira, may he merit a long and good life, has waged war in the name of true Jewish Orthodoxy![21]
>
> He stands like an iron wall and fights against apostasy, despite great rabbinical opposition. He has succeeded in replacing the existing Orthodox office in the Ruthenian section of Carpathia with a new one with him in charge.[22]
>
> *As befits a leader of Israel*
>
> > To our great sorrow, Munkács has, for the past several years, become a town of refuge for false prophets—that well-known gang led by the ------" (the rabbi of Belz), whom Rabbi Spira denounced to the authorities, and had expelled from town "because he has turned Judaism into an eternal heap of ruins."[23]

However, after we got rid of that nuisance, his hypocritical disciples remained—everyday they shed the blood of our sainted rabbi, and their ------ looks on and does nothing. After that, the Spinker (better called "the Shtinker") [the rabbi from Spinka] has settled here to undermine the authority of our rabbi and teacher, whose precepts and decisions we are bound to follow—the Spinker's household members make their own "court" here, Heaven forbid.[24] If that were not bad enough, a second person has arrived, who calls himself the Ziditshover Rebbe and acts the same way.[25] Our master and teacher, may he merit a long and good life, complains loudly and publicly in the synagogue that all this is making this a town full of idolaters.[26]

The time has come for countrywide elections. Our rabbi and teacher has organized a Jewish party, headed by the attorney Dr. Sandor Kroó, in order to preserve our faith, kick the hypocritical majority out of town, and strengthen the power of our rabbi and teacher. The abovementioned party leader has taken this arduous work upon his shoulders, with both of his brothers acting as guarantors: 1) Mr. Beinesh Kroó, president of our community, who has worked as hard as he can to banish the Spinker and the Ziditshover and close their *yeshivot* and "houses of learning," which rightly, despite the best efforts of wicked Jews acting against the will of our rabbi and teacher, have not yet succeeded. 2) His second brother Mr. Ya'akov Kroó, longtime director of the National Health System, who works for the good of all. Our rabbi and teacher, may he merit a long and good life, wishes him to become the Jewish mayor of Munkács. However, as a punishment for our sins, the wicked who call themselves the Hasidim of Belz, Spinka, Ziditshov, Vishnitza, Sighet, and many other towns, unite at every opportunity to weaken our sacred strength.[27] Now they have attracted many minor rebbes, who are—to our rabbi and teacher, may he merit a good and long life—as important as a corn husk, but are carrying rabbinical correspondence between communities urging them to vote for list number eleven, led by the known agitators Mendel Gutman and Mosheh Tatshar. May the Lord judge them for making such an abomination in Israel! Against the will of the greatest man of his generation! This is the work of ------" (referring to Rabbi Dushinsky, leader of *Agudat Yisrael* in Jerusalem) "and the *Oberlerner* from Chust, who is campaigning to make Mosheh Tatsher a delegate."[28]

Doesn't everyone know that Dr. Sandor Kroó is much more qualified to be a delegate than Gutman and Rosenfeld? These evil hypocritical Hasidim confirm the Orthodoxy of their own candidates, declaring that, by contrast, Dr. Kroó and his colleagues desecrate the Sabbath and eat pork. Even if this were true, does a Jewish delegate have to be kosher? No!—all he needs is intellect! To sit and eat with Polish noblemen, who are government ministers, and by so doing improve the lot of all Jews. Only the Kroó family are capable of doing this. Do they really want Gutman and Rosenfeld, with their beards and sidelocks? Our president is also not a kosher Jew. Exactly because he frequents coffeehouses, he accomplishes what our rabbi and teacher, may he merit a long and good life, requires from us (to expel the rebbe of Belz). Soon he will succeed, and his brother will be voted in as a delegate, so that he can expel the Spinker and his hundred horse-tailed yeshiva foals.[29]

On the Sunday noted below, our rabbi and teacher, may he merit a long and good life, and Dr. Sandor Kroó will deliver talks outlining their program in the Great *Beit Hamidrash* in Munkács, clearly stating that all good Jews must vote for Dr. Sandor Kroó and that all wicked rabbis, who speak with forked tongues and do the opposite, are "cursed, because they do not uphold the words of the law by carrying it out."[30]

We implore followers of other rebbes not to allow themselves to be seduced by leaders who don't seek the truth. They are false, idolatrous prophets, who wish to lead you astray from the true Jewish path. All Jews who really seek the truth are followers of our master, rabbi of the entire Diaspora, the Holy and Pious Chaim Elazar Spira, may he merit and long and happy life, and will vote for the top of the ticket, Dr. Sandor Kroó. Jews, have mercy on our rabbi and master, may he merit a long and happy life, who is persecuted on all sides by a clique of evil men who call themselves Hasidim! Assist the victory of his chosen representative and protector, thus speedily leading to full redemption by his plenteous mercy and righteousness!

(Signed) The Hasidim of Munkács

In the name of the Jewish republican party administration.

This is only one of the many billets-doux of the Munkács Hasidim, from the establishment of the saintly and pious Rabbi Chaim Elazar Spira, may he merit a long and happy life. The proclamation is extremely interesting for many reasons. It comes from the "holy chief rabbi of the entire Diaspora," and expressly permits politics to trump religious orthodoxy, allowing eating of pork and drinking nonkosher wine with Polish noblemen. The aim of the organizing political party is to close all houses of learning and kick out the *bokhers* with their "long horses tails."

I ask you—where else in the world is the darkness of hypocrisy as black as this?

Another proclamation, this time against the Munkács Jewish gymnasium:

> *Warning!*
> Concerning entrance into Zionist dens of iniquity!
> We hear with greatest anguish that the leprous rash emanating from the cursed Zionist lair (punishment for our many sins) has allowed the devil to successfully place an empty-headed Jewish abomination as head of schools and gymnasia to entice young souls into heresy and apostasy, etc. In 1922, we already issued a strict ban against attending these schools which are full of heretics, etc. Wherever you call yourselves Jews, guard yourselves from their dens of iniquity. The Torah itself commands you not enter them. Have pity, have mercy on your sons and daughters—the last remnants of our people—so as not, God forbid, to lose them from amongst us. Do not go to these dens of iniquity—where the Zionist heresy is spewed out![31] Those who avoid those terrible places will avoid shame and disgrace, improve their reputations, and bring blessings and goodness upon themselves.
> Munkács, this Sabbath eve of the Hebrew year 5686 (1925).
> Signed by five rabbis and *beth din* heads.

We must conclude that the express purpose of the Munkács Jewish gymnasium is to "entice the souls of pupils into heresy, etc. etc."

The tyrannical bitterness of the "saintly and gaonic rabbi" must be comprehended in all its fury, to fully understand the obstacles lying in the way of those laboring here in the darkness of Egypt, to establish a Hebrew high school, in which "Satan holds sway."

It is obvious that several apostles are at work here, men who stand, like a mighty fortress in the middle of local political currents, eyes directed upwards: toward Hebrew education.

This storm of local and national politics tosses even the strongest to and fro, devouring the national will. Political leaders couldn't care less about principles: for them the national idea which they espouse, and for which they fight, is nothing but a ladder to reach the parliament in Prague. Of course, some of these "lion cubs" are "converts by coercion," unconnected to—and even opposing—any national Jewish ideal and Hebrew culture. They are "allowed" to be voted in as Zionists, just so long as they get the necessary number of votes, when necessary.[32]

But even such as these cannot stop the flow of progress. Munkács and its surroundings have been cursed by a Satanic decree, giving rise to a new generation unafraid of the Hasidic Savanarola and his proclamations.[33]

It happened by chance that, in this exact town, "Spiraville," a young pioneer from the Land of Israel was visiting his parents. He arrived in the *beit hamidrash* of the Hasidic tyrant on *Tisha Be-av*, and saw his mouthpieces and cronies joining others of their ilk playing like mischievous babies, throwing thistle heads at each other.[34] On seeing this, the pioneer rose and cried out to the gaonic leader:

"You make me a laughingstock for mourning the two lost Temples. You should be ashamed of yourselves, making sport of one the greatest national disasters in the history of the Jewish people! May your names and memories be blotted out, like Amalek![35] You dare pour scorn on Zionism and Zionists, accusing us of desecrating the Western Wall! Pfui!"

He spat on the floor, and left.

Deathly silence in the *beit midrash*.

The saintly rabbi stood, eyes bulging and mouth wide open. In any other case of such insolence, the Hasidim would have gutted the arrogant man like a herring. But this time was different.

An old man all the while silently observed the scene: no one knew who he was and he has since disappeared from history: he must have been one of the itinerant beggars. He rose and said:

"Happy are we to have merited hearing God's reproach. This was surely Elijah the Prophet Himself speaking!" He walked up to the Holy Ark, kissed the curtain, and left, weeping quietly.

A young man with short trousers, bare knees, and unkempt hair blowing in the wind. Certainly no one has seen Elijah the Prophet in such a guise.

If he did, it would have had to have been in Munkács.

The saintly rabbi continued his lamentations, making sure to include mourning for Munkács in his *Tisha Be'av* mourning for Zion.³⁶ An added tragedy had occurred: Munkács Zionists had succeeded in naming one town street after Yehudah Halevi, a second after Bialik.³⁷

"Woe unto us that we have been so defiled!" The pious, learned rabbi wept crocodile tears. "Two streets in our town, and in the Nation of Israel, have become a ruin and a desolation!³⁸ One bears the name of the heretic Bialik, the other that of his brother-in-law the heretic Yehudah Halevi!"

A sensational discovery in the annals of the Jewish people! Bialik is Yedudah Halevi's brother-in-law! Amazing!³⁹

Chapter 23

The Holy Operetta[1]

The God of Clowns has reserved a special privilege especially for me: a wedding in the sacred confines of the Holy Light's private dwelling.[2] The wedding of his only daughter to a silken yeshiva *bokher* saved, may God protect us, from the clutches of the evil Zionists: a highborn biblical scholar, son of one of Poland's most important rabbis.[3]

Once the agreement was sealed, and the wedding confirmed, Rabbi Spira's "ministry of finance" went to work, enlisting the assistance of the entire civilized world for the good of the wedding, which must be held with "pomp and circumstance such as the world has never seen." "Taxes" began to be levied on Hasidim, cronies, and those that belonged to neither category. In an "emergency," why would the Light of the Diaspora—may he live a long and good life—and his cronies examine the source of money? Does it matter that it comes from those he had previously cursed, excoriated, and excommunicated?—The source is unimportant, only money matters. Their rabbi and teacher—long may he live—is, thank god, a modest man. He relinquishes his honor and that of the Holy Torah, and defiles his pure hands with the money of Zionists, *mitnagdim*, and other impure demons—may God spare us—but only to encourage Torah study and observance as if at the *hilula* of a saintly rabbi, obligating rich and poor to contribute together, using their money for holy purposes, as it is written: "silver and gold purify *mitnagdim*," etc.[4] In this way, his ghoulish emissaries dressed in sacred garb went from house to house, using a mixture of fear and authority to cow the entire area, collecting a fortune for the "wedding of the century," as they pronounced it, words dripping with holiness. Week after week, Munkács/Mukachevo and the surrounding region echoed with premarital party tumult. All the miserable, poverty-stricken villages, sick with nutritional deficiencies from a diet only of corn, wailing with want, for whom a piece of bread (that is to say, corn or wheat) was an occasion for celebration and only granted to a privileged few. All these dismally poor people collectively opened their "granaries" and donated generously to the Moloch from Munkács, who cast a spell over these primitive wretches terrified of his holy curse.[5] They were even more afraid of him than illiterate superstitious Ruthenians are of the Virgin Mary and all the saints combined. The torrent of terrible curses and obscenities emanating from Rabbi Spira's *beit midrash* pulpit hung in the air like a gleaming sword of Damocles over everyone in the valley: Carpathian Jewish women shook their aprons out and searched their rags for money: they even stole to be able to bring gifts to their great teacher's daughter's wedding to avoid falling under the terrible curse that he proclaimed in public:

"If a woman is impregnated, conceives, and is about to give birth—but follows false gods, is drawn to those who hate us, and does not donate all she can to raise a pure sacrifice to the Lord—the curse of the Lord will come upon her and her unborn offspring! She will surely miscarry in great pain and, if perchance she does give birth, her cursed offspring will die like a dog before the mother's eyes and receive a donkey's burial outside the city walls in shame and disgrace![6] Amen! Amen!"

To "raise a pure sacrifice before the Lord"—was, of course, the wedding table in the house of the sainted Rabbi Spira!

Which woman can withstand the fear of God, endanger her life and that of her unborn child, or a child that is already born? How can she not wish to prevent the baby from dying like a dog and being buried like a donkey outside the city walls because of her guilt?

This sword of Damocles saw gifts carried in from the poor to the rabbi's house for weeks. Theft in Carpatho-Ruthenia is not counted as one of the world's worst transgressions. However, even by their standards, a real plague of theft—from poultry to objects of every shape and description—broke out before the Great Event: utensils from stores, provisions, cloth face masks, heifers from the cowshed, even baby clothes and cradles in honor of the saintly rabbi's future heirs—may many be born from this blessed union! Receipts from "tax and customs" included everything known to man, all for that most godly and modest of men, the Holy Light, thanks be to God.

The wedding day finally arrives. The streets of Munkács are jammed with thousands of people, who have streamed in from all parts of Carpatho-Ruthenia for the privilege of witnessing this great event. Journalists, photographers, cinematographers—all invited by the great Hasid to grant them his blessing and—by the way—negotiate the price for a photography permit. He promises that he will give of himself—in other words, "the radiance of his holy countenance, which no son of man has yet been permitted to photograph." One photographer is cunning enough to actually extract a photograph fee from the Sage of Munkács, by hinting at the strict prohibition against photographing an Orthodox Jew. The reporter—Munkács born—receives in effect bribe money.—It takes one piece of iron to blunt another!"[7]

All this hustle and bustle is not for nothing, of course. This wedding is of such importance that it justifies loading the bride's marriage table so high that gifts overflow into other rooms, rendering the original large gift hall invisible. Even gifts that expressly transgress negative Torah commandments are present! The Holy Light's commandments trump everything! Crowds stand jam-packed in the streets of the town and its suburbs, in offices and stairs with a view, on roofs, at windows, on trees, rocks, telephone and telegraph poles, Suddenly the sound of solemn *shofar* blasts are heard in the distance, a proclamation in the form of a symphony of sounds in solemn harmony, as if shouting for joy from the castle turrets, for all to hear: she's coming![8] Then—miracle of miracles—something than no man on earth expects to see: we are privileged to witness with our own eyes! Jewish hearts expand and overflow with unheard of ecstasy—a troop of horsemen—cavaliers on spectacular, galloping horses. Riders dressed in splendid colors, uniforms as befit a king's bodyguard, glittering in the sunlight with precious stones of the high priest's breastplate: rubies, topaz, and emeralds; garnets, sapphires, and diamonds; opals, agates, and amethysts; aquamarine, onyx, and jasper—all set in gold, with gold-encrusted buttons, buttonholes, hooks, and flowers.[9] They blow golden and silver *shofars* and trumpets, and the three ritual *shofar* blasts resound everywhere—*tekiah, shevarim, teruah*—as directed by the Holy Spirit. Everything—singing and accompaniment—is molded into a heavenly symphony of praise, merged into a reverent prayer directed to our teacher, the Hasid of Hasidim, repeated at various times by the assembled prayerful audience.

Each man begins with the six introductory psalms to the morning service; each man reciting his section loudly, and gradually the pieces of individual passages join together: first to second, second to seventh, seventh to twenty-second, resulting in a sacred confusion of riotous exaltation. The first man bursts out: "What is our strength, what is out heroism?";[10] the second replies: "His delight is not in the strength of the horse";[11] the fourth claps his hands with joy: "Terror and dread will fall on them";[12] the seventy-first praises thankfully: "You have redeemed us from the house of slavery";[13] the forty-fifth explains; "And every firstling of an ass you shall redeem with a lamb";[14] the twelfth prays devotedly: "Many openings and hollows";[15] the thirtieth asserts: "We do not know what to do."[16] The rabbi honors them with words of consolation: "I wash my hands in innocence."[17] One of his Hasidim replies: "In fact, urine may well serve this purpose!"[18] This carries on until half the day has passed— in holiness and purity, poetry and singing accompanied by trumpeters on fiery horses galloping together. Behind this glorious column—the king finally appears, "the enlightened one from on high," the great rabbinical Sage of Sages, head of the entire Munkács diaspora, in glorious person, sitting in Elijah's holy chariot, in sacred contemplation, turning his holy countenance to the impertinent dogs and *mitnagdim*—crushed and eaten up with envy—bestowing holy smiles upon photographers and those being photographed alike, so as to give the image of his radiant face to the whole world, and raise the normally idolatrous theatergoing public to sanctity.[19]

After him—may God preserve him—units of his royal bodyguard, keepers of his court, follow in royal majesty, followed by the carriage of bride and groom, ushers, and bridesmaids, their enormous baggage train, both sets of in-laws, relatives, and all the Hasidim and God-fearing folk of the Munkács Jewish community. The procession of common folk flows behind them like a river in awe and reverence of the Sage of Sages, dancing as if escorting Sabbath the bride, with inspiration from both upper and lower worlds.

Happy the eyes that have witnessed all this!

Happy the eye of the Jew who is privileged to see, in its original splendor and glory, the magnificence of Jerusalem's king of Carpatho-Ruthenia, who has changed, overnight, exile to redemption, slavery to freedom, mourning to festivity, and darkness to great light.[20] But there is another side, as reported by those impertinent dogs, personified in the bribed reporter—may the Lord blot out his name and memory for eternity—who, in the garbage he calls a newspaper, has laid bare the soul of the land, with his forked tongue:

> On Rabbi Spira's orders, wedding organizers hired all the play and operetta costumes and musical instruments from the surrounding theaters—paying cash on the nose. They then dressed up the Hasidic youths and silken *bokhers* in the rabbi's yeshiva and placed them on emaciated gypsy nags to create the horse guard escort of the rabbi's court. The young boys stuck their sidelocks behind their ears, and the rabbi gave permission to cut all beards—even sidelocks—so as to fulfill the mitzvah of increasing the praise, splendor, and glorification of the Torah.

Someone who has not seen this holy "spectacle" has never experienced a sacred operetta. Only the non-Jews present quietly suppressed their laughter, and left the tumult, shaking their heads with a whisper of compassion: "So these are your great ones, O Israel!" One of Rabbi Spira's opponents let the words slip out: "In memory of Israel's destruction."

One cannot know what is greater in this blessed valley of the Carpathians: the wretched poverty, or—perhaps even worse—the spiritual darkness.

Those same Carpathians, whose soul Ilya Ehrenburg and Ludwig Renn thought they had penetrated and described as they thought that it was.[21] What a mistake—they never witnessed this wedding: they didn't see anything. They also didn't see:

How a daughter of Israel, helped by her young children, buries her dead bastard infant in the garden behind the house. To ensure than none open their mouths to tell the father, she cuts off their ear lobes as a warning.

How one of the Hasidim suddenly disappears from the synagogue on Yom Kippur between the afternoon and concluding prayers—to steal his neighbor's fat goose, aided by his wife.

How a Hasid's son sets fire to the village cowshed to chase away the mourners at the body of the love of his life. When alone with her corpse in the house, he embellishes to her what he has done: "Look how the Jews set one another's houses on fire—just because of envy and needless hate."

How the old Hasid of over eighty years old kicks his seventy-six-year-old wife outside so she will not disturb him from screwing the *shikseh* milkmaid.[22]

How—how—

When Itzik-Elye, imprisoned fifteen years ago for murdering a rich farmer and stealing his money, is let out of jail, he—a murderer and thief—is amazed at how good conduct has been corrupted in the village of his birth and its surroundings.

The cradle of my childhood, groaning in an agony of confusion and distress from all possible indecencies listed by police detectives against the bums and garbage of mankind. People who have never in their lives sent a letter without evil rumors and news of corruption—about someone who died a strange death, someone who divorced his wife, lost in court, sickened with a fatal disease, was thrown into jail, etc. Never a single good word, ever.

All his life, my grandfather stood in this valley of sorrow, like a living conscience, trying to convince his brethren of their transgressions. Before his death, he said:

"The nation has to give rise to an Ahab in the form of a community head or rabbi, and also a prophet of rebuke."[23]

Well, half of the prophecy has come to pass: Ahab has appeared in the guise of a teacher and pedagogue, an exalted sage. But the prophet is late in coming, and has not yet appeared. In place of a pit, punishment awaits this modern-day Jeremiah within the pages of a Jewish newspaper.

Woe to the person who knocks on the seventy-seven pillars of Carpatho-Ruthenia!

Let a Hebrew writer dare to touch, even in the smallest way, on any of their institutions and their deficiencies—at once the Zionist newspapers emblazon the words:

"Be very careful of the Hebrew writer!"

The objections of educated Zionist youth are of no use. The Zionist editor who sits in his comfortable office hundreds of kilometers away from this valley of hell has no idea about what is happening in the Carpathians, where fear of God replaces common humanity, and rules in two forms: the Hasidim call it religion, the *mitnagdim* call it nationalism.

How does the old saying go?

You can't make a silk purse out of a sow's ear.

Chapter 24

The Canaanite Servant

I report this matter without explanation.

A certain Jew from the town of Uzhhorod[1] near my suffering birthplace, published the following announcement in the newspaper:

> Servant offer:
> Life has robbed me of everything and I have no more strength to fight for my daily bread. I am prepared to sell myself as a servant to someone who will give me the opportunity to support my family and not see them in constant despair.[2] I am an educated man of thirty-seven, previously employed in an "intelligent profession." I am qualified for all manner of work, from servant to private secretary and wood-cutter. Please contact the editor under "Canaanite servant."

The words "Canaanite servant" indicate that the writer of the message is a Jew. The letter cannot be translated into a known European language, but the facts are glaringly European.

Chapter 25

Spain the Healer

I have read in the newspapers that the Spanish republican government has arranged a program to encourage Jews to immigrate to their country. It only applies to merchants and those with a profession or trade "capable of injecting new blood into Spain's moribund trade and industry." The ministry of trade has sent a special delegation to Rusinski (Carpatho-Ruthenia) to prepare Jewish immigration from this dirt-poor region to Spain at the earliest possible opportunity. The delegation is headed by Spanish representative Unamuno, who has recently written a newspaper article about it.[1]

> Successive royalist governments have allowed our industrial and trade situation to deteriorate catastrophically. We, the people of the Spanish Republic, wish to rectify this situation by encouraging talented Jews to immigrate to our country. We are well aware that the word "Spain" elicits a negative response in Jewish hearts, because of the tragic memory of the Jewish expulsion at the end of the Middle Ages. But we, out of a desire to educate our people in a spirit of humanity and progress, will heal this wound. Up to now, with a quiet but considered approach, we have successfully helped 180 Jewish families from Yugoslavia immigrate to our country. We have settled them in different parts of the country: Madrid, Valencia, Saragossa, Bilbao and Granada. We emphasize that this is not an issue of sentimentality; our aim is not to care for impoverished Jews or correct injustices perpetrated by our ancestors during the Inquisition. Our aim is purely altruistic, but we hope that our action—whose implementation combines our needs with those of Jews, who because of

poverty and overcrowding cannot exercise their talents where they are—will be well received by world Jewry.

In addition to men of industry and commerce, we also wish to encourage the immigration to our country of small business owners and artisans, who will also help improve our lagging economy.

How will the Europe of barbarians respond to this civilized gesture? Will it permit Spain to desecrate the "national ideal"?

Chapter 26

Charoset[1]

His Nastiness, the Holy Gaon from Munkács has established an extensive school system throughout Rusinski and Slovakia, the two areas of the Carpathians adjacent to the High Tatra Mountains. If it were possible to collect all the hot air spewed out by these gaons (and which rabbi is not a gaon?) against Zionism, and also against each other, a lexicon of unparalleled value would result.[2] Formerly, a rabbi who cast an evil eye on the livelihood or honor of his friend would at least look for some sort of pretext, or flowery phrase, to conceal his intention. For instance, he'd find something new in the Torah, and put his own personal interpretation on the passage's direct, allegorical, derived, or secret meaning, proving without any possible doubt that rabbi so-and-so, rabbinical authority so-and-so, is the most impure of the impure, a biblical and rabbinical ignoramus, and a thief to boot.[3] Meanwhile, he would express his sadness in 1001 languages for his "sorrowful duty to make a derogatory, but true, remark about a fellow member of the house of Israel. But, to tell the truth, what can be done when—as punishment for our many sins—a boor and transgressor is found in our midst?" When I was still a child people still had a kind of courtesy, and fear of what non-Jews would say.—But today? Today—their real intentions are revealed, their masks stripped off, violence is permitted, and the great ones of Israel lie, slander, curse, and insult, with high-sounding rhetoric (as befits educated men), take revenge, and bear grudges like slithering snakes. All this from the depths of their ultra-Orthodox souls.

They don't wrap themselves in cloaks of self-serving holiness to investigate the minutiae of whether *kashrut* laws are diligently adhered to.[4] No: for these learned sages, their domain of biblical exegesis relates to "*kashrut* in manufacture of toothpaste, which has to adhere to the strictest possible rules; soap, which is permitted for use even before a ceremonial meal; shoe polish, produced under strictest supervision of the head of the *beth din*—may he merit a good and long life—meticulously preventing even a hint of anything forbidden, God forbid, in its manufacture."

I read an announcement somewhere that the Paris king of cosmetics, such as face powder and rouge, Mr. Coty, makes sure that all his products are made "under strictest rabbinical supervision.[5] This assures that the daughters of Israel use only strictly kosher products. God forbid that their eyeshadow or lipstick should contain anything forbidden." As it is written: "Charm is deceptive, and beauty is fleeting; but a woman who fears the Lord is to be praised"; "It will be pleasant in their ears, and they will be blessed for it, Amen."[6] Coty and the rabbi from Munkács: two peas in a pod. The rabbi who infuses the "fiery crusaders" with his spirit of piety and holiness, and the rouge-and-eyeshadow king, who provides holy female soldiers in the battle against the current crop of heretical rabbis, and against Zionism.

Young Zionist maidens—who call themselves pioneers, may the All-Merciful protect us—are strictly prohibited; they are excommunicated, reviled, subject to the vilest curses and barred from entering the woman's section in the synagogue—God forbid. But Orthodox maidens and self-righteous young women are allowed to dye their hair, powder themselves, pile on the makeup, and dance the Charleston and Dakota bare-legged.

Like attracts like: wild Europe, and wild but pious and gaonic rabbis, who have turned Czechoslovakia into a bubbling cauldron; Hasidim beat each other, pluck each other's beards out, denounce each other to the government beneath, and excommunicate each other to the All-Highest above; Hottentots attacking each other with spears. But, while European Hottentots have certain borders which they do not cross, our Jewish Hottentot brethren spew part of their venom across borders, if the need arises. No government on earth would levy import taxes on such rabbinical products as proclamations, prohibitions, curses and insults of all sorts, and excommunications. Everything is as it should be, God is in his Heaven, and all's right with Israel.

In the Carpathian-Tatras portion of walled-in Slovakia, righteous Munkács on its eastern border—which proscribes the establishment of the Land of Israel out of *reverential awe*—and holy Pressburg in the west, which does the same thing, but in the name of Torah—a Jewry exists, which with the correct leader could hasten our redemption by several years.[7] It is difficult to describe what the concept "Land of Israel" means to our brethren here. Amongst the crowds of simple folk, and also those who are well-to-do, a new Israel-oriented youth has arisen, which contains the seeds of endless blessings for our land and ourselves. These youth are ten times more valuable because for them the land of Israel is a refuge for their idealistic souls, full of deep disgust for immoral, barbarous Europe. They have an even deeper hatred for the costume party represented by fashionable assimilation, which has been going on for generations and is only recently being revealed in its true colors. This new generation has a right to take its place at the top of the Jewish ladder, amongst influential landowners, victorious army generals, high government bankers, ministers, and officials, great and small. These Jews have over the years—and this is not a joke—included highly placed, influential priests whose families have, for various reasons, been baptized or apparently baptized.

I emphasize the above in order to explain:

A person's self-respect doesn't depend only on his private feelings. It is also a collective question, whether he is an integral part of the nation as a whole. Whenever I see a Jew who stands on the minutest point of honor, makes sure he sits next to Bialik, photographed reverently facing east, or is voted onto a committee where he can be of no possible use, I immediately examine his family and the Jews from his town and the country from which he comes.[8] This pathological lust for respect is typically Jewish: Jews search for rehabilitation not only in what they were never in a position to do until now—for example sit at the same table with a high officer—but also in what their nation has not yet been able to provide—a place of honor for Jews at table with princes and potentates. Herzl has cited the Jewish thirst for status, as one of the main reasons for redemption in the Land of Israel.[9]

This is not only a desire for respect, but the well-known Dostoyevskian principle: a desire to rule.[10] The desire for respect may often be absurd and grotesque, but it does no harm. By contrast, the desire to rule is potentially dangerous to the community. The idea of an "upstart on horseback" is destructive even when it seems constructive.

The Jews of Slovakia and Rusinski, despite the poverty in Carpatho-Ruthenia, want nothing to do with this "respect." In fact, it has nauseated them from the first moment the spirit of "redemption" touched them. This explains the fanaticism of the followers of *Brit Shalom*, which is really the extreme, exaggerated wing of those who completely renounce honor and exercise of authority.[11]

My hatred for political parties does not blind me to reality. It is no coincidence that I couldn't find a single member of the pioneers-in-preparation of *Hashomer Hatzair* in Slovakia and Rusinski, who hasn't abandoned the possibility of an organized home life—regardless of whether their families were rich or poor.[12] It must be borne in mind that poverty in Carpatho-Ruthenia (in effect a Mandated territory of Czechoslovakia), is much worse than in Slovakia, where it is hard to find a Jewish pauper in need of medical care.[13] *Oberlander* Jews have lived comfortable lives for generations, in all the usual trades and professions.[14]

Parents turn to me with anguished pleas: for God's sake, save their children from this madness: they are leaving their comfortable parental home, their studies, security, and a shining future! And look at what their sons are doing? They are at the preparatory stage, doing slave labor, like installing and cleaning municipal toilets, and making do with four crowns a day for food.

Four crowns—when one Palestinian pound buys 165 crowns!

In the middle of twentieth century Europe!

Like, during the era of civilized Rome—monks "immigrated" to—and some were born in—isolated monasteries in the middle of the Libyan and Egyptian desert, like Paul of Thebes.[15]

Today—in the middle of civilized Europe—pioneers are preparing to emigrate to Palestine, to become modern-day anchorites living in the middle of the Canaanite desert.

Tanks, airplanes, Nobel Prizes, Rodin's art—even Vatican Radio—are of no use to ancient Rome.[16]

War chariots, circuses, amphitheaters—not even the Peace Palace in the Hague, the glorious statues of Zeus, the Palace of Athena and Venus, daubed by Coty with red paint, and decorated with all Barbara Gould's art—none of these can save Europe.[17]

Moses atop the pyramids.

Jesus atop the Capitoline Hill.

Herzl atop the Tower of Babel.

Did Herzl ever dream of a new religion?

Even Moses our teacher never dreamt of such a thing: all he wanted was to redeem his small nation from the yoke of Egyptian slavery.

Even Jesus the young yeshiva *bokher* didn't dream of a new religion: he just took the suffering of his small nation on his shoulders—suffering under the "terror" of Rome and the "blindness" of Judah.

Every crazy laugh directed at (or in the name of) Heaven is followed by the voice of the Lord from the human heart.

The old beggar was right. In response to the mockery by the disciples of the sage of Munkács mourning the destroyed temple "Elijah the Prophet" appears in the guise of a pioneer with short pants, spits on them, and emigrates to Israel.

A religion based on "childlike" faith—that pays no heed to overblown voices of enlightenment, warnings about the future, logic, and the lamentations of parents and loved ones—is necessary for human creativity.

The world will not be redeemed from its miserable state by the G.P.U., but rather by the simple faith of those rotting in the prisons of Siberia.[18] The Land of Israel will not be built by political infighting, but by the religious faith of the young female apostles who are preparing for the trip.

These young girls, scattered all over the Carpathians and the High Tatras, are its tender, fertile building blocks.

In every little village and town, Jews attached to the building of a new homeland can be found, who dream up ways and means to ensure the success of this enterprise.

I meet a Jewish homeowner who has made care and cultivation of the *Wachholder* [juniper] his life's work. He writes his name and address in my notebook: "Theodore Wister, Nove Mesto."[19] I should please introduce this plant into Israel. This plant has many uses: it contains sugar, its fruit makes good preserves, and juniper oil has many health benefits.

I write everything down and promise to convey these suggestions to my friend the revolutionary botanist Avizohar in Jerusalem, an old apostle who works for nothing.[20]

Another Jew has, during the past five years, drunk only Rishon Letzion wine.[21] A typical Hungarian Jew, for whom the drinking of wine is a very serious business, not just an obligatory Sabbath and festival mitzvah.

Here is an entire family, whose men for many years have only worn expensive ties from Israel. They have a "pioneer" middle man in Tel Aviv who buys locally manufactured carves, and sends them to the family.

Here is a bourgeois young woman who orders stockings from Israel.

Here is a rich Jewish breeder who breeds and sells pedigree dogs. Every last dog in his large "herd" understands only "pure" Modern Hebrew. Non-Jewish noblemen acquire hard-to-find apprentices from him—their job is to teach dogs instructions in Hebrew because without these the dog cannot be trained.

Here is a simple tailor from the town of Bardejov, who writes a letter to the "commodity" factory in London, requesting that it sends him no more British merchandise until the British government has the safety and security of Mandated Palestine under control![22] This simple tailor understands more than all our nation's self-important philistines combined!

Out of nowhere, I receive a parcel of Pesach *charoset* from my old religious friend Mr. Pasmanik, a Tel Aviv egg seller, manufactured by Moshe Volodarski in Bnei Brak.[23] The *charoset* is wrapped in special paper to protect it from any *chametz*.[24] The following note is written on the wrapping paper:

> This *charoset* is good to eat and pleasing to the palate; there is no greater or more pleasant way for young and old to honor the festival days. Apart from appreciating and getting to know the produce of the Holy Land, our sages have explained (Pesachim 10; Mishnah 3) that eating *charoset* is a mitzvah. Its manufacture also gives work to several Jewish souls. May we by doing this merit full redemption speedily in our days. Amen.

The charoset factory has received *kashrut* approvals from every possible gaonic rabbinical group, irrespective of sect or degree of religiosity. Rabbis Kook, Sonnenfeld[25] Menahem Nachum Twersky of the Chernobyl lineage, our master and teacher Rabbi Schneerson the Lubavicher, Rabbi Vaslabodki chief of the Hevron *beit din*, Rabbi M. M. Epstein, and many others—may they all merit good and long lives.

The parcel creates a sensation in the town and surroundings. If I had received it a month or so before Pesach, I could have ordered more for the holiday. As it is, a furious fight for the few precious portions of *charoset* that are available ensues—between both those in favor of, and against, Zionism (there are practically no Zionism-haters here). Finally, it is sold for the benefit of the Jewish National Fund—a true victory for Israel! Opponents of Zionism contributing to the Jewish National Fund box![26] Who heard of such a thing?!

If only the land of Israel could manufacture sufficient amounts of the endless liturgical items necessary for the diaspora—prayer books, tefillin, tallitot, mezuzot, etc.; food and drink for Sabbaths, festivals, weddings, and circumcisions—unbreakable bonds between the entire religious world and the Land of Israel would be forged.

Just think how more useful *Keren Hayesod shaliachs* would be in the *charoset* trade than they are now—heaping trials and tribulations on the suffering new *yishuv*![27]

Is that not so?

Charoset is not only a memory of mortar, but what has been built with mortar. Think again of what the "imprisoned girl" said in Vienna:

"Dictatorship! That's what we need! Dictatorship! To build factories to manufacture *charoset* and Sabbath candles!"[28]

Dictatorship—that understands the current yearning for religion and the spirit of true apostles, that doesn't allow young pioneers to be perverted, once they are in the land Israel, into future epicurean idealism!

Better one portion of *charoset* than a hundred of food aid![29]

One of the richest local Jews enquires in the synagogue whether he could arrange for someone to say *kaddish* at the Western Wall after his death. He will pay whatever is asked of him.

An itinerant beggar, passing through the area over Shabbat, hears him and says:

"Really? Why doesn't anyone else worry about such an important issue?! Everyone knows how poor I am, but I would save all my life for someone to say *kaddish* for me at the Western Wall. Ai, Ai, Ai—"

Had I tried at the moment, I could have collected "*kaddish* money" for every beggar at the wall for an entire year.

Chapter 27

The Legend of Alliance

> The blood of our fornication is no more ours,
> Anyone who wishes can take our place,
> We have used up our potency with sins.
>
> The fiery rage of ages has not strengthened us,
> The world-furnace has melted us,
> We will be lost, since we have lost ourselves.
>
> —Endre Ady[1]

This bitter prophecy from Hungary's greatest poet-prophet accompanies me like a jeremiad throughout my travels in mountainous Slovakia. It echoes in response to our astonishment at the New European Order. This is not a political problem per se, but its foundation lies in politics. How is it possible that Hungary, after 1,000 years of rule, has lost all these ancient regions, including Slovakia?

I'm convinced that no one—not even poets who, "whispering in the assembly of nations," observed the war and its repercussions—has studied this issue properly. I, at any rate, have neither seen nor heard anyone doing so. The nub of the matter is that not one of the countries defeated in the Great War has been punished so cruelly and terribly as Hungary.

Hungary—as is well known—wanted this war less than any other nation. Its prime minister Graf Tisza tried with all his strength to prevent the outbreak of war. Only his great loyalty and personal devotion to Kaiser Franz Joseph compelled him to finally agree with the "heroes" who prevailed upon the old kaiser to present Serbia with such an uncompromising démarche—the match that lit the fuse of the European tinderbox.[2]

And yet, this same nation was forced to pay for a lost war by national destruction on a scale unlike anything previously seen in European history. From more than 250,000 square kilometers (a lot more: I believe than the number is closer to 325,000), poor, mutilated Hungary has now shrunk to a country of about 70,000 square kilometers. Almost all its natural and human riches have been torn away, regions over which it had ruled over for over 1,000 years.

But its tragedy cannot be measured merely in terms of natural riches.

Travel the length and breadth of the mountains, valleys, and towns of Slovakia, dear readers, and you will see lofty fortresses—untouched, half-, or completely destroyed. If you add the history of their world, the mausoleums of their heroic Hungarian nobility, and the artistic treasures they contain, you come up with a 1,000 year historical epic unmatched in the annals of European history. The entire foundation of Magyar culture—which today provides plays, actors, and producers for stages and theaters around the entire world, from Berlin to Hollywood—is *rooted in these fortresses and draws its origin from them.* Each fortress is surrounded by a legend, an epic poem, drama, or Hungarian novel. Join all of these together and you will find the "testament" of this small nation, which arrived here 1,000 years ago from somewhere in the Mongolian steppes—suddenly, on thundering hooves, with the splendor of conquering kings, blood seething for new conquests.[3] These strange, Turan-Mongolian people, conquered the entire area, Latins and Slavs together.

Each victory was crowned by a song, each war by a picture, and each defeat—by renewed creativity. Take Moritz Jókai, for example: one of the greatest Hungarian novelists—known the world over for his roughly 200 great novels, plays, and stories which have become the pride not only of his native country but of all Europe and beyond.[4] Each one of his novels is in realty a magical fantasy about one of these fortresses, either in Slovakia or Transylvania.

I think that only a Jew is capable of understanding the "destruction of the Temple"—an event even worse than destruction of concrete possessions. Was the Temple not the essence of the stubbornness of a clique of destructive hooligans that caused Rome to overthrow Judea more ferociously than all other conquered peoples combined? Had the

Rome of wise Horatian philosophers understood this, perhaps it would still exist!⁵

Because what is the loss of concrete possessions around storied strongholds compared to the loss of their concealed spiritual and cultural treasure?

Woe to the nation that has lost the capacity to absorb knowledge! Woe to the spirit of culture, that has lost itself! It has become like an emperor without clothes.

Like the culture of the wretched people of Israel.

Now, I understand what Endre Ady meant when he wrote the lines: "As it was once written in a book, / By Erdély's ancient, melancholy prophet, / Searching for kinship with the Jews."

A tragic alliance, an alliance of mourning and desolation!

Study Adys lines carefully: "The blood of our fornication is no more ours, / Anyone who wishes can take our place."

They contain the entire tragedy of this Turan-Mongol tribe.

The Magyars are an atavistic, warlike people, a nation of knights and heroes in the true sense of both words. A nation that knows not only how to conquer, but also how to govern, by tradition of any government, over generations. The claim that Hungary governed by oppressing small nations and minorities is a claim of war, not philosophy and logic. Let any ruling nation that doesn't behave in this way cast the first stone at Hungary. The real reasons for Hungary's downfall lie in the methods of modern warfare, by which the glorious heroism through which they conquered over so many generations has been rendered obsolete: that same attribute that Ady called "the blood of fornication," that blood which boils for great events, conquests, victories, and drunken victory odes.

But this blood has slowly dissipated during the last few generations of "civilization," and the few drops that have remained are valueless. What is the value of the "blood of fornication" compared to the mathematical calculation of artillery, airplanes, and poison gas?

What is heroism worth at a time when London can be destroyed within only an hour?

"Anyone who wishes can replace us."

How true: anyone with the ability and wherewithal to wage modern mechanized war, can flatten and squash all the bravery, strength, and courage in the world like a bug.

I come back to those Jerusalemite hooligans—Roman courage could not stand against the "rebellion mania" of the heroes of Masada. But one thing that the Romans had, and the defenders of Masada did not, were the engines of Titus, which the "joy of humanity" invented, built, and bequeathed to his people before he died.[6] These ballistas and siege machines—the machine-guns and tanks of their day—were the instruments that spelled Judea's final doom after fierce and prolonged fighting—out of all proportion to its tiny size—against the might of Rome.

These same war machines have created new borders, not only in peace, but also in war. Both sides have tried to undermine each other—to undermine war itself—thereby creating the foundations of a new world. A world that opens its eyes and sees that bloody wars of the past must be replaced by covenants of bread and salt between all the small and medium-sized nations: this is especially important when they live side by side, as brothers who suffer and till the soil together. Emphasis should be not laid on the number of different European nationalities and their separate needs. Just the opposite: their boundaries should be blurred to recognize what a blessing they could be to each other if they lived as one large family, sharing land and creative talents. The victorious Entente should not colonize the conquered region with their own sons and daughters—this will be of no use on the Day of Judgment. Because, once again, war will come, and each small nation will join one of the strong ruling nations and, once again, the victor will not hold a referendum with its artillery and tanks. A cannon does not ask—it answers. When the war is "strangled by its own fuel"—again the question of numbers will not decide, but rather that of shared interests in the form of one European economic unit.

"The fiery rage of ages has not strengthened us."

Hungary's near-term redemption will not come from scraps of paper stubbornly proclaiming catchphrases like "we will never yield" fastened onto every door and gate. Historical eras of hooliganism are transient: not because of shame due to lack of morals, but through wisdom and understanding of the dividends of peace. That same Europe that rejects all culture, also has a civilization of science: of physics, chemistry, fuels, gases, and aeroplanes, that forces it towards peace.

The warlike nature of these beautiful Hungarian fortresses has dissipated, and what remains is—culture, which will draw renewed strength from the coming European economic union.

An excellent symbol for the above is the "red hill" fortress of Rozsnyó Rožňava and the grave of the handsome Dénes Andrássy.[7] The late count himself is the embodiment of what should occur in the not-too-distant future.

Here is his gentle life story:

Count Dénes Andrássy fell in love with a Czech girl who wasn't a member of the nobility, but a stage actress, daughter of a learned professor.[8] The count's family strenuously objected to this "mixed marriage," and finally the count abandoned them, to live in splendid isolation with his beloved wife.

His happiness did not last long because his wife died very young. The count arranged a funeral for her, the likes of which had never been seen before, even amongst Hungarian nobility. Afterwards, he built a mausoleum for his wife and himself out of purest marble, the dome inlaid with pure gold mosaics. The eastern wall consisted of a mosaic image of his wife's guardian angel, neck decorated with pearls and the most precious stones. Inside the mausoleum were two marble sarcophagi, his and hers. On top of the sarcophagi stood the sculpture of a dog, a symbol of his faithfulness to her.

His wife had a small pet dog. When she died, the count hired a maid to look after the dog until it died. He erected a small memorial statue on its grave, made by one of Germany's greatest sculptors. The statue stands outside the mausoleum.

On entering the mausoleum and looking around, one is seized with an indescribable sadness at this demonstration of the great love by a man for a woman. Only a Hungarian count is capable of such wild, romantic love.

The source of this is—a Czech woman.

A day will come when all the hidden wealth in this mausoleum will have no real value. Even today, the Czech government doesn't dare touch it and will not do so even if, God forbid, its national bank is near bankruptcy. This, even considering the fact that several banks could be saved by this National treasure.

It is not innate wealth that will remain for generations to come, but rather innate happiness.[9] There will come a time when people will come from the four corners of the earth to see the true Hungarian soul mirrored in the pure, eternal love that the count had for his wife. I am sure that

Romeo and Juliet were also interred in a mausoleum of pure gold. A day will come when even the mercantile, penny-pinching British will not be measured by gold, but by the pure and faithful love of Romeo and Juliet. Woe to Britain if future generations will measure it merely by its wealth!

It would be a pity if Hungarians took these things as solace or consolation. As a sign of eternal thanks to the country of my birth, I want to share with them what I myself have learned, as a member of the world's most tragic nation. When the Romans surrounded and were choking the life out of Jerusalem, and it became clear to all that they would destroy the Temple, our sage Rabbi Yohanan Ben Zakkai stole into their presence with a request that he might be allowed to leave the city and join Yavneh and its wise men. And so it was: the Romans destroyed the Temple, our most holy building—but its spirit remained in Yavneh and its inhabitants.[10]

The real tragedy in all this is that two intelligent and talented peoples (the Magyars and Czechs), who together could redeem the whole of Europe, are still at each other's throats.[11]

Count Dénes Andrássy was the first to remove this hate and replace it with an unrivalled temple to love.

He waits in his marble tomb, to see positive results, in both peoples, of his love for his Franciska.

The count's family opposed the unfortunate Franciska not because she was not of noble birth, but rather because she was a Czech—and such a malady is incurable.

There is much more to love than to hate in the Czech nation.

Graf Andrássy swore eternal love, but only a nation is eternal.

The time has come to remove all scarecrows from the Hungarian border and allow them to make a better living.

What is our Old Testament but one great epic based on our national geography? Hungary has created its own testament, through its own rich tradition of literature and art: one great geographic epic about its glorious nation and peoples. This epic is indestructible: if Hungary became wise enough to combine with Czechoslovakia in a friendly economic union, why even dream of making war against them?

Graf Andrássy's legend of union must stop just being a story.

Our own Jewish epic also demands a union.

Because war always brings harm, and union only good.

Chapter 28

The Rear Echelon

In the Slovak town of Nitra I visit the gaonic Rabbi Dr. Schweiger, head of a scholarly, enlightened Jewish congregation.[1] I tell him about the trouble I have had with rabbis who anathematize the Jewish National Fund collection box because it replaces the one for Rabbi Meir Baal HaNes and interferes with the livelihood of the *kolel*, which hammers Torah and fear (of the Lord) into its students by loveless rote.[2]

The learned, sharp-witted rabbi replies:

"Go ask them: they have been supporting the Jerusalem *kolel*, and its way of beating Torah and fear of the Lord into willing and unwilling heads, for 150 years—how many biblical or Talmudic gaons has it produced during this time? Not one! Surely they should have produced at least one Torah gaon? How many learned Biblical books containing something new have they hammered out during this time? Not one! Surely, during all this time, they should have managed to publish at least one book that might have been of use to the Diaspora? Now, think about how many gold coins have been put into the Rabbi Meir Bal HaNes box during these 150 years, and what we have received for this largesse? Not one gaon, not one Torah or Talmud commentary! Any book of substance has appeared not from the learned *kolel*—hammering in hairsplitting day and night—but rather from the 'evil demons' on the other side. Books with new Torah insights, and books on Kabala, have appeared from the *yeshiva* of the Zionist Rav Kook. I also hear that Rabbi Yehoshua Kasowsky's book of Mishnaic concordances sits in a place of honor on the table of the 'Ashkenazi Council'—another Zionist 'captive.'"[3]

The rabbi concludes:

"Please tell them, in your name and mine, that the *kolel* shouldn't use words of the Holy Torah purely as an excuse to hammer in legalistic hairsplitting. An entire yeshiva of learned men should have been capable, during a period of 150 years, of finding something new!"

Words that goad like sharp spurs.

I arrive in Bratislava, the glorious city of Pressburg, with a feeling of awestruck respect, as if the Lord had commanded me to take my shoes off before I enter the sanctum sanctorum.[4]

I have not visited Pressburg for the last twenty-five years, but understand well the level of responsibility inherent in my lecturing here on the Land of Israel. Pressburg is used for lectures by various *shaliachs* and other leaders. But a lecture by a Hebrew author, writing in the holy language—and one, to boot, who has learned Torah and fear of the Lord at the feet of gaons of the Pressburg school—these two things are enough to stir the pot a little. My lecture in Munkács is fraught with danger. The gaon Rabbi Spira, that great detractor of Zionism, was in Israel at the time, but before he left he arranged for a hundred of his disciples to be present at my talk. I was warned to watch my words, and not, God forbid, say anything against the honor of the great gaon. These noble and pious disciples know no legal compassion, so it would be better if I sought police protection.

I did not ask for police protection because I know Munkács and its way of doing things thoroughly. At the most dangerous moment, all I needed to say to them was:

"Tell your respected and pious rabbi that his honor is in grave danger! Tell him, that there is still time to repent! The greatest of all dangers awaits him: he is beginning to look ridiculous, and we are distressed to see this, in such a Great Man of Israel. This is an auspicious time to mend his ways, repent, and return to the right path. He has travelled to Israel, and the greatest of all mitzvot would be for him to help Jewish settlement in the Land of Israel, not pontificate against it!"

This was enough to make Rabbi Spira's disciples look as though they were standing on hot coals. They looked at me with astonishment, whispering to each other:

"What chutzpah! How dare he!"

Finally they came to me, one by one, as secretly as they could, to discuss "the matter" out of pure curiosity. Who is this young man from the village of Ó-Dávidháza, Reb David's grandson, who speaks such "pure" modern Hebrew?[5]

Things in Pressburg the Glorious are different. Here, Hasidim "burning with sacred fire" are replaced by educated and enlightened city dwellers. Both Torah and enlightenment are combined, without anathemizing the one or the other.[6] As they say here, "there is room on the head for more than one set of tefillin."

It was Rosh Hashanah. I entered the great synagogue, to hear the gaonic rabbi, the great grandson of the *Chatam Sofer*, and the grandson of the *Ktav Sofer*.[7]

The sermon lasted about an hour and a half.

It was pure torture, a punishment to sit through.

He expounded on some passage or other for one and one-half hours. I certainly don't remember the text itself, but I will never forget two words, "Holy Torah," which the learned sage repeated no less than 632 times. Both Dr. Joseph Fish and I can attest to that: we counted carefully.

Just think: six hundred and thirty-two times during ninety minutes!

We started to count when it became obvious that the words were being used too many times, so a few times were obviously missed.

I attempted, after the tumult of words of this great homiletical masterpiece, to find a trace of sense: perhaps on the surface, maybe a hint, midrashic, or secret meaning.[8]

Nothing: nothing at all.

Just the Holy Torah, the Holy Torah, and nothing but the Holy Torah.

I remember Rav Kook's profound sermons, and my mind is set at rest:

"These types of gaons are not dangerous enemies. All of us know that the Torah is holy, we perhaps more than most: so what harm is there in his reminding us of this again and again and again? Let him—after all, it's true."

The amazing thing is, that rabbinical sermons in Pressburg have been thus limited in style and scope for generation upon generation. Thousands of educated, enlightened people listen to the same old thing, repeated ad nauseam in the same old way. In the meanwhile, civilizations destroy and are destroyed, built and brought down, huge wars shake the very foundations of the earth, pogroms, expulsions, persecution of every kind, borders become blurred, and new countries appear at every side. And these same educated, enlightened people listen with rapt attention to these same lame, uninspired, boring, heartless words from the pulpit, without a single new word that comes from the heart of a suffering Jew.

"Are they not real, their bruises? Why is their prayer false?"

Bialik did not direct his questions to people like this, who appear indifferent to Israel's sufferings, and feel no moral compunction in what is occurring.

"And spitting thee, strange incense they will bring."[9]

It's of no use, and represents no clear and present danger to their daily lives. It is rather the Zionists—those who eat, drink, and sleep their ideal—to whom these words bring potential danger and pain.

It's difficult for such people to listen to a true accounting of a Land of Israel working, suffering and standing guard on uncountable front lines: enemies, malaria, politics, and unemployment. It's difficult for them to understand that Zionism was not created for their own particular livelihoods or careers, and that they are not doing their duties as faithful Jews. It's difficult for them to hear words that transfix and absorb the Jewish masses: our sacrifices that cannot be even guessed at from afar, our monastic lives cut off from all beauty, creature comforts, and proper rest—all the things that fill the lives of people living here.

Very interesting: all the different anti-Zionists parties listen to my talk and either say nothing or speak in opposition, with justified or unjustified objections—but always courteously and respectfully. The only scathing critique of the "talk by the German-Zionist poet" is from the head of the Jewish National Fund agency, who writes in the official Zionist newspaper that "the Hebrew poet cursed and insulted the sages of the Talmud as well as Maimonides, of blessed memory!"[10]

The deliciousness of this little matter, is that the editor in question wasn't even present at the talk by the "Hebrew poet" and that the reporter who wrote the article couldn't understand a word of the language in which the "Hebrew poet" spoke.

The ear bashing that the editor received the next day, during one of the frequent meetings of the Zionist Council, didn't help one bit:

"I came, I saw, I spoke. I am not in the habit of repeating myself."

I find out the hidden explanation for all this a few days later: "The visiting lecturer did not find time or need in his busy schedule to visit the local head of the Jewish National Fund. That is why the Zionist official didn't attend the lecture—even before the day of his visit."

Communication between the front line and rear echelon is difficult.

I find the solution to many Zionist "riddles" in this great city, mother of Jewish learning. The key which opens all locks is the local political machinery. This great windmill grinds all forms of Zionist energy into flour to make bread, baked with the "holy fire" of the old apostles. The bread, however, is tainted: it is the product and symbol of the whole futile process, contaminated by the local Jewish establishment's constant fear of antisemitism and mockery by Jewish and non-Jewish anti-Zionists.

If it were not for this fear, there would be no anti-Zionists in the world.

Herzl forgot about three obstacles to the establishment of an independent State of Israel.[11]

Fear, in case—in case—in case—

Teachers for whom politics brings money and respect.

Zionists who contaminate their ideals with regional and local diaspora politics.

I know of no other country in the world that is more fertile ground for the propagation of Zionism than Czechoslovakia. The Czechs are the most intelligent and educated of all Slavs, with a well-developed sense of nationalism. Not only their old president—whose good sense is celebrated throughout the land—but also his government officials understand the importance of a Jewish State in Israel.[12] Rusinski has recently become part of the Czechoslovak state: the geography of countries in which Diaspora Jews live is of paramount importance to us. Our icebreaker in these northern climes is the Maggid from Munkács, king-despot of the Eskimos, ruler of a kingdom of fat, slippery seals.

The ship is breaking the ice with great gusto.

Woe to the icebreaker with an Eskimo skipper, who plays evil, damaging tricks and lets the foxes into our henhouse.[13]

One thing surprises me: even the most ardent Zionists, fighting their war with one, united front and national discipline, don't mix their ideals with socioeconomic realities. A second-generation apostle, an exemplary Zionist and human being—a dentist with a large and distinguished clientele—tells me that he has never, in his long career, ever had a single Zionist patient. The same applies for lawyers and other professions.

In every case, Zionism is regarded as vulgar idol-worship.

Instead of serving as a positive and constructive learning academy for "Hebrew work" in the Diaspora (this, apart from its other uses).

In the town of Piešťany, a well-known Slovak spa town, I meet one of the victims of speculation in Israel. Dr. Rosner, a Zionist from the old days, and owner of a splendid sanatorium. He is a learned man from a good family—his father participated in the production of Hebrew newspapers. His house is a medical gathering place/conference center for guests from Israel. An entire catalogue of people from Israel visit him and—to his great pride—are cured from their various maladies.

I ask him if he is considering emigrating to Israel. He has great difficulty answering and sits suffused in sanatorium-style silence for a while. He finally bursts out with the sad story of his bitter disappointment. He visited Israel intending to buy a piece of land in Tiberias and with various professional plans. In the end he was left without land or money, having been sold a bill of goods.

Not one national or communal organization lifted a finger to help.

Not even for a God-fearing apostle. The revered, upright Budapest apostles didn't help him either.

After everything, he remains exactly as he was before—an apostle: dreaming about the Land of Israel, a faithful contributor to *Keren Hayesod* and loyal supporter of the Jewish National Fund. He wants to bring in a Hebrew teacher for his sons from Israel—preferably a Yemenite.[14]

A Jew has no luck—another example.

But more than luck—we lack Jews who are *menschen*: with character, rectitude, dignity, a sense of the real meaning of right, responsibility, and decorum.[15]

When I return to my wretched birthplace, a Magyar pushes an ode in memory of the "poet" Joseph Trumpeldor into my hands.[16] He is a simple farmer, who has been seized with poetry and rhetoric: Janos Récsei.

"Please don't forget my name."—I won't forget—Janos Récsei.

His knowledge of all the details of Trumpeldor's life, and especially of his death, is amazing—a detailed epic poem filled with veneration for the hero of Tel Hai!

"Jews have written so much about the heroes of Hungary—it's time for a Magyar to write about a Jewish hero"—he says to me with a diplomacy from which our own political wheeler-dealers could learn a great deal.

Chapter 29

The Beacon of Light

Europe is currently gripped by a wild, ravening hunger, hidden by a thin fig leaf with the beautiful name of nationalism. But this fig leaf, produced by the French Revolution to adorn *liberté, egalité, fraternité*, has, by now, become a transparent, convenient cover for any European cannibal who sees his tribe's happiness in war, separation, hate, and the defeat and destruction of neighboring rival enemy tribes. If this is the case for old, great, and strong nations, how much more so for small nations who have joined together as a result of the war and stand guard on their independence and freedom. In these smaller nations, the "national ideal" dances a *Walpurgisnacht* of noble, upright principles secure in the rightness of their cause. What they really mean is: "We can only be built on the ashes of our neighbors." All the tribes of Europe agree on the license to devour their neighbor, with the authorization of a lofty ideal.

But it's well known that Satan is a great jester. He always leaves us with a contradiction. "Not necessarily: the opposite is also possible! Human nature has no fixed laws!"

Its symbol is old Tomáš Masaryk, president and founder of the Czechoslovak Republic.

From all the praises heaped on this man, who serves as a beacon of light in a Europe gone mad, one suitable sentence should be extracted, to engrave on the foundation of a giant statue, erected in his honor: "Priest of the Most High in the house of Baal that is the jungle which is twentieth century Europe."

I travel the length and breadth of breathtakingly beautiful Czechoslovakia, with a constant inner feeling of observing two things at once. On one hand, man's evil impulse, always ready to burst forth from the untamed masses demanding what they see as their primeval rights. On the other, Masaryk's tender yet firm hand, using man's good impulse as a powerful subjugative force to prevent the eruption of man's primitive desire to destroy and burn. Imagine—a hero of national freedom and independence, who rules not with the demagoguery of hate, destruction, and nationalist ferocity—but with the redemptive spirit of the socialist ideal, which educates and builds bridges of trust between hostile tribes, nations, and simple human beings just because they are human beings, not necessarily members of the same nationalities. The republic combines three Slavic peoples: Czechs, Slovaks, and Ruthenians, all with a commitment to mingle, combine, and melt into one healthy, complete people—in other words, to become what they have always been—a Slavic nation protecting its independence and developing its manifold talents of a *mission civilisatrice*.[1]

And yet: instead of a sense of effort and unity, I sense a desire among them to be separated by raucous, warlike demands for "national autonomy"—in other words, tribal independence. Of course, this African tribal desire rests upon the praiseworthy, positive support of each of the three group's national culture, typified in their own individual language—really, dialectal differences in the same original language, which (they feel) rise to the level of their own national language! Thus, linguistic unity does not rule, but is replaced by dialectal differences. The humorous-sad thing about all this is, is that wretched Carpatho-Ruthenia, with hardly ten original songs and stories in its own "language," lives—even today—in the same primitive state as natives of the Solomon Islands, with their primitive Yakut-like shamanist beliefs in spirits and hobgoblins.[2] They leave their gardens dirty, don't trim the seedpods and branches from their fruit trees unless ordered to do so by the authorities, and only send their children to school out of fear of fines and imprisonment. If their children become ill—it depends on what costs more: the doctor or the priest-undertaker. These "people" also demand a separate nation: autonomy! At least the Slovaks have their own type of culture: beautiful dances, celebrations, and national poetry, separate customs and clothes, despite speaking just another Slavic dialect, not a separate language. But what do the Ruthenians have in the way of national culture or poetry? Nothing. What they do have are their nauseating "Hungarian" songs inherited together with an entire throat disease of garbled Hungarian words. Passing through the village, they bleat their cacophonous "songs" without a trace of taste or melody, with a total of three unmusically monotonous high-pitched harmonies to which even the most daring village boy wouldn't add a fourth, nor attempt to somehow turns this racket into something remotely resembling music.³

By all means give such a people national autonomy! Look how different and special they are! It's beneath their dignity, God forbid, to assimilate into the Czech nation! Why should they? Look how well the Carpatho-Ruthenian village youth are progressing with the spirit of the times! On Sundays and holidays, girls wear silk stockings, city dresses, with powder and lipstick, even mascara around the eyes! Naturally, they don't bathe, even during summer—their leaders, instead of adopting customs of the Czechs, steeped in European culture and talent of every kind that fertilizes every aspect of national life—instead of learning and teaching it, they want national autonomy and independence just the way they are!

Masaryk gives them national autonomy. But in the meanwhile he has to watch them with the eyes of Argus and hands of Shiva: they still believe in the Jewish blood libel and, if they could, would wisely and seriously push their legal system—which is progressing so well under the current regime—back to the Middle Ages. This would be accompanied by radio programs by "Zionist revisionists" describing all the grisly details of the blood libel.⁴

Masaryk, and his pupil Minister Beneš, two decent and respected men in the midst of a European jungle, two heroic national freedom fighters, who loathe nothing more than envy, national hatred, and the leprous filth that accompanies these two evil feelings.⁵

Slovakia is showing signs of dangerously unruly national behavior. But Tomáš is old, well advanced in age.⁶

How many millions pray fervently and fearfully for this dear man's long life, and the welfare of the Czechoslovak state, eyed jealously by a steel-fanged Germany, ready to swallow it whole?

"Alas, who shall live after God has appointed him?"⁷

I am sitting with the author Karel Čapek and ministerial advisor Joseph Paliwitz, talking about the "old gentleman."⁸ Talking?—I am the only one talking: they are sitting in silent awe of the father of the Czech Republic. Their silence betokens an apprehensive prayer:

"If there is a God in Heaven, let us not see, with the death of the 'old gentleman,' extinction of our magical beacon of light!"

Their light? No—this prayer applies to the whole of Europe.

Chapter 30

The Intoxicating Darkness

I am stuck in the imbroglio[1] that is "the New Europe," turned inside out by the Great War, and searching for an isolated spot to sit and observe it objectively—just the way it is—from afar. I need to escape this primeval jungle and not be dragged after its dance of death, to be able to analyze it with a clear mind. This is very difficult because I feel a sort of intoxicating darkness enveloping me from top to toe.[2] A wonderful opium-laced rosy darkness covers everything: reactionism, glorying under the name "national ideal"; negligence, covering bloodlust in the name of pristine humanity with the silken gloves of social democracy; despair in the younger generation, who already realize that they have been born merely to die in the next war. They amuse themselves with sport, bridge, and other idle, vapid pursuits, everything done at warped speed, like the crazy desire to exceed the world speed limit. After all, "Eat, drink and be merry, for tomorrow you will be sent to the front to die!"

This dark cloud spreads its "artistic" wings, intoxicating all the senses (but especially the eye) with its sensuality, radiant beauty, and splendor.

It is called: *moving pictures*.[3]

Moving pictures represent the final and complete victory of civilization over its companion-in-suffering—culture.

These two sisters have been at unending, merciless war with each other for countless generations. They are not—as we thought in error—daughters of enlightened, evolving mankind, twin sisters, helping one another in the war for existence and progress. We assumed that civilization is the daughter of *consciousness*, aspiring to comfort and material benefit. It is the daughter of the thinking brain, creating and nurturing logic, science, mathematics, and all other types of knowledge. Its only purpose is to prepare a fertile cradle for its sister "culture," which in turn aspires to the beautiful and noble—aims without material purpose, *daughter of the subconscious*, the dream that soars heavenwards. All man's efforts are directed to creating a comfortable life, with automobiles, cleanliness, hygiene, building, and all other instruments of science. The sole purpose of these efforts is to help culture on its difficult path forward. So, in sum, both civilization and culture have the same aim: the creation of a New Man—enlightened, noble, moral, and wise, who realizes that the highest happiness is a life of beauty, peace, and creativity.

How wrong we were! This is a very old, powerful war and we either didn't or couldn't recognize it. The aim of civilization is the exact opposite: to help barbarians create new implements for bloodletting and creating vicious competition, splitting apart, not uniting us— to give the evil inclination full rein in achieving its ancient goal: war, war, only war.[4] Poisonous gases instead of rocks and stones, long-range cannons instead of arrows and javelins, airplanes instead of hand-to-hand combat, and prisoner of war camps in which to inflict a thousand agonies on unarmed prisoners, instead of the simple taking of scalps.

Twentieth-century civilization has found the perfect tool to ensnare, disable, and defeat an enemy culture; to bind it with silken cords and subdue it with intoxicating beauty. The powerful combination of the new art: silent and talking pictures, which stretch their satanic wings over every type of culture and artistic device.

Its success is overwhelming and complete.

Movies have already achieved their main goal: the destruction of honest, artistic criticism. The "new criticism," courtesy of this new and improved form of art, is based upon the fact that during the past several years all that was good has been neutralized by the *taste of the masses*. Who today remembers that before the war every literary beginner knew the basic rule: anything that finds favor with the masses has no genuine artistic value? Great and genuine aesthetic values have never penetrated the heart of the masses, and never will. No creation worth its name—in literature or any other art form—has ever been welcomed initially by the general public. It takes a long time and a great deal of effort—some of it secretive, devious, and indirect—to educate the masses even minimally in enlightenment and aesthetics.

Today, every new creation is counted in two types of millions—the millions who watch or read and the millions the creator makes from his "great works of art." The true yardstick by which a movie is measured is: the millions who come to see it and the money paid by large movie factories to the indentured servants who create it. What can be more logical than the new and "surprising" phenomenon of the "creator" who earns millions from his "art"? Instead of the old ethical principle, that the true artist doesn't hire himself out for daily service, a *new plutocracy* has been created, with a new class of millionaires—a company of gypsies, empty-headed bohemian clowns, new capitalists, who know that everything—they themselves, their creations, but especially artistic critique—is for sale to the highest bidder.[5] Never before have we experienced the sentimental, saccharine effusion and sweet-smelling incense that now drenches an "actress" like Greta Garbo or one of the other average Hollywood starlets. Garbo's acting is also something new. Up till now, we have known that art has one great characteristic: *revelation*. It reveals to humanity what the man in the street looks at, but only sees clearly—and that with some surprise—when revealed to him by the artist: "I see: yes! Of course! All my life I looked at it, but I didn't see!!" In this way, an actor of genius can reveal what even a talented writer has not properly clarified with the written word. For this reason, acting has up till now studiously avoided all forms of false pathos, recitation, and superfluous movement which *covers* the essential humanity of the central theme instead of dissecting and revealing it. We are swamped with banality, accompanied with sighs, tears, pious proclamations—everything that the masses utilize in their daily lives. But there is nothing new under the sun. While, in the era before moving pictures, artists created their own methods of expressing the laughter and tears of the human condition, Miss Greta Garbo uses vulgar pathos, body movement, and her gravelly voice known and recognized by all, influencing all! All, that is, except the true artist, the enlightened person who knows the meaning of real art, which reveals and creates, instead of spouting forth platitudes.[6]

Imagine an amateur stage production, replete with provincial pathos, named the "Sale of Joseph."[7] The play features a small-town seamstress in the leading role, which, before the movie era, would not have helped the heroine's career one little bit. In fact, the theater director would have advised her to go home, help her mother in the kitchen, marry a good boy, have children for the fatherland, and not bother the stage with anymore rubbish. But now, this type of thing is all the rage with Greta Garbo and her fellow starlets, in the sanctum sanctorum of twentieth-century art.

Of course, there is another way to attract an audience: sexuality. Who thought of asking if the heavenly Eleonora Duse, Komissarzhevskaya, or Sarah Bernhardt were beautiful or not? Eleonora Duse—who in only one performance plumbed the depths of pain and joy for her audience, leaving them feeling as if a storm had hit them days after the performance—was ugly in a way that cannot be imagined today! But who saw this when she was on, or even off, the stage? And she didn't spend thousands of dollars on publicity like Garbo, who continuously announces that "she wants to be alone."[8]

A typical comparison: Duse's fiery love affair with D'Annunzio didn't stop him from reporting the intimate details of their relationship in a sensational novel, which desecrated her to such a degree that she was forced to run away to America, where she died in want and penury.[9]

Let us now compare Duse with Greta Garbo, beloved of the great director Moritz Stiller, who both discovered her and made her a world-famous star out of passionate love.[10] She booted him out straight after her first success, driving him to an early grave; but before she did, she made sure to have married him, thereby inheriting his estate when he died young. When the head of his impoverished family in Helsingfors asked her for a small amount of financial assistance to help them out of dire straits, she gutsily stood by the letter of the law and they got nothing.[11]

Quite obviously, none of this has anything to do with the real artistic value of "the Divine Greta," who has replaced the old attributes of artistic integrity and worth with something new—"sex appeal," in other words, pure erotic attraction. We now have a new element in art: it is to be hoped that the modern Leonardo da Vinci will recognize the fundamental importance of a sexy body when he paints his new Mona Lisa.[12]

The new plutocracy has created its own geniuses—handsome men like Rudolf Valentino, John Gilbert, and Maurice Chevalier.[13] A week ago, when I was in Prague, I saw how hysterical the crowd was for a mere glimpse of Chevalier. The artistic machine grinds out new plays every month in the same sausage casings, where great artists plumb the depths of tragedy in a single night, and new stars are born at every turn.

A young, beautiful woman has only to demonstrate the tiniest bit of talent—and she is already crowned a star. Poor Eleonora Duse aspired to that title only after years of study, searching, suffering, and self-doubt.

There are some real artists in Hollywood—for example, Norma Shearer, who acts with talent, depth, and modesty; or Joan Crawford, who surrenders herself entirely to her roles.[14] But neither can begin touch the little finger of the great Garbo, the "holy ascetic, who wants to be alone," and will soon enter a nunnery. The tragedy lies in the fact that movies attract us through our love of art exactly because they contain in them seeds of highest culture: the culture of the eye and the ear together, the synthesis of rhythmic beauty of which we have never before dreamed.

Civilization has thus expertly destroyed our cultural values, the object of countless previous generations. It intoxicates us in all sorts of ways, educating us in the new culture of the jungle; the heroism of war, sporting events that turn men into beasts of prey in the name of sacred nationalism; admiration of every governmental defilement such as the rule of money; thoughtless enjoyment, in the presence of mass hunger; government by the new cinema-affiliated plutocracy, assisted by "stars" in the name of art and culture; the combination of sex appeal and happy endings, always protecting against desecration, God forbid, of the white race which must remain pure at all costs. After all, "East is East, and West is West, and never the twain shall meet."[15]

The cinema: the new rule of stupidity and sadism. The cinema, to which a cultured man is drawn like a moth to a flame, which burns out any spark of comprehension of artistic creativity or protest against European barbarism.

In the first rank of these stands Adolph Zukor, creator and head of "Paramount."[16] A man of generous and noble character, a distinguished, moral Jew, with whom few can compare in our twentieth century. If only he could place ethical above technical and financial progress, and the rule of Mammon!

We wander in intoxicating darkness, indulge ourselves in false dreams of amazing technology, and don't feel how this satanic civilization is undermining the ground beneath us and slowly returning us to the jungle. A few movies can be called artistic: the Christian films of Germany and Moscow, which are still made with an eye to searching for meaning and not just the sexy musicality of Marlene Dietrich in *The*

Blue Angel.[17] But who knows how long these two countries will be able to maintain their high cultural standards, without being overpowered by the unerring good taste of the "Great Ziegfeld," who understood exactly what the twentieth century needs—sex gods and goddesses, who attract millions of viewers and dollars—but died of a broken heart after losing everything in the 1929 Wall Street crash.[18]

Five great victories for the cinema:

Victory of the masses over individual genius.

Victory of taste of the masses over artistic criticism.

Victory of advertising over talent.

Victory of money over art.

Victory for the European jungle of submerged over demanding taste.[19]

Sooner or later, this powerful instrument of mass education must surely come to serve its original mission: to raise the standard of the masses, not bring us down to their level.

Some film directors already show signs in this direction. Civilization is fulfilling its original mission: a struggle of culture over money.

Physics, chemistry, and technology will bring peace to the world.

The cinema will, kicking and screaming, eventually bring the victory of true artistry to the world—but not yet.

Chapter 31

Conscience

Prophets have bequeathed us the great inheritance of optimism: obstinate faith in the possibility of man's rehabilitation and elevation to a life of enlightenment and morality. Faith is not blind or insipid, dependent only on the personal wishes of the individual prophet. The real driving force here is that, whenever individual people or society do something low and stupid, signs of morals and conscience reappear: good wins over evil, shame over wickedness, and we are encouraged to believe that at the end of days the wolf will lie down with the lamb.[1]

Europe's conscience—confused by hate and war—is sprouting forth again phoenix-like around two great twentieth-century figures, who act as a life raft in the present sea of blood and chaos:

Einstein and Huberman.

The unique regard in which Einstein, the brilliant theoretical physicist, is held centers more on his awakening of the conscience of humanity than maybe even his scientific greatness.[2] Probably less than ten of the 2 billion people in the world really understand Einstein's theories: maybe we have exaggerated and the number is really a hundred. No matter what the number, is it enough that many appreciate his scientific achievements, which don't improve their individual lives in any way? Since when has the world appreciated something so theoretical, built from neither concrete matter nor spirit?

We are not talking about his theory of general relativity here. The unique aspect of Einstein's personality that Europe grasps as a sort of alibi is his absolute sense of human morality.[3] His personality stands like a mighty rock in the ocean of barbarism that is our twentieth century. It is no fleeting fancy, but rather an integral part of the personality of a wise, enlightened man of peace, such as we have not encountered in a very long time. This mighty moral faith in the New Man is no less powerful and secure than his new physical equations of relativity: any attempt to obfuscate them through pure science, professional envy, or antisemitism is met by a confident smile of complete belief in his truths.

"What will happen," Einstein was once asked, "if the scientific community stands against your theory of relativity and say that it an error?"

"Nothing," he answered with a smile, "it will never happen."

That smile reflects Einstein's personal and ethical *Weltanschauung*: a universe not only of general relativity, but also of humanistic ethics. He is the first moral philosopher in history who—*horribile dictu*—is not against the death penalty! Is that even possible? Can a moral man—and a Jew at that—condone legal execution? Can he agree with our sages of blessed memory that "if a man rises up to kill you, rise earlier, and kill him first?"[4] Can he take the part of David against Goliath, but still support the hanging of Haman and self-defense by revolver against a potential murderer—a monster who could break out of the prison in which he is incarcerated to rob and murder children, Jewish and non-Jewish alike?[5] Can society agree that it is not only allowed but obliged to remove such monsters—who more resemble microbes than man, and who stand in the way of civilized happiness and progress—from its midst? Even a humble microbe has the right to exist in God's world: what Jew would logically suggest that all microbes be separated and imprisoned for their own protection? But what if the microbe has a human face—the face of a monster?

It's not Einstein's incomprehensible theory of relativity that draws him so irresistibly to the ordinary man in the street; but rather his ethical principles, set out in his essay "The World As I See It," which should serve as a short catechism for enlightened man of the twentieth century. Our wretched degenerate world, sunk to the lowest depths of depravity, claws at this man's conscience by its fingernails. His prophetic, even more than his scientific, soul serves as an island of rescue to drowning men whose moral compasses have capsized in a sea of blood. It announces: "We are cultured men who know how to honor genius!" Einstein's Jewishness also plays a role: "We do not differentiate between Jew and non-Jew."

The second great personality is Bronisław Huberman, the great violinist beloved by the entire world for his art.[6] Here too his sublime artistic talent is not the main reason for his high regard, but rather the moral foundations which underpin his character. Huberman the philosopher-dreamer, the pan-European seer of a new beginning, the redemption of today's barbaric Europe from pogroms, wars, and constant vicious competition. Huberman's artistic genius is absolute, secure, and all conquering, comparable in its own way to Einstein's scientific genius. A child could write down the number of those who can distinguish between Huberman's mastery of the violin and that of other violin prodigies. Huberman's faith in the enlightened belief of the New Man in a better world is engraved into his soul and conscience as if in marble. You will not find this in critiques of his music, but rather in private interludes with him and his conversations with different journalists and art critics. It is no accident—that he is a Jew.

Hope is not lost:[7] a spark of shame still burns in stinking, unclean, barbaric Europe, and where there is shame there is hope for redemption.

Anyone who even appears to appreciate the value of Einstein and Huberman can still be saved and there is hope for his redemption.

But who knows how long this relationship will last?

Who knows if the conscience of Europe—and indeed of the entire world—will tire? The cult of "national idealism" holds great power and gradually conquers even the most active conscience—that of the youth, into whose inexperienced hands the prophets of this new cult are handing control, especially in the halls of science.

This is one of novelties in the New Europe: to ensnare the youth with the lust to rule.

An example: in the city of Timișoara in the New Romania, mothers arranged a large public meeting to protest the prosecution of the war, which was devouring the population.[8]

Who broke the meeting up with clubs?

Why, university students, of course!

Einstein and Huberman—I cannot get away from their similarity to the "great light" and "small light" described in the creation chapter in our current shadow world.[9]

I find a third meaningful citation during my travels in the Carpathians. We stop for a glass of slivovitz in a meager village tavern. The bartender is unnerved by the "unnamed" city guests and produces—as if from a hidden crevice behind the stove—his daughter, a young woman of about twenty, to welcome us in a city manner. A complete surprise: she could be the French minister of culture's private secretary. She introduces herself—Sarah Brand. Without asking who we are, she brings us into her room, another total surprise. Imagine if you will—a miserable little mountain village, dark in a dozen different ways, but especially materially and spiritually, in a rickety wooden house with leaky thatched roof that is home to hundreds of nesting birds. And in this setting—a small palace, sparkling white furniture, individually painted walls, a small but well-chosen library. She is the village kindergarten teacher.

She presents us with the "honor of the house"—smiling, but silent. Like Little Briar Rose in the children's story. A small album with a handmade leather cover lies on the table. I ask permission to look through it. There it is—on the sixth page:

"Wagner: 'I believe in God and Beethoven.'"[10]

"Somebody: 'I believe [feminine] in the God of Israel and Einstein.'"

I have found what I am looking for.

I want to reward her for the favor:

"Copernicus revealed the 'what'—Kepler revealed the 'how'—Newton revealed the scientific 'why': what happened in the past to cause the present state of affairs—Einstein is revealing the future purpose of things and perhaps even the 'who.'"[11]

Upon hearing this, she says, with a happy smile and a warm, deep, maternal voice

"Happy is the person who reaches these conclusions."

Her eyes brim with tears of joy.

Chapter 32

Homeward Bound

When I leave Prešov, an important Jew from Slovakia says to me: "We understand your longing for the Land of Israel. I envy you that, not only because you are finally living in the land of our forefathers, but principally because you live in the company of fellow Jews, occupied with the politics of their homeland, Israel. When you return home, please tell the relevant person(s): 'We implore you to send out a categorical imperative that forbids our own Zionists from meddling in the affairs of the countries in which they live. They can get involved if there is a real and personal need: they can even go up to the ministry if they so desire—but *not* in their role as Zionists. They must not debase our national ideal, to become the servant of any type of national politics. This kind of meddling causes international chaos. The civic duty of every Zionist is to fight for the interests of the country in which he has been born. You know what that means at the moment, especially in a balkanized Central Europe where almost each neighboring country growls and bares its fangs at the other.'"

Words of great wisdom.

I have not mentioned my longing for Israel during the past three or four months, despite it having become an almost physical force. This nostalgia is something new to me. Twenty years ago, I was a typical son of the homeland in which I was born and educated—from sweet nursery songs to mighty songs of big city tumult, air resonating with the evanescent sounds of birds in the Hungarian fields and plains. Then, as well, I traveled overseas for long periods of time: but with the normal attachment to the homeland in which my family still lived.[1] I was never drawn to my home with the almost physical force that is now the case with the Land of Israel.

I have not mentioned this up to now because I am a Hebrew writer, and a Hebrew writer is forbidden any form of sentimentality in the service of pure, sacred seriousness. No matter how hard you try, you will not find any clear relationship between cheap sentimentality and romanticism worth its name in our literary, art, or music critiques.—We are an ancient people, who shy away from childish things.

"Pfui! It isn't pleasant here!"

During the last few months I haven't found my place here, despite traveling from town to town and landscape to landscape to the rhythm of clacking railway wheels mixed with the joyous almost audible sound of fields bursting with a fertility strong enough to make me forget the Zionist songs which have no association with my experiences here at all.

What draws me so strongly to the Land of Israel?

Is it my intimate circle of friends—who are not here?

Is it my "fan club," with colleagues sitting next to each other like evil demons, secretly hating each other?

Is it the many political parties to which I make a point of not belonging, because I cannot partake of their portion of hatred?

Is it our political freedom?

Is it the bare mountains and hills and gritty valleys blazing in a fiery glow?

Is it Jerusalem with its monastery bells and chanting from mosques, secretly incubating venom?

Is it the burning land of collective farmsteads, sweating in the sun, gradually being tamed by the sacred returning Diaspora planting new trees in a hitherto untilled land?

Or is it Tel Aviv—yes, despite everything, is it perhaps Tel Aviv?

Could it just be Tel Aviv, with all its deficiencies, dusty streets, houses which are gradually taking on the shape of a Jewish mystic priestess in the old city of Kiev?[2] Yes, it's that same Tel Aviv that pulls me back with unbearable longing.

It's not because my little family—my wife and daughter—sleep in one of those houses. That is another small chapter in my book of longing for the Land of Israel. I miss Tel Aviv for an entirely different reason: at the present time, Tel Aviv is the only Jewish settlement in which there is a small taste of the ingathering of exiles. Jerusalem is under crafty

Ishmaelite rule and the shadow of the New Rome, lying in ambush for the Jewish people.

In the *moshavot* the farmers rule, in contrast to the *kevutzot*, where people have no work, and neither cares about the other.³

Tel Aviv blurs all these artificial boundaries, blending them into a truly Israeli harmony. Even if not all Jewish, it certainly is all Israeli.

One can do without many of its "Israeli" smalltown characteristics:

For example, one can do without the widespread familiarity, by means of which each prying neighbor knows exactly what is happening in every corner of the neighborhood.⁴

One can do without the good neighbors' concerns about the welfare of my wife and family: they are so worried about my family that they expound on all my faults and defects to my friends, and on their many faults and defects to me. Real disciples of Aaron, loving peace and pursuing peace, dispensing domestic tranquility wherever and whenever they can!⁵

One can do without God's Holy Cossacks, who delay the coming of the Messiah by using their holier-than-thou *shofars* to announce the coming of Shabbat like a military *Zapfenstreich* [*Proverka* in Russian], whose terror exceeds even that of the Hitlerites to differentiate between good and evil.⁶

One can do without the municipal street cleaner, who instead of sweeping the streets, sweeps the dust into our bedrooms through the open windows.

One can do without the type of spiritual "janitor" who, instead of cleaning out the cobwebs in the community, educates them to do without theater, music, and other forms of art, but only concern themselves with Diaspora-related activities.

One can certainly do without stores in which bankrupt people are taught how to buy on credit with accumulating interest.

One can do without a lot in Tel Aviv, but not without the city itself. Tel Aviv is, at the moment, our only institution that symbolizes hope for an independent state, sometime in the future.

The enemies in the city hall and *Histadrut* office—bureaucrats all—are not the ones who control Tel Aviv.⁷

Tel Aviv is controlled by the hundreds of children's strollers in Israeli streets.

Tel Aviv is controlled by the seashore, sculpted in myriads of colors mixed together without regard for sex or political affiliation.

At night, Tel Aviv is controlled by coffee houses such as Sheleg Levanon; at whose tables people sit playing chess and philosophizing on pure art.

What is the noise of Vienna compared to the noise of my Tel Aviv?

What are the streets of Europe compared to broad Allenby Street, the narrow market of Nahalat Binyamin, Herzliyah, tree-lined Bialik Street, and imperial Rothschild Boulevard?

What is the Eiffel Tower compared to the Dizengoff Clock Tower?

What are Budapest's gloomy policemen compared to policeman Kupferstein, whose smile illuminates the roads for automobile drivers?

What is the combined politics of continental Europe compared to the commotion of Tel Aviv elections in which I never participate because it's so much nicer to observe this glorious Jewish spectacle from the sidelines?

Yes, our elections—but why should I participate when whatever we decide doesn't tip the scales, because we are not free?

These elections are the same thing for which attorney Rapkach envies me: "Fellow Jews, occupied with the politics of their homeland."

It would be better if politics were not the main topic, influencing everything—at least when no elections are being held.

I understand the man's envy.

This is the same community of families placed here by Herzl to found the new Jewish State.[8]

Tel Aviv's strong nostalgic pull even extends to European ascetics because it also contains a small taste of self-flagellation, if one feels the need. In Europe there already exist statistics on how many women poison themselves to death and how many turn themselves into invalids through various diets. Tel Aviv still doesn't have these civilized accoutrements. I myself have absolutely no need for such statistics. As for me, these women can peg out without fancy statistics, and it wouldn't worry me one bit if they get a donkey's burial outside the walls of the city.[9] The actress Leah Rosen—who is currently tormenting the high echelons of Vienna Jewish society with her stinging prophecies about the Land of Israel—is a beautiful woman, although she is not exactly tall or skinny.[10]

When I kiss her in front of everybody after my lecture, I am the envy of every Don Juan in the city.

This kiss from Leah Rosen is the crowning glory of all I have received for the 116 lectures that I have given during my time in Europe and leaves me with a feeling of fulfilment on the ship back home.—Despite everything, it's worthwhile to be a Hebrew author and lecture on the Land of Israel.

It's also worthwhile to lecture in Tel Aviv, and elsewhere in the Land of Israel, about the wild and savage Europe that I found on my return after a seventeen-year absence—after the Great War.

Let me summarize:

Splendors, decorations, blinding colors—stained glass, glittering roofs, gargoyles.

Jazz, drums, idle chatter, deafening noise, jungle dances.

Clothing scanty to the point of nudity, with bananas instead of fig leaves covers, and pasted-down forelocks.

Eastern-style forest dweller hospitality, together with the cult of war—the cult of Hunnic skulls and Bedouin blood vengeance.

The cult of sport, bridge, and children's games in the hands of earnest-looking adults—from table games to yo-yos in streets and houses.

Bedouin-like tattoos on women's bodies—the cult of manicures and rouge.

The cult of tasteless artforms: idolized fetishes at home and abroad—children's dolls, people, dogs, cats, bears, and monkeys serving as amulets and protection against the danger of the evil eye; table knocking to ward off the evil eye. All this, not only in the career of stars, but also in the most serious world of all—high finance and politics.

The cult of dictatorship—everyone searching for a "leader," a tree on which to be hanged, an ethnic, tribal leader. Grave desecration in a war of useless, pointless hate, without goal or practical purpose.

The romance of a "matter-of-fact" approach to love, but not to morals, literature, and art, together with "Eat, drink and be merry, for tomorrow we die."

In the midst of this tumult, beautiful and nauseating at the same time, the powerful, primitive desire—invisible to the community—for shared life, love, and happiness on a primeval level.

Etc., etc., etc.—all the signs that I leave others to define and complete.

In summary, we can hope to see and experience many wonderful, unheard of things in the near future: first and foremost, legalized cannibalism, especially of the same race, but on the other side of the border.

To complete this beautiful image, sometimes high priests of the new religion appear in the midst of this barbarity: Monseigneur Carl von Ossietzky, Cardinal Albert Einstein and Missionary Bronisław Huberman—who stand in imminent danger of being barbecued on a spit, their roasted flesh eaten with gusto.[11]

Only now do I really understand the sweet, intoxicating song from the Viennese cabaret Femina, sung by the great Mimi Shorp, bathed in the glow of eternal longing.[12]

> You, ape-man with arrow and drum,
> I love you to death.
> You are black and comely
> And I am very pale.
> You bring me gifts—
> Skulls and tin mirrors
> I put them on,
> And go out dancing wildly.
> You are a murderer, a sweet devil,
> I love you to death.
> You are black and comely
> And I am very pale.

Hurrah Mimi Shorp! Hurrah Europe! All roads lead to Bushmanistan!

I travel happily and joyfully, with this song in my heart, on the ship home, accompanied by the noise of the ship's engines and the waves.

But, as it turns out, my destiny as a Hebrew writer comes back to haunt me, placing me in the company of the same people who had previously shown interest in the relationship between the Diaspora and Israel and its culture. A young passenger is dressed like a Russian commissar, with good boots.[13] He comes up to me and, without any reason, says to me with malicious spite:

"Yes, yes, I heard what you said in your lecture—I heard."

"What did you hear?" I am afraid. "What did I say? Perhaps something that you didn't like?"

"Yes, I didn't like how you spoke about the entire Land of Israel as the front line."

"So what?" one of the travelers asks.

"Why must I repeat what I have said already?

To me:

"Try to say that in the Land of Israel!"

I bite my tongue: God in Heaven, what have I said that cannot be said in the Land of Israel? Am I forbidden from saying that Israel is one large battleground, the front of a war against haters, malaria, unemployment, and recalcitrant nature? How can saying this be forbidden?

Who is this young man?

He is filled with hate and disgust.

The kind of hate which I have not felt during the past year.

Finally the first secret is revealed: I am a known revisionist![14] Aha!

The second secret: "I'm a known Bolshevik! Aha!"

My first insult, on behalf of of my beloved Land of Israel.

And the second—because of its name?

No—because of party affiliation. Only internal party politics can sting so sweetly.

Till today I don't know the name of that youth in the commissar's uniform: I just remember that he had a ruddy complexion and unpleasant eyes.

A vigorous argument breaks out over religion on the ship.

A Jew with an expensive fur coat begins to spew poison on those who profane religion in the Land of Israel. When asked:

"Why does the hunger and employment in Israel not upset you to this degree?"

The man with the fur exclaims:

"How do you know that it doesn't upset me?"

They say to him:

"If you were able to save a few pioneers from the shame of hunger, would you sacrifice this fur coat?" They grab the coat.

"Yes!"—he says. "Tell me who is in need, and I'll give it to him."

As luck would have it none of us on the ship are in need of his coat at the present time.

The next day, we are requested to collect a small amount of money before we leave the ship: one of the passengers is a few pounds short of the disembarkation fees.

The Jew with the fur coat is the first one to refuse.

We all contribute freely—he requires security for the requested half a pound.

How good to hear the ship's siren!

It whistles at chaotic Europe.

We've arrived in Tel Aviv.

Notes

Introduction

1 Department of Literature, Tel Aviv University.
2 Hayim Nahman Bialik (1873–1934), Hebrew national poet.
3 United Israel Appeal. Official fundraising organization for Israel founded in 1920 to provide the Zionist movement with resources for Jews to establish a Jewish state in Palestine.
4 Miklós Horthy de Nagybánya (1868–1957), Hungarian admiral and statesman, who became the Regent of Hungary. He served as Regent of the Kingdom of Hungary between World Wars I and II and throughout most of World War II, from 1 March 1920 to 15 October 1944.
5 Uri Zvi Greenberg (1896–1981), Israeli poet and journalist; Abba Ahimeir (1897–1962), journalist, historian, and political activist. *Brit Habiryonim* was a clandestine, self-declared fascist faction of the Revisionist Zionist Movement in Mandatory Palestine, active between 1930 and 1933 founded by the trio of Abba Ahimeir, Uri Zvi Greenberg and Yehoshua Yeivin (1891–1970).
6 *Numerus clausus* (closed number) was one of many methods used to limit the number of students who may study at a university. In many cases, the goal of the *numerus clausus* was simply to limit the number of students to the maximum feasible in particularly sought-after areas of studies. In historical terms, however, in some countries, *numerus clausus* policies were religious or racial quotas, both in intent and function.
7 Avner Holtzman, *Romanim Hatiyudiyim shel Avgdor Hameiri* (The Documentary Novels of Avigdor Hameiri) (Tel Aviv: Dvir, 1989), 271–295.
8 The first English translation of this novel appeared a few years ago: Avigdor Hameiri, *Hell on Earth*, trans. and annot. Peter C. Appelbaum (Detroit: Wayne State University Press, 2017).
9 Avigdor Hameiri, *Of Human Carnage. Odessa 1918-1920*, translated and ed. from the original Hebrew *Ben Shinei Ha'adam* by Peter C. Appelbaum (Middeltown, RI: Stone Tower Press and Boston, MA: Black Widow Press, 2020).
10 Portions of *Halomot Shel Beit Raban* (Dreams of Heder Children) were published as *Halomot Shel Yatom* (Dreams of an Orphan) in the literary journal *Hatekufa*. The sections chosen by Ya'acov Cohen, the editor at the time, did not include characters such as Hector the Dog, Yossi the Parrot, Silver Maria, and Monkey-Faced

Peter. These characters were introduced to the public ten years later, in 1932, when *Halomot Shel Beit Raban* was published in its entirety in Hameiri's book of collected poems *Sefer HaShirim* (Tel Aviv: Hotsa'at Am-Hasefer, 1932).

Translator's Introduction

1. Avigdor Hameiri, *Masa Le'eropa Hapera'it. Rishmei Agav Anakroniyim* (Tel Aviv: Va'ad Hayovel, 1938).
2. Genesis 12:1. "The Lord said to Abram, 'Go from your country, your people and your father's household to the land I will show you.'"

Prologue

1. Zalman Shneur (1887–1959), prolific bilingual Yiddish and Hebrew poet and writer. The poem "Yeme Habenayim Mitkarvim" was published in 1913 against the background of the Beilis blood libel trial, the approaching rebrutalization of European civilization and reemergence of a visceral, "medieval" antisemitism.
2. This did not prove to be the case. Jews that escaped into Spain were safe from the Nazis. Francisco Franco (1892–1975), Caudillo of Spain, did not persecute them.
3. An untranslatable pun: Greta *garbaim* is Greta "with the stockings." Hameiri is confusing Garbo with Marlene Dietrich in *The Blue Angel*. Both women were androgynous. Hameiri is (perhaps purposely) wrong: Garbo never married.
4. Elizabeth Bergner (1897–1986), European actress of Jewish origin.
5. Gustav Fröhlich (1902–1987), German actor and film director. He landed secondary roles in a number of films and plays before landing his breakthrough role of Freder Fredersen in Fritz Lang's 1927 film *Metropolis*. Fröhlich was married to Hungarian opera star and actress Gitta Alpár, with whom he had a child, but the marriage was dissolved in 1935 because Alpár was Jewish and the marriage was considered un-German in Nazi Germany. Aryan Germans were not obliged by law to divorce their Jewish spouses, and most did not. It was illegal, however, to marry a Jew or Jewess, as well as to have carnal relations with them.
6. Hebrew daily *Doar Hayom*.
7. David Lloyd George (1863–1945), British Liberal politician and prime minister 1916–1922.
8. Émile Édouard Charles Antoine Zola (1840–1902), French novelist, playwright, journalist, the best-known practitioner of the literary school of Naturalism, and an important contributor to the development of theatrical naturalism. A major figure in the political liberalization of France and in the exoneration of the falsely accused and convicted army officer Alfred Dreyfus, encapsulated in the renowned newspaper headline "J'accuse."

Chapter 1. Drama

1. A Jewish way of mocking a concept by repeating it with altered initial consonants.
2. 1 Kings 19:12.
3. Fourth line of "Hatikvah" (The Hope), Israeli national anthem.

4   Hebrew *chalutz*, meant as a pioneering immigrant to the Land of Israel.
5   In Hebrew, to immigrate to the land of Israel is *la'alot* (to ascend); from Israel to anywhere else it is *laredet* (to descend). Immigration is *aliyah*.
6   Maimonides (Rabbi Mosheh ben Maimon) (Rambam) (1135–1204): medieval Sephardic Jewish philosopher who became one of the most prolific and influential Torah scholars and writers of the Middle Ages, also a preeminent astronomer and physician.
7   Exodus 16:3.
8   See Exodus 16:31.
9   After Numbers 20:2–5.
10 Exodus 17:7.
11 Isaiah 66:8.
12 Genesis 42:3. "To buy grain from Egypt."
13 Genesis 42:2.
14 Exodus 16:8.
15 Exodus 16:10.

Chapter 2. A Scattering of Exiles

1   Before the the swamps were drained and irrigation was introduced, malaria (spread by *Anopheles* mosquitos) was very prevalent, especially in the Galilee.
2   The old *yishuv*, or *kolel*, consisted of ultra-Orthodox Jews who had continuously resided in the Land of Israel for many centuries before the onset of Zionist *aliyah* and consolidation of the new *yishuv* by the end of the First World War. Each group of European Jews established their own *yishuv*.
3   A series of demonstrations and riots in late August 1929, stirred up by Mohammed Amin Al-Husseini, Grand Mufti of Jerusalem (1895–1974), when a long-running dispute between Muslims and Jews over access to the Western Wall in Jerusalem escalated into violence. Riots took the form, in the most part, of attacks by Arabs on Jews accompanied by destruction of Jewish property. During the week of riots from 23 to 29 August, 133 Jews were killed by Arabs and at least 200 others were injured, while at least 116 Arabs were killed and 232 were injured, the vast majority by the British police while trying to suppress the riots During the riots, seventeen Jewish communities were evacuated.
4   *Rebbetzin*: rabbi's wife. *Midrash*: a genre of rabbinic literature which contains anthologies and compilations of homilies, including both the exegesis of Torah texts and homiletic stories and sermons, as well as legends and occasionally even laws, which usually form a running commentary on specific passages in the entire Old Testament.
5   Young Guard: a socialist-Zionist, secular Jewish youth movement founded in 1913 in Galicia, Austria-Hungary; also the name of the group's political party in the *yishuv* in pre-1948 British Mandate of Palestine.
6   *Agudat(s) Yisrael*: Ultra-Orthodox political party opposed to Zionism, which felt that a Jewish state could only come about by Divine intervention.
7   Until the advent of National Socialism, the German film industry was amongst the most advanced in Europe.
8   John Gilbert (1899–1936): silent film star known as the "Great Lover."

9   During the 1929 Palestine attacks, rioting in Safed culminated in the massacre of eighteen to twenty Jewish residents on August 29, 1929.
10 *Kevutza*: precursor of the modern kibbutz commune.
11 Annual recital of *kaddish* (prayer for the dead) at *yahrzeit* (anniversary of bereavement).
12 *Keren Hayesod* (United Israel Appeal) was established at the World Zionist Conference held in London on July 1920, to provide the Zionist movement with resources needed for the Jewish people to return to the Land of Israel. It came in response to the Balfour Declaration of 1917, which stated that "His Majesty's government view with favor the establishment in Palestine of a national home for the Jewish people." Hameiri is being sarcastic: such money would have been used by the ultra-Orthodox rabbinate for their own purposes, unrelated to the founding of a Jewish State, as they abominated Zionism.
13 Quorum of ten adult Jewish men necessary to hold an Orthodox service.
14 Modern Hebrew was, from its inception, meant to be spoken with a Sephardi accent but, until the establishment of the State of Israel, most prayers were (and in some communities still are) recited with the old Ashkenazi accent.
15 *Maftir*: additional reading from the prophets after each weekly or festival Torah reading. This (and the Torah reading itself) was traditionally recited in old Ashkenazi Hebrew pronunciation.
16 Hundred Gates: one of the oldest settlements (established in 1874) outside the walls of the Old City, and ultra-Orthodox. Men living there traditionally still have long beards and pray in the old Ashkenazi manner, many refusing to accept Modern Hebrew as a spoken language. The Galician Jew is different on two major counts.
17 Jeremiah 16:7.
18 Approximate number of Jews living in Israel under the British Mandate of Palestine in 1930.

Chapter 3. A Telegram on Credit

1   Rachel Luzzatto Morporgo (1790–1871), said to be the first Jewish woman to write poetry in Hebrew under her own name in 2,000 years. Her works were often dismissed because she was a woman.
2   Sir Moses Montefiore (1784–1885), British banker, financier, and philanthropist (particularly to the Holy Land).
3   Rachel Bluwstein Sela (1890–1931), Hebrew-language poetess who immigrated to Palestine while it was still under Ottoman rule.
4   Communal settlement: during prestate Israel.
5   A former region in the south of Asia Minor, between Lycia and Cilicia, extending from the Mediterranean to Mount Taurus (modern-day Antalya province, Turkey). It was bounded on the north by Pisidia and was therefore a country of small extent, having a coastline of only about 120 kilometers with a breadth of about fifty kilometers.
6   Herod the Great (73/74 BCE). In 41 BCE, Herod and his brother Phasael were named as tetrarchs by the Roman leader Mark Antony. They were placed in this role

to support Hyrcanus II. Later, Antigonus, Hyrcanus' nephew, took the throne from his uncle with the help of the Parthians, and Herod fled to Rome to plead with the Romans to restore Hyrcanus II to power. In Rome, he was unexpectedly appointed King of the Jews by the Roman Senate. He went back to Judea to win his kingdom from Antigonus. After three years of conflict, Herod and the Romans finally captured Jerusalem and Herod sent Antigonus for execution to Mark Antony. Herod took the role as sole ruler of Judea and the title of *basileus* (βασιλεύς, "king") for himself, ushering in the Herodian, and ending the Hasmonean, dynasty. Hameiri errs, in that Octavian (to whom Herod subsequently switched allegiance) only became Augustus Caesar after Mark Anthony was defeated at the Battle of Actium in 31 BCE.
7   Vladimir (Ze'ev) Jabotinsky (1880–1940), Russian Jewish revisionist Zionist leader, and founder of the *Irgun Zvai Le'umi* (revisionist Zionist paramilitary organization that operated in Mandate Palestine between 1931 and 1948); Chaim Weizmann (1874–1952), chemist, Zionist leader, and Israeli statesman, who served as president of the Zionist Organization and later the first president of Israel. Jabotinsky's more extreme views and methods alienated him from moderate leaders such as Weizmann and most members of the new *Yishuv* (Zionists of late Ottoman rule and British Mandate).
8   Two early Jewish settlements. Local Hebrew newspapers: *Doar Hayom*. *Ha'aretz*, *Davar*.
9   An untranslatable joke. *Tashlich* is a Jewish rite, performed on the afternoon usually of the first day of Rosh Hashanah, in which participants symbolically cast off their sins of the previous year by gathering along the banks of a river, stream, or the like and reciting prayers of repentance. The verb *lehashlich* means "to cast or throw out."
10 Nonkosher.
11 Formerly part of the Habsburg Empire, annexed by Italy after the end of the First World War.
12 Twelve bloody battles were fought between the Austro-Hungarian and Italian armies in World War I, mostly on the territory of present-day Slovenia with the remainder in Italy along the Isonzo River on the eastern sector of the Italian Front between June 1915 and November 1917. After the Central Powers lost the war, Trieste was annexed by Italy.
13 Olives are bitter until cooked; olive oil is tasteful and healthy; the olive tree doesn't shed its leaves; olive trees can easily resist drought, diseases, and even fire—their roots regenerate the trees even after the ground is destroyed. Therefore they live for many years.
14 Postwar Hungary lost two-thirds of the former Kingdom of Hungary to newly formed and existing surrounding nations, principally Romania.
15 "Before a proselyte, even unto the tenth generation, insult not an Aramean" (Sanhedrin 94a).
16 The Hungarians originate from the Ural Mountains region, between the Urals and the Volga.
17 Hungarian Jews such as Bèla Kun and Tibor Szamuely founded the Hungarian Communist Party, and were responsible for the 133-day-long Hungarian Soviet Republic in 1919. Hundreds were killed in the so-called Red Terror and subsequent White version.

18 Ben Zion Mossensohn (1878–1942), teacher and principal of Herzliyah gymnasium, public figure, and one of the founders of Tel Aviv.

Chapter 4. The Dawn of Europe

1 Miramare: a nineteenth-century castle on the Gulf of Trieste near Trieste. Semmering: a town in the district of Neunkirchen in Lower Austria famous for its skiing and as a health resort. When the Semmering Railway was completed in 1854, it brought many tourists from Vienna for skiing trips.
2 "Blessed are You our God King of the Universe, who has granted us life (*shehecheyanu*), sustained us, and enabled us to reach this occasion."
3 "Anim zemirot" (I shall sing sweets songs) is a Jewish liturgical poem sung in some synagogues at the end of Shabbat and on holiday morning services. Formally, it is known as "Shir hakavod" (Song of glory).
4 Before the First World War, passports were not essential to pass from one European country to another.
5 Leviticus 1–3.
6 Newly formed after the collapse of the Austro-Hungarian Empire.
7 Niam-Niam: the Azande, an ethnic people from North Central Africa.
8 Tungus are peoples who speak Tungusic languages. They inhabit Eastern Siberia, and are recognized as distinct from Mongols and Turkic peoples. Igbos: indigenous people from Southern Nigeria. George Bernard Shaw (1856–1950): Irish playwright, critic, and polemicist.

Chapter 5. The Viennese Smile

1 *Blumenmarkt*: flower market.
2 Almost nothing—0.012 of one Palestine pound (lira).
3 *Wienerisch*: Vienna dialect.
4 Hayim Nahman Bialik (1873–1934): Israel's national poet. Avraham Avronin: (1869–1957) Jewish grammarian and Hebrew-language writer.
5 "Wien bleibt Wien" is a well-known march by Johann Schrammel (1850–1893). There is no operetta of that name that I could find and the march does not have a text, so the origin of the words is unclear.
6 Johanna (Hansi) Niese (1875–1934): one of the most popular actresses of the Austrian monarchy.
7 William Wordsworth (1770–1850), "Ode: Intimations of Immortality from Recollections of Early Childhood."
8 Savielly Tartakover (1887–1956): grand chess master and author.
9 The Vienna Woods area northwest of Vienna.
10 In part due to coal burning and lack of ventilation.

11 Vega is the brightest star in the constellation of Lyra, fifth brightest star in the night sky, and second brightest star in the northern celestial hemisphere, after Arcturus (a star in the constellation of Boötes). Algol: a bright multiple star in the constellation of Perseus.
12 Eight years before the *Anschluss* in 1938.
13 Symbols of wickedness (1 Kings 15–22; 2 Kings 9:30–37).

Chapter 6. The Eye and the Ear

1 *Fabula* and *syuzhet* are terms originating in Russian Formalism and employed in narratology to describe narrative construction. The *fabula* is the raw material of a story and *syuzhet* is the way a story is organized.
2 Eleonora Duse (1858–1924): Italian actress generally regarded as one of the greatest actresses of all time.
3 Untranslatable wordplay: *kisharon* (talent); *shikaron* (intoxication).
4 The word Hameiri uses here, *rei'noa*, denotes silent films. *Kolnoa* denotes talking pictures.
5 *Lyrisches Intermezzo* (1822–1823): a set of love poems by Heinrich Heine (1797–1856), some of which were set to music as *Dichterliebe* by Robert Schumann (1810–1856). Heine's style, seemingly superficial on the surface, conceals deep and equivocal truths, and nothing is as it first seems (an accurate description of outward sexual expression in upper-class prewar Vienna). Accurate translation of Heine's poetry is almost impossible.
6 Eugenie John (Marlitt) (1825–1887). Popular German novelist of the nineteenth century.
7 Anastasiya Alekseyevna Verbitskaya (1861–1928): Russian novelist, playwright, screenplay writer, publisher, and feminist.

Chapter 7. The Prisoner

1 Method of musical composition devised by Arnold Schoenberg (1874–1951); Mimi Shorp (1905–1974), Austrian actress and singer; Max Reinhardt, born Maximilian Goldmann (1873–1943), one of the most prominent directors of German-language theater in the early twentieth century; Paula Wessely (1907–2000), Austria's foremost actress after the end of the First World War.
2 "He who watches over Israel will neither slumber nor sleep" (Psalm 121:4).
3 Theodor Herzl (1860–1904): father of modern political Zionism. When Herzl died, he was buried in the Döbling cemetery, Vienna. In 1949, his remains were moved from Vienna to be reburied on the top of Mount Herzl in Jerusalem, named in his memory.
4 The *Keren Kayemet LeYisrael* (Jewish National Fund) was founded in 1901 to buy and develop land in Ottoman Palestine (later, land under the British Mandate

for Palestine, and subsequently Israel and the Palestinian territories) for Jewish settlement.
5   Lemberg (Lviv, Ukraine) was the site of violent pogroms during the latter half of November 1918. After the war, most of Galicia's Jews fell under control of Poland, ruled by Marshal Józef Piłsudski (1867–1935) from 1918–1922 as "chief of state," and from 1926–1935 as de facto leader of the Second Polish Republic.
6   An untranslatable pun: *zaken* (beard); *zakan* (old man).
7   Hameiri is being sarcastic: the assimilated Jews of Vienna were, to put it mildly, not well disposed to the traditional, Orthodox Jews of Galicia, who flooded Vienna as refugees during the war.
8   See chapter 2, note 12.
9   Micha Josef Berdyczewski (1865–1921) Ukrainian-born writer of Hebrew, journalist, and scholar. He appealed for Jews to change their way of thinking to free themselves from the dogmas of Jewish religion, tradition, and history. but is also known for his work with premodern Jewish, myths, and legends. Some of his short stories are well known.
10 Communal settlement: during prestate Israel, the word was used in reference to communal life. For many years, *kevutza* collective settlements were distinguished from kibbutz settlements in that they intended to remain small and mainly agricultural, whereas the larger kibbutz was intended to expand with agriculture, industry, and other productive pursuits. The two were ultimately merged into kibbutz settlements.
11 Hameiri may also be referring to the many divisions in the Zionist and non-Zionist allegiances of the Jewish youth of Vienna; also the many political ideals and potential parties in the British Mandate of Palestine. Jews are a contentious people.
12 Leviticus 19:18.

Chapter 8. Our Two Faces

1   A historical region in Eastern Europe, bounded by the Dniester River on the east and the Prut River on the west. Today Bessarabia is mostly (approx. sixty-five percent) part of modern-day Moldova, with the Ukrainian Budjak region covering the southern coastal region and part of the Ukrainian Chernivtsi Oblast covering a small area in the north.
2   For celebrations, Hameiri sarcastically uses the word *hilula*: celebrations at the death of a saintly rabbi.
3   Theodor Herzl (1860–1904): father of modern Zionism.
4   Pinchas Rutenberg (1879–1942), Russian engineer, business man, political activist, and founder the Palestine Electric Company (forerunner of the Israel Electric Corporation); Abraham Isaac Kook (1865–1935), Jewish thinker, halakhist, kabbalist, a renowned Torah scholar, and the first Ashkenazi chief rabbi of British Mandatory Palestine; Esther Raab (1894–1981), Hebrew author of prose and poetry, known as the "first Sabra poet"—she escaped from Sobibor in 1943; Hannah Rovina (1888–1980), the original "First Lady of Hebrew theater"; Yehoshua Bartonov (1879–1971), one of the earliest actors at the Habimah Theater.
5   See chapter 2, note 12; chapter 7, note 4.

6   Alfred Moritz Mond, First Baron Melchett (1868–1930): British industrialist, financier, and politician. In his later life he became an active Zionist; Rufus Daniel Isaacs, First Marquess of Reading (1860–1935), was a viceroy in India (1921–1925), barrister, jurist, and the second practicing Jew to be a member of the British cabinet (the first being Herbert Samuel). He was a founder member of the Palestine Electric Company.
7   *Geheimrat* was the title of the highest advising officials at the Imperial, royal, or princely courts of the Holy Roman Empire, who jointly formed the *Geheimer Rat* reporting to the ruler. The term remained in use during subsequent monarchic reigns in German-speaking areas of Europe until the end of the First World War. The English-language equivalent is privy councilor.

Chapter 9. With the Almighty's Help

1   Theodor Herzl (1860–1904): father of modern Zionism.
2   Exodus 32:9.
3   Chapter 7, note 4.
4   Second municipal district. Heavily Orthodox Jewish section of Vienna before the Holocaust.
5   Quorum of ten adult men.
6   The Seventeenth of Tammuz is a Jewish fast day commemorating the breach of the walls of Jerusalem before the destruction of the Second Temple. It marks the beginning of the three-week mourning period leading up to *Tisha Be'av*, the Jewish day of national mourning and fasting, which commemorates the fall of both temples, the expulsion from Spain, and many other tragic events which fell on the same day. The First World War began on *Tisha Be'av*. The period between the two fast days is called *Bein haMetzarim* (between the straits—i.e. Between the Days of Distress or the Three Weeks). Some form of abstinence, such as not eating meat, is traditional during this period.
7   An opprobrious epithet for a non-Jewish woman (abomination).
8   If a man is found lying with a married woman, then both of them shall die (Deuteronomy 22:22).
9   Yebamoth 61a.
10 Citron, used on Sukkot, the Feast of Tabernacles.
11 Hameiri is being sarcastic. Hasid: "righteous man."
12 Officially appointed and trusted commissar-type functionaries of the Jewish Section of the Communist Party formed with Lenin's consent in the first years of the Soviet Union (fall 1918), until it was disbanded together by in the late 1930s The Yevsektsiya (Евсекция) deemed Russian Zionist organizations to be counterrevolutionary and agitated for them to be shut down. Delegates to the Zionist Congress in March 1919 complained about administrative harassment of their activities—not from government agencies but from Jewish Communists. At the Yevsektsiya's second conference in July 1919, it demanded that the Zionist organizations be dissolved. After an appeal from the Zionists, the All Russian Central Executive Committee issued a decree in that the Zionist organization was not counter-revolutionary and its activities should not be disrupted. The campaign continued, however. In 1920, the first All-Russian Zionist Congress was disrupted

by members of the Cheka and a female representative of the Yevsektsiya. At its third conference in July 1921, the Yevsektsiya demanded the "total liquidation" of Zionism. They particularly fought against the sixth Chabad Rebbe Yosef Yitchak Schneersohn, who urged his followers to resist to their last drop of blood attempts to uproot religion which went against Communist ideology, causing many of them to be arrested and sometimes killed, and eventually led to the arrest of the rebbe himself in 1927. The Yevsektsiya attempted to use its influence to cut off state funds to the Habima Theater. branding it counterrevolutionary. The theater left Russia to go on tour in 1926, before settling in Mandatory Palestine in 1928 to become Israel's national theater. It was disbanded as no longer needed in 1929. Many leading members of the theater were murdered during the Great Purge of the late 1930s, including Chairman Dimanstein.

13 See chapter 2, note 12.
14 *Techinot* are woman's prayers for pregnancy, prior to immersion in a *mikvah* (ritual immersion bath) and other occasions. *Tze'nah u-Re'nah*—sometimes called the Women's Bible, is a Yiddish-language prose work from the 1590s whose structure parallels the weekly Torah portions of the Pentateuch and *maftirs* (additional readings) used in Jewish worship services.
15 Of highest intellectual quality.
16 Swedish-born Austrian actress (1905–1974).
17 Hameiri is being sarcastic. The original quote is: "About Zebulun he said: 'Rejoice, Zebulun, in your going out, and you, Issachar, in your tents'" (Deuteronomy 33:18).
18 A traditional Jewish beef or chicken stew, simmered overnight for twelve hours or more and eaten for lunch on the Sabbath. *Cholent* was developed over the centuries to conform with Jewish laws that prohibit cooking on the Sabbath. The pot is brought to a boil on Friday before the Sabbath begins and kept on a hotplate or placed in a slow oven or electric slow cooker until the following day.
19 Yosef Chaim Sonnenfeld (1848–1932): rabbi and cofounder of the *Edah HaChareidis*, Haredi (ultra-Orthodox) Jewish community in Jerusalem during the years of the British Mandate of Palestine and vigorous opponent of the Zionist ideal. Abraham Isaac Kook (1865–1935): Orthodox rabbi and first Ashkenazi chief rabbi of Mandatory Palestine, Jewish thinker, halakhist, kabbalist, and renowned Torah scholar. Contrary to popular belief, Rabbi Sonnenfeld and Rav Kook, although differing vigorously in many ideals, worked together.
20 *Le Rire* (Laughter): successful French humor magazine published from October 1894 through the 1950s. It appeared as typical Parisians began to achieve more education, income, and leisure time. Interest in the arts, culture, and politics intensified during the Gay Nineties. It was the most successful of all the *Journaux Humoristiques*.
21 Immanuel ben Solomon ben Jekuthiel of Rome (Immanuel of Rome, Immanuel Romano, Manoello Giudeo) (1261–1328): Italian-Jewish scholar and satirical poet. Immanuel brought the Italian sonnet form to Hebrew literature, and in this respect he is justified in saying that he exceeded his models, the Spaniards, because he introduced alternate rhyme instead of single rhyme. He also excelled in inventiveness and humor. In his old age, during a sojourn in Fermo, he collected his Hebrew poems in the manner of Yehudah Alharizi, producing a *diwan* (collection of poetry) entitled *Mehaberot*. Out of gratitude to his generous friend, he put these poems in a setting that made it appear as if they had been composed entirely during

his stay with him in Fermo and as if stimulated by him, though they were really composed at various periods. The poems deal with all the events and episodes of Jewish life and are replete with clever witticisms, harmless fun, caustic satire and, at times, frivolity. The Hebrew idiom in which Immanuel wrote lends a special charm to his work. His parodies of Biblical and Talmudic sentences, his clever allusions and puns, and his equivocations are such linguistic gems that it is almost impossible to translate his poetry into another language

22   Brightness: book of Jewish mysticism.
23   Communal settlement.
24   Traditionally, only the high priest used the Name of God (*hashem hameforash*) in the Temple on Yom Kippur day. After the destruction of the Temple, the Name became forgotten.
25   Hameiri appears to be speaking about the riots of August 1929.
26   A fund originated by European Torah scholars in 1796 to provide assistance to struggling Jews in the Land of Israel. Rabbi Meir Baal HaNes (Rabbi Meir the Miracle Maker) was a Jewish sage who lived in the time of the *Mishna*. He was considered one of the greatest of the *tannaim* (teachers) of the fourth generation (139–163). His wife Bruriah is one of the few women cited in the. He is the third most frequently mentioned sage in the *Mishna*.

Chapter 10. The Dust of Criticism

1   This might be a reference to Palais Lobkowitz, the site of the premier of Beethoven's Third ("Eroica") symphony.
2   Israel is sensu stricto part of the Asian continent.
3   Rab said to R. Kahana: "Flay carcasses in the market place and earn wages and do not say, 'I am a priest and a great man and it is beneath my dignity.'" (Pesachim 113a).
4   The world to come.
5   This probably refers to the Deutscher Arbeitersängerbund, although I could not find reference to the conductor.
6   No details could be found about his.

Chapter 11. Sicarii

1   The term *Sicarii* refers to the extremist section among the Zealots who were active at the time of the destruction of the Second Temple and so named for their daggers (called *sicae*), with which they assassinated Jewish moderates, whom they considered to be too sympathetic to the Romans. In the Talmud, the word means terrorists or robbers, and is applied only to Jews. The Sikarikin escaped to Masada not from the Romans but from their Jewish brethren. During the rebellion; they did not fight the Romans but instead robbed neighboring Jewish villages. During the 1930s, when Hameiri was writing this text, the group of maximalist Zionists called *Brit Habiryonim* (Uri Zvi Greenberg, Abba Ahimeir, and others) started making numerous references to this historical group, with Ahimeir even publishing a manifesto entitled "Megilat Hasikarikin" (The Sicarii Scroll, c. 1930). In this chapter,

Hameiri reveals his familiarity with this idiom and sympathy towards this extreme militarist version of Revisionist Zionism.
2   Béla Kun (1886–1938), Hungarian Jewish Communist revolutionary and politician who de facto led the short-lived Hungarian Soviet Republic in 1919.
3   *The Tragedy of Man* (Hungarian: *Az ember tragédiája*) is a play written by the Hungarian author Imre Madách (1823–1864). It was first published in 1861. The play is considered to be one of the major works of Hungarian literature and is one of the most often staged Hungarian plays today. Many lines have become common sayings in Hungary.
4   Theodor Herzl (1860–1904), founder of modern Zionism.
5   Bava batra 16b: "A man is not held responsible for what he says when in distress."
6   Zechariah 2:4.
7   Ski resort ninety kilometers from Vienna.
8   The word "kingdom" is borrowed directly from Uri Zvi Greenberg. This is one of the numerous comments made throughout the book that reveal Hameiri's indebtedness to Greenberg and his unique, hawkish brand of Revisionist Zionism (considered extremist by mainstream Zionists at the time).
9   Franz Joseph was not universally popular in Hungary, even after 1867.
10 After the 1867 *Ausgleich* (Agreement), Franz Joseph became emperor of Austria and king of Hungary.
11 After the end of the short-lived Hungarian Soviet Republic in 1919: most of whose leaders were Jews.
12 *Numerus clausus* (closed number) was one of many methods used to limit the number of students who may study at a university. In many cases, the goal of *numerus clausus* was simply to control the number of students in particularly sought-after areas of studies. In historical terms, however, in some countries, *numerus clausus* policies were religious or racial quotas, both in intent and function.
13 Uri Zvi Greenberg (1896–1981), Israeli poet and journalist. In his poem "Sikarikin," Greenberg calls for armed action instead of passive resistance against acts of antisemitism (invoking the spirt of Masada). Hameiri's comparison of the Sikarikin with the Awakening Magyar movement after the failed Hungarian Soviet State in 1919 is strange in view of the latter's antisemitic nature. Perhaps this, and Hungarian literary and artistic examples praising riots, is an effort to laud action over inaction, no matter against whom.
14 The 1920 Treaty of Trianon left Hungary as a landlocked state approximately one third its prewar size, with forty percent its prewar population. Its principal beneficiaries were Romania, Czechoslovakia, and Yugoslavia. Hungarian statisticians wrongly included Croatia-Slavonia in their statistics, in order to make Hungarian losses at Trianon look even more catastrophic.
15 Another poem by Greenberg.
16 Eleazar ben Simon (Yair) was a Zealot leader during the First Jewish-Roman War, who fought against the armies of Cestius Gallus, Vespasian, and Titus.

Chapter 12. Journey to Ruin

1   Hebrew: "Is this really Naomi" (Ruth 1:19). An expression for when someone or something is seen that has undergone great change.

2   Jean Patou (1880-1936)—fashion designer; Mauboussin—French jewelry firm started in 1827; Société Cartier—French luxury goods company, which designs, manufactures, distributes, and sells jewelry and watches, founded in Paris in 1847 by Louis-François Cartier (1809-1904).
3   Isaiah 3:18-23: "In that day the Lord will snatch away their finery: the bangles and headbands and crescent necklaces, the earrings and bracelets and veils, the headdresses and anklets and sashes, the perfume bottles and charms, the signet rings and nose rings, the fine robes and the capes and cloaks, the purses and mirrors, and the linen garments and tiaras and shawls."
4   Hameiri is being sarcastic. The word he uses, *hilula*, means the celebration at the death anniversary of a righteous man.
5   Wordplay between *osher* with an aleph (happiness) and *osher* with an ayin (riches). The words sound the same because the two letters are silent.
6   Lajos (Ludwig) Nagy (1883-1954): writer (especially of short stories) and publicist.
7   Between June 1921 and January 1924, Germany underwent a period of hyperinflation which caused much suffering and political instability. By the time Hameiri visited in 1930, the new rentenmark had been well stabilized.
8   Harold Sidney Harmsworth, First Viscount Rothermere (1868-1940): newspaper magnate, who strongly supported a revision of the Treaty of Trianon in favor of Hungary. On 21 June 1927, he published an editorial in the *Daily Mail*, entitled "Hungary's Place in the Sun," in which he supported a detailed plan to restore to Hungary large pieces of territory that it lost at the end of the First World War. This boldly pro-Hungarian stance was greeted with ecstatic gratitude in Hungary.
9   Barbara Gould was a well-known cosmetics queen—famous in the United States and Europe—from the 1920s through the 1940s, specializing in women's personal care products, including signature perfumes, nail polishes, facial creams, bath salts, makeup, and lipstick. Hameiri appears to be using her as a symbol for all contemporary fashion icons.
10 Untranslatable wordplay. Hameiri is sarcastically referring to the biblical laws of *pe'ah* and *shichecha*. *Pe'ah*—corner of the field left for the needy to harvest; *shichecha*—crops that are harvested and bundled, but then forgotten in the field; these are also left for the needy. The Hebrew word *pe'ah* can either mean sidelock or the corner of a field, as described above. Religious Arabs sometimes have beards but with a clean-shaven upper lip, to remind them of how the Prophet Muhammad wore his own beard 1400 years ago.

Chapter 13. Blond is Beautiful

1   Original: *Mahalat hatzahevet*—untranslatable play on words meaning jaundice or the disease of turning yellow. This overly wordy chapter presents two opposing trends that paradoxically exist simultaneously in Hameiri's eyes: the European fascination with the "savagery," "primitivism," and "vitality" of Africa and the adoration of Aryanism, as reflected in the cult of blond hair. Despite his extreme language, Hameiri does not despise gypsies or blacks, etc.: he ironically exposes these inclinations among the European nations, perhaps as an indirect explanation of their rooted antisemitism. France is presented as the font of "progress" and

tolerance and America—despite the Constitution and Bill of Rights—as a nation of racial intolerance.
2 Jean-Jacques Rousseau (1712–1778), Francophone Swiss philosopher whose political philosophy was central to the Enlightenment in France and beyond. As such, he was an important influence on the ideas behind the French Revolution. In the *Discourse on Inequality* and *The Social Contract*, Rousseau argues that mankind has fallen from a pure "state of nature" into the corrupt condition of modern society.
3 Elisabeth Rachel Félix, also known as Mademoiselle Rachel (1821–1858), French actress; Sarah Bernhardt (1844–1923), French stage and early film actress, regarded as one of the finest actresses of all time.
4 Josephine Baker (1906–1975), black American entertainer, activist, and French Resistance agent. Her career centered primarily in Europe, mostly in her adopted France. Apart from France, Europe's interaction with blacks—from the United States or Africa—was scant in the 1920s and 1930s.
5 Claude Debussy (1862–1918), French impressionistic composer whose music is noted for its sensory content and frequent usage of nontraditional tonalities. Other contemporary French composers (e.g. Satie, Poulenc) also included jazz and non-European tonalities in their compositions.
6 Benjamin Disraeli (1804–1881), British politician and writer who twice served as prime minister; Otto von Bismarck (1815–1898), conservative Prussian statesman who dominated German and European affairs from the 1860s until 1890 and served as minister president of Prussia from 1862 to 1890.
7 Max Nordau (1849–1923) was a Zionist leader, physician, author, and social critic. Hameiri is referring to Max Nordau, *Paradox* (Leipzig: Elischer, 1885)—*Paradoxes: From the German of Max Nordau*, trans. J. R. McIlraith (London: Forgotten Books, 2012).
8 Vilma Bánky (1901–1991), Hungarian-born American silent screen actress; Greta Garbo (1905–1990), Swedish-born American actress of the 1920s and 1930s; Charlotte Susa (1898–1976), German-born silent screen actress signed as a (failed) rival to Garbo. This section is not uniformly accurate: Bánky, Garbo, and Susa had dark hair, and Jeanette MacDonald (1903–1965) wasn't a blonde, but a natural redhead. Hameiri is also being disingenuous because of the general use of hair dyes in the 1920s and 1930s. Jean Harlow, for example, had ash-blond hair, dyed platinum blond. The exaggerated use of the phrase "Blond is beautiful" is tongue-in-cheek, doubtless a reaction to the "Aryanization" of Europe.
9 Also inaccurate: Chaplain had no Jewish antecedents. He had black hair which turned white with age.
10 Clara Bow (1905–1965), star of silent screen and talking pictures; Brigitte Helm (1906–1996), German actress. Clara Bow was not a blonde.
11 Anita Loos (1889 –1981), American screenwriter, playwright, and author, best known for her blockbuster comic novel *Gentlemen Prefer Blondes* (1925), followed two years later by *But Gentlemen Marry Brunettes*. Another example of Hameiri's irony.
12 Mae Murray (1885–1965), American actress, dancer, film producer, and screenwriter, was indeed blonde.
13 Not found.
14 The Hebrew word *Madiari* can be split into *Madi* (Magyar) and *Ari* (Aryan).

15 Asher Zvi Ginsburg (1856-1927), Hebrew essayist and one of the foremost prestate Zionist thinkers. Known as the founder of cultural Zionism. Hameiri is referring to an essay by Ahad Ha'am, "Avdut Be-tokh Cherut" (Slavery Within Freedom) published in Russia in 1891. See Ahad Ha'am, *Slavery in Freedom*, trans. Leon Simon (Whitefish: Kessinger Publishing, LLC., 2010). It rejects the reproach that the Zionists, especially in Eastern Europe, are backward-oriented compared to their Western European brethren and, because of this backwardness, keep hold of the old concept of the Jews as a nation. The article was a response to another article titled "Eternal Ideals" printed in the Russian Jewish monthly journal *Voshkod* (Dawn) by Simon Dubnow.
16 Ernő (Ernest) Szép (1884-1953), Hungarian Jewish poet, writer, and journalist.
17 Erzsébet Simon (1909-1977), winner of Miss Europe 1929 (best known as Simon Böske) Maurice de Waleffe (1874-1946), Belgian-born French journalist who founded the Miss Europe pageant after having founded the Miss France beauty pageant a decade earlier.
18 Scandinavians and Dutch are ignored.
19 The Übermensch of Friedrich Nietzsche (1844-1900) was one who conquered himself, not others.
20 Hameiri uses the word "Indians." The Romani people originated from the northern provinces of India.

Chapter 14. The Costume Party

1   2 Samuel 2:14: "And Abner said to Joab, Let the young men, I pray thee, arise and play before us."
2   2 Samuel 2:26: "Must the sword devour forever?"
3   Chilling irony in view of the legitimacy given the Nazi regime by permitting the 1936 Olympics to be held in Berlin.
4   Lajos Gellért (1885-1963), Hungarian actor and writer.
5   Chapter 2, note 12.
6   Oscar Beregi Sr. (1876-1965), Hungarian film actor; Max Reinhardt (Maximilian Goldmann, 1873-1943), one of the most prominent German theater directors of the twentieth century—cofounder, with Hugo von Hoffmansthal (1874-1929, of Jewish extraction) of the Salzburg Summer Festival after the First World War.
7   Not found.
8   Hameiri is being sarcastic. Counts György Apponyi de Nagyappony (1808-1899) and Gyula Andrássy de Csíkszentkirály et Krasznahorka (1823-1890) were senior Hungarian ministers under the prewar Austro-Hungarian monarchy.
9   Henri-Léon-Gustave-Charles Bernstein (1876-1953), French playwright associated with the Boulevard Theater.
10 After Leviticus 19:18.
11 Rabbi Akiva was a *tanna* (teacher) in the latter part of the first century and the beginning of the second century CE, and a leading contributor to the *Mishnah* and *Midrash*; Simon bar Kokhba (d. 135 CE), Jewish leader of what is known as the Bar Kokhba revolt against the Roman Empire 132-136 CE; Benedict (Baruch) Spinoza (1632-1677), Dutch philosopher of Sephardi Portuguese origin, considered one of the great rationalists of seventeenth-century philosophy;

Heinrich Heine (1797–1856) German-Jewish poet and essayist; Karl Marx (1818–1883), Jewish-born philosopher, social scientist, historian, revolutionary, and founder of the theory of communism; Benjamin Disraeli (1804–1881), twice British prime minister; Moses ben Maimon (Maimonides, 1135–1204), medieval Sephardic Jewish philosopher, who became one of the most prolific and influential Torah scholars of the Middle Ages. In his time, he was also a preeminent astronomer and physician; Moses Mendelssohn (1729–1786), German Jewish philosopher to whose ideas the *haskalah* (Jewish enlightenment) of the eighteenth and nineteenth centuries is indebted; Yehudah Halevi (c. 1075–1141), Spanish Jewish physician, poet, and philosopher; Rabbi Shlomo ben Yitzhak (Yitzhaki/Rashi, 1040–1105), medieval French rabbi and author of a comprehensive commentary on the Talmud and entire Old Testament. Acclaimed for his ability to present the basic meaning of the text in a concise and lucid fashion, his works remain central to contemporary Jewish study; Elisabeth Rachel Félix, also known as Mademoiselle Rachel (1821–1858), French actress; Sarah Bernhardt (1844–1923), French stage and early film actress, regarded as one of the finest actresses of all time.
12 Béla Salamon (1885–1965), Hungarian actor, comedian, and theater director.
13 Tomás de Torquemada (1420–1498), Spain's first Grand Inquisitor; Johannes Pfefferkorn (1469–1523), antisemitic German theologian and writer who converted from Judaism; Győző Istóczy (1842–1915), nationalist Hungarian politician, lawyer, and leading antisemite; Saint John of Capistrano (1386–1456), Franciscan friar and Catholic priest who incited violence against Jews; Karl Lueger (1844–1910), antisemitic mayor of Vienna and founder of the Austria Christian Social Party; Vyacheslav Konstantinovich von Plehve (1846–1904), director of Imperial Russia's police and later minister of the interior—blown up by revolutionaries; Caligula (12–41 CE), Vespasian (9–79 CE), and Titus (39–81 CE) were all Roman emperors. Vespasian was the father of Titus, who presided over the destruction of the second Temple in 70 CE.
14 Rufus Daniel Isaacs (1860–1935), First Marquess of Reading, a British Liberal politician and judge, who served as lord chief justice of England, viceroy of India, and foreign secretary,
15 Theodor Herzl (1860–1904), founder of modern Zionism.
16 Shylock, the moneylender in Shakespeare's the *Merchant of Venice*. Act 3, scene 1.
17 "I believe": thirteen principles of the Jewish faith, formulated by Maimonides in the twelfth century; "I accuse": Hameiri is probably referring to "J'accuse," the article published in 1898 in the newspaper *L'Aurore* by Emile Zola about the Dreyfus affair.
18 Saint Elizabeth (Erzsébet) of Hungary (1207–1231), symbol of Christian charity.
19 Chapter 2, note 12.
20 Géza Feleky (1890–1936), Hungarian Jewish journalist and writer.
21 Israeli wines.
22 Herzl died in 1904.
23 The First Zionist Congress was convened in 1897 by Herzl in Basel, Switzerland.
24 Yoysef (József) Holder (1893–1944/45), one of Hungary's most important Yiddish writers and poets; in his youth, also a writer of Hebrew poems.
25 Derogatory epithet by which a Jew calls a non-Jew.
26 Proverbs 27, 22: "Crush a fool in a mortar with a pestle along with crushed grain, yet his folly will not depart from him."

Chapter 15. A Hebrew Novel

1. Count István Tisza de Borosjenő et Szeged (1861–1918), Hungarian politician, prime minister, political scientist, and member of the Hungarian Academy of Sciences. The prominent event in his life was Austro-Hungary's entry into the First World War (which he initially opposed) when he was prime minister for the second time. He was assassinated during the Chrysanthemum Revolution on 31 October 1918—the same day that Hungary terminated its political union with Austria. Tisza supported the dual monarchy of Austro-Hungary and was representative of the then liberal-conservative movement.
2. Sigmund Freud (1856–1939), Austrian neurologist and father of psychoanalysis.
3. Frigyes Karinthy (1887–1938), Hungarian author, playwright, poet, journalist, and translator. He was the first proponent of the "six degrees of separation" concept, and the first to translate the Winnie the Pooh stories (Micimackó) into a Hungarian that many say is better than the English original.
4. Edgar Allan Poe (1809–1849), American writer of short stories of the macabre; H. G. Wells (1866–1946), English writer of history, politics, social commentary; Leonid Nicolaievich Andreyev (1871–1919), writer, playwright, and father of Expressionism in Russian literature; Edward Bellamy (1850–1898), American author, socialist, and utopian.
5. Frigyes Karinthy, *Krisztus és Barabbás* (Budapest: Dick Manó, 1918).
6. Yehoshua Yeivin (1891–1970), Maximalist revisionist; Shmuel Yosef Agnon (1888–1970), central figure in modern Hebrew fiction, who shared the Nobel Prize for literature with Nelly Sachs in 1966. *Brit Habiryonim* (Alliance of Thugs) was a clandestine, self-declared fascist faction of the Revision Zionist Movement in Mandatory Palestine, active between 1930 and 1933, founded by Abba Ahimeir (1897–1962), Uri Zvi Greenberg, and Yehoshua Yeivin. For Sikarikin, see chapter 11.

Chapter 16. Frozen in Time

1. Albert Einstein (1878–1955), German-born theoretical physicist who developed the general theory of relativity; George Bernard Shaw (1856–1950), Anglo-Irish playwright, critic, and polemicist; Martin Buber (1878–1965), Austrian-born Israeli Jewish philosopher best known for his philosophy of dialogue and his book *Ich und Du* (I and thou); Karl Liebknecht (1871–1919), German socialist and cofounder with Rosa Luxemburg of the Spartacist League and the Communist Party of Germany, best known for his opposition to the First World War in the Reichstag and his role in the Spartacist uprising of 1919.
2. Judah Leon Magnes (1877–1948), Reform rabbi.
3. Franz (Ferenc) Molnár (1878–1952), Hungarian-born dramatist and novelist.
4. Baron Lajos Hatvany (1880–1961), Hungarian writer, critic, journalist, and literary scholar, patron of literature, and champion of Modernism. Hatvany was a leftist, liberal thinker, who believed in the values of democracy. These beliefs were not welcome in Hungary after the dissolution of the Austro-Hungarian monarchy; consequently, he had to leave the country twice. After participating in the 1918 bourgeois-democratic revolution as a member of the Hungarian National Council, he moved to Austria and Germany until 1927. When he returned to Hungary that

year, he was tried for defaming the country, as he had sharply attacked the regime of Regent Miklós Horthy (see below) that emerged in Hungary after the suppression of the 1919 Communist Revolution. Sentenced to one and a half years in prison, he was released for health reasons after serving nine months. Count Mihály Ádám György Miklós Károlyi de Nagykároly (1875–1955) was briefly Hungary's leader from 1918 to 1919 during the short-lived First Hungarian Republic. He served as prime minister between 1 and 16 November 1918 and as president between 16 November 1918 and 21 March 1919. Endre Ady (1877–1919), one of Hungary's greatest lyric poets.

5   Miklós Horthy de Nagybánya (1868–1957), Austro-Hungarian admiral and statesman who served as Regent of the Kingdom of Hungary between World Wars I and II and throughout most of World War II, from 1 March 1920 to 15 October 1944.
6   *Al Chet*, the public confession of communal sin recited many times during Yom Kippur eve and day as part of the *viddui* (confession).
7   *Dina d'malkhuta dina* (Aramaic: the Law of the land is the law), is the halakhic rule that the law of the country is binding, and, in certain cases, is to be preferred to Jewish law. The concept of *dina de-malkhuta dina* is similar to the concept of conflict of laws in other legal systems.
8   Sándor Pál, Jewish member of the ruling party in the Hungarian parliament, who in 1926 persuaded Primer Minister István Bethlen to consent to the representation of the major Jewish congregations in the upper house, as a sign of liberality.
9   Yosef Chaim Sonnenfeld (1848–1932), ultra-Orthodox rabbi and cofounder of the *Edah HaChareidis* in Jerusalem during the years of the British Mandate of Palestine.
10 See chapter 2, note 12.
11 Leon Trotsky (Lev Davidovich Bronshtein, 1879–1940), Marxist revolutionary and Soviet politician who engineered the transfer of all political power to the Soviets with the October Revolution of 1917; founding leader of the Red Army.
12 Akiva ben Yosef (50–135 CE), leading *tanna* (teacher) of the latter part of the first century and the beginning of the second century.
13 Johannes Pfefferkorn (1469–1523), German Catholic theologian and writer who converted from Judaism and then actively preached against it.
14 Institute for full-time, advanced study of the Talmud and rabbinic literature.
15 Rabbi Abraham Isaac Kook (1865–1935), Orthodox rabbi, first Ashkenazi chief rabbi of the British Mandate of Palestine, Jewish thinker, halakhist, kabbalist, and renowned Torah scholar.
16 *Glatt*—strictest possible.
17 Talmud Torah schools were created in the Jewish world, both Ashkenazi and Sephardi, as a form of parochial primary school for boys of modest backgrounds, where they were given an elementary education in Hebrew, the Scriptures, and the Talmud; Ben-Zion Meir Hai Uziel (1880–1953), Sephardi chief rabbi of Mandatory Palestine from 1939 to 1948, and of Israel from 1948 to 1954; Shlomo Aronson, Ashkenazi chief rabbi of Tel Aviv; Rambam—Maimonides (Rabbi Mosheh ben Maimon, 1135–1204).
18 Oral Law.

19 Berakhot 24a. Orthodox Jews are generally not permitted to hear women sing. The Talmud classifies this as *erva* (nakedness).
20 See chapter 7, note 4.
21 Voluntary payment to the Roman Catholic Church that goes directly to Rome; Rabbi Meier BalHanes boxes, meant only for Orthodox charities, against (at the time) the establishment of a Jewish State.

Chapter 17. The Baptists

1 Hameiri uses the word *baptistim* (plural) or *baptizers*. I have interpreted this word as "New Apostles." This long, complex chapter, laced with references to early Zionism, reflects Hameiri's growing disillusionment with how the Zionist movement in and outside Israel has strayed from its original roots. It also reflects his deep distaste for the ultra-Orthodox and their emissaries sent out to gather money not used for its purported purpose.
2 Ukrainian-born Shaul Tschernichovsky (1875–1943), one of the great modern Hebrew poets, associated with nature poetry. As a poet, he was greatly influenced by the culture of ancient Greece.
3 Throughout this chapter, Hameiri uses the word *baptistim* to denote the original apostles of Herzl and Nordau's Zionist ideal. They go out and preach the gospel of Zionism in the same way as Christ's apostles preached the gospel of the Risen Christ.
4 Theodor Herzl (1860–1904), founder of modern Zionism.
5 Zionist songs. "Neither Dew nor Rain" comes from David's lament for the deaths of Saul and Jonathan (2 Samuel 1:21).
6 In the Hagadah, a tale is told of a group of rabbis who discuss the Exodus from Egypt all night, until their students come and say to them: "Rabbis, the time has come to recite the morning *shema*." Hameiri is sarcastically comparing the exodus from Hungary and other European countries to the Exodus from Egypt.
7 The Hebrew word *tevilah* (dipping) can mean either "baptism" or "Jewish ritual immersion."
8 Probably Robert Lachmann (1892–1939, died in Jerusalem), a German ethnomusicologist, linguist (German, English, French), musicologist, orientalist, and library official, who establish a center of oriental music and the Archive for Oriental Music in Jerusalem.
9 Named after Yohanan Ben Levi of Gush Halav (John of Gischala), who became a chief zealot commander in the Jewish revolt against the Romans in the Galilee and later in Jerusalem.
10 Chaim Weissburg—Zionist writer and journalist from Transylvania; Tzur Shalom—Town in the Haifa area, in the Gulf of Acre, which became a center for sport in northern Israel
11 Hameiri includes himself among the original "apostles" of Zionism.
12 Rabbinical emissary designated to collect funds for Israel in the Diaspora. Not known for their honesty.

13 The (old) *yishuv* is the term referring to the body of Jewish residents in Palestine, before the establishment of the State of Israel. The term came into use in the 1880s, when there were about 25,000 Jews living across Palestine, then comprising the southern part of Ottoman Syria; it continued to be used until 1948, by which time the number of Jews had increased to about 700,000.
14 The Jewish Agency for Palestine (1929–1948), which replaced the Palestine Zionist Executive as the agency charged with facilitating Jewish emigration to Palestine, land purchase, and planning the general policies of the Zionist leadership. Hameiri is sarcastically comparing the "dictatorship of the proletariat" with the "dictatorship of the *sochnut*."
15 Genesis 14:1–8.
16 Untranslatable comparison between Elam and *lehitalem* (ignore or disregard).
17 Untranslatable comparison between Shinar, *noar* (youth) and *lena'er* (to shake off).
18 Untranslatable pun between Ellasar, *El* (God) and *lasur* (to turn away, leave).
19 *Goyim* can also mean non-Jews.
20 Shmaryahu Levin (1867–1935), Zionist activist in the Russian Empire, then in Germany and the United States; member of the first elected Russian parliament for the Constitutional Democratic Party in 1906.
21 Chapter 7, note 4
22 The Maccabee World Union was founded in 1921 with the purpose of forming one umbrella organization for all Jewish sports associations. The Budapest branch was founded in 1906.
23 Koppel Reich (1838–1929), Orthodox chief rabbi of Budapest.
24 Shimon Bacher, poet and Hebrew translator; Yehudah Aryeh Blau, teacher at the Budapest Rabbinical Seminary (banned from teaching by Orthodox rabbis).
25 The Treaty of Trianon (1920), which, among other things, awarded Transylvania to Romania; it was a source of great bitterness in Hungary. Bessarabia, a province between Romania and Russia (including Ukraine) was the most open to Zionism and especially socialist Labor Zionism. By 1920, 267,000 Jews lived in Bessarabia, which was second at the time only to Palestine in the number of Jewish farmers, many of whom emigrated to Palestine to found new settlements. Most of Bessarabia now lies within modern day Moldova.
26 Now known as Haifa Bay.
27 Sites of fierce fighting during the 1929 Palestinian riots.
28 Max Nordau (1849–1923), Zionist leader, physician, author, and social critic. Cofounder of the World Zionist Organization together with Theodor Herzl, and president or vice president of several Zionist congresses.

Chapter 18. Mosaic

1 Ritual circumcisers.
2 Heves Kornél (1870–1945, murdered in the Holocaust). *Av Beit Din*: chief of a Hungarian rabbinical court invested with legal powers in a number of religious matters.
3 Tarnów (modern-day Poland).

4   A form of parochial primary school created for boys of modest backgrounds, where they were given an elementary education in Hebrew, the Scriptures (especially the Pentateuch), and the Talmud.
5   Opprobrious epithet for non-Jews.
6   Dezső (Desider) Szabó (1879-1945), Hungarian linguist, writer, and intellectual antisemite; considered one of the pioneers of Magyar populist literature. His novel *Az Elsodort falu* (Village adrift) was considered sensationalist at the time, shocking polite literary circles due to its description of racial violence against Jews and Danube Swabians (the ethnic German-speaking population). At the time Hameiri wrote his book, Szabó was notorious for his antisemitic views, but had also become an outspoken critic of the fascist Arrow Cross Party-Hungarist Movement that was growing in power. The town where he was born, Kolozsvár or Klausenberg (present-day Cluj-Napoca, Romania), was originally part of Hungarian Transylvania, ceded to Romania at the Treaty of Trianon in 1920.

Chapter 19. My Two Souls

1   Israel is, strictly speaking, on the Asian continent.
2   Hebrew: *shechinah* (dwelling or settling)—the manifestation of God's presence on Earth.
3   Ignác Goldziher (Yitzhak Yehuda Goldziher, 1850-1921), noted Hungarian Jewish scholar, considered one of the founders of modern Islamic studies in Europe. Goldziher's belief that study of Bedouin life and folklore could be used as a vehicle to understand the Old Testament was predicated on the suggestion that the modern Bedouins' ancestors could be the ancient Israelites. These theories had a strong impact on early Zionist thinkers, especially during the First and Second Aliyot
4   Assyrian: Babylonian.
5   Cluj Napoca (Romania).
6   When Romania entered the war on the side of the Entente in August 1916, it was invaded by the German Army, under General August von Mackensen. Additionally, a short war between Hungary and Romania preceded the Treaty of Trianon, which ceded Transylvania to Romania.
7   The Székelys (or Szeklers) are a subgroup of the Hungarian people, who live in the valleys and hills of the Eastern Carpathian Mountains, corresponding to the present-day Harghita, Covasna, and parts of Mureș counties in Romania. Originally, the name "Székely Land" denoted the territories of a number of autonomous Székely seats within Transylvania. The self-governing Szekler seats had their own administrative system and existed as legal entities from medieval times until the 1870s. The privileges of the Székely and Saxon seats were abolished and seats replaced with counties in 1876. Along with Transylvania and the eastern parts of Hungary proper, Székely Land became a part of Romania in 1920, in accordance with the Treaty of Trianon.
8   Wallachia is a historical and geographical region of Romania situated north of the Lower Danube and south of the Southern Carpathians.
9   Turan (the word is of Iranian origin): fictitious area in Central Asia. The original Magyar tribes allegedly (but not factually) migrated to Europe from Turan in Central Asia; Trajan quelled the kingdom of Dacia in two campaigns (101-102 CE,

105–106 CE) and absorbed them into the Roman Empire. Romanian is therefore a Romance (Latin) language with a strong Slavic influence.
10 Endre Ady was born in Érmindszent, Szilágy County (part of Austro-Hungary at the time; now a village in Satu Mare County, Romania,
11 From Ady's poem "A Szétszóródás Előtt" (Before the Dispersion).
12 Prison (cistern) during the period of the First Temple, in which Zedekiah imprisoned Jeremiah (Jeremiah 37).
13 Ady died in January 1919. Immediately after the war on 1 December 1918, the province of Transylvania, following Bessarabia and Bukovina, united with the Old Kingdom of Romania. The Social Democrats fell in March 1919 in favor of Béla Kun's Communist Party. The Red Army fought several wars against Romania and Czechoslovakia. The destruction of the Hungarian Soviet Republic and the Romanian occupation of parts of Hungary proper, including its capital Budapest in August 1919, ended the war. Romanian troops withdrew from Budapest in November 1919, and the Treaty of Trianon in June formally ceded seventy-two percent of Hungarian territory (including Transylvania) to Romania.

Chapter 20. The Living Scarecrow

1 Untranslatable pun: *zoche* with a chaf means "merit, deserve"; *zoche* with a chet means "move, change." The two words sound the same and can only be distinguished by the spelling.
2 Ion I. C. Brătianu (1864–1927), Romanian political leader, prime minister of Romania for five terms, and foreign minister on several occasions. Brătianu's political activities after the First World War, including part of his third and fourth term, saw the unification of the Old Romanian Kingdom with Transylvania, Bukovina, and Bessarabia.
3 Cleopatra probably means Queen Marie of Romania; Mark Anthony is President Woodrow Wilson. Another example of Hameiri's sarcasm.
4 Short primer: abbreviated version of the *Shulchan Aruch* (the codified list of 613 commandments for an Orthodox Jew).
5 Constance Drexel (c. 1884/1894-1956), naturalized American and groundbreaking feature writer for US newspapers. She returned to Europe soon after the end of the war, first to cover the Paris Peace Conference and then to cover and participate in the conference of the International Conference of Women and International Woman Suffrage Alliance (which succeeded in obtaining a woman's equality clause in the Covenant of the League of Nations).
6 *Siebenbürgen* (German).
7 Pun on *palcha* (crop cultivation) and *pulchan* (religious ritual).
8 A subgroup of the Hungarian people living mostly in the Székely Land, now in Romania.
9 *zhyto* (wheat); *zhyty* (to live).
10 Genesis 2:5.
11 The original reads: "*Fumotul intersis.*"
12 Octavian Goga (1881–1938), Romanian politician, poet, playwright, journalist, translator, and antisemite.

Chapter 21. The Messiah's Entreaty

1. Isaiah 21:2.
2. Sighetu Marmației, birthplace of Eli Wiesel.
3. Moldavia is a historical region, and former principality in Eastern Europe, corresponding to the territory between the Eastern Carpathians and the Dniester River. An initially independent and later autonomous state, it existed from the fourteenth century to 1859, when it united with Wallachia as the basis of the modern Romanian state. At various times, Moldavia included the regions of Bessarabia and all of Bukovina. The western half of Moldavia is now part of Romania, the eastern side belongs to the Republic of Moldova while the northern and southeastern parts are territories of Ukraine.
4. Alexandru C. Cuza (1857–1947), Romanian far-right politician and theorist. A recurring theme of Cuza's writings was that the Jews had been collectively working to ruin Christian nations, especially Romania, because of what he believed to be a Jewish "genetic code." Cuza founded the National Christian Union in 1922. The new party found inspiration in fascism and the Blackshirts, and from 1921 used the swastika as its symbol—already connected to the antisemitic Nazi Party in Germany.
5. The life of King Carol II of Romania (1893–1953) was marked by numerous scandals. His continued affairs with Magda Lupescu—a woman of Jewish extraction—obliged him to renounce his succession rights in 1925 and leave the country. His second wife Princess Helen of Greece and Denmark eventually divorced him in 1928. His father King Ferdinand died in 1927 and Carol's five-year-old son ascended the throne as Michael I. Carol returned to Romania in 1930 and replaced the regency that had been in place. He was forced to abdicate in 1940.
6. Tedescu in the original.
7. Cluj Napoca.
8. See chapter 2, note 12.
9. Rabbi Joel Teitelbaum (1887–1979), head of the Sighet-Satmar Hasidim and a fierce opponent of Zionism.
10. "That so-called doctor" refers to Herzl. Haman was the evil antagonist in the Book of Esther, who, according to the Old Testament, was a vizier in the Persian Empire under King Ahasuerus and attempted to organize the slaughter of all Jews in the kingdom.
11. A Socialist-Zionist, secular Jewish youth movement founded in 1913 in Galicia, Austro-Hungary; also the name of the group's political party in the *yishuv* in pre-1948 British Mandatory Palestine.
12. Romanian Yiddish socialist newspaper, started in 1896.

Chapter 22. My Birthplace's Agony

1. *Cheder*: Literally "room." A traditional elementary school teaching the basics of Judaism and the Hebrew language; Munkács—Mukachevo, Ukraine. In Hameiri's time, it was part of Austro-Hungarian Carpatho-Ruthenia; *beit hamidrash*—Jewish study hall located in a synagogue, yeshiva, or other building.
2. Stare Davydkovo, Ukraine.

3   Rabbi Yochanan said in the name of Rabbi Shimon ben Yehotzadak: "By a majority vote, it was resolved in the attic of Nitzah's house in Lod that in every (other) law in the Torah, if a man is threatened, "transgress and not suffer death," he may transgress and not suffer death—except for idolatry, incest (including sexual licentiousness) and murder" (Sanhedrin 74a).
4   Tribes that inhabited Canaan and Gaza before arrival of the Israelites. The Hebrew word *kaftor* also means "a button."
5   Many superstitions have been a part of Jewish life through the ages. One is to spit three times in reaction to something especially good or evil.
6   Hameiri is being sarcastic: by *Perizzite* he means non-Jew.
7   On the second night of Rosh Hashanah, it is common to eat a "new fruit"—a fruit that participants have not tasted for a long time.
8   According to the Table of Nations (Genesis 10), the Hivites are one of the descendants of Canaan, son of Ham. Hameiri is being sarcastic again.
9   More biblical sarcasm. Zaphnath-Paaneah is the name, as stated in the Bible (Genesis 41:45), given by Pharaoh to Joseph.
10 Ecclesiastes 1:2.
11 One Austrian crown was made up of 100 heller. One Palestine pound was made up of 1,000 mils. In other words, practically nothnig.
12 Opponents of Hasidism (singular: *mitnaged*).
13 H. G. Wells (1866–1946), author of *The Time Machine* and *War of the Worlds*.
14 Plural of "tallit."
15 Yosef Chaim Sonnenfeld (1848–1932), ultra-Orthodox rabbi and cofounder of the *Edah HaChareidis* Jewish community in Jerusalem during the years of the British Mandate of Palestine.
16 The *Gemara* is the component of the Talmud comprising rabbinical analysis of, and commentary on, the *Mishnah*. Zionist *Mizrachis*: religious Zionist organization founded in 1902 in Vilnius at a world conference of religious Zionists. Rabbi Elazar Spira (see below) was violently opposed to this group.
17 Chaim Elazar Spira (1868–1937), one of the rebbes of the Hasidic movement of Munkács. As the one of the most extreme rabbis in post-First World War Europe, he was estranged from many other major Hasidic rabbis, whom he considered apostates. He regarded any form of Zionism as apostasy. However, many leaders of Hasidism looked to him as one of the greatest scholars and leaders of the twentieth century. Many great rabbis, though not formally referred to as the "gaon [genius] of ------" are often lauded with this honorific as both a mark of respect and a means to indicate their greatness in the field of Torah learning.
18 *Beth din*—rabbinical court of Judaism. *Agudat Yisrael* began as a political party representing Orthodox Jews in Poland, originating in the *Agudat Yisrael* movement in Upper Silesia. It later became the party of the ultra-Orthodox population of Israel. It was the umbrella party for almost all Haredi Jews in Israel during the British Mandate.
19 Josiah C. Wedgwood (1872–1943), British labor and liberal politician.
20 Lord Arthur Balfour (1848–1930), British foreign secretary and author of the November 2, 1917 Balfour Declaration.
21 Before the entire culture was destroyed in the Holocaust, the Jews of Carpatho-Ruthenia comprised a large number of Hasidic groups, who frequently quarreled with one another.

22 Ruthenians (Rus people) are a separate Slavic cultural and linguistic group who live in southwestern Ukraine, eastern Slovakia, southeast Poland, northeast Hungary, and northwestern Romania. In Austro-Hungarian parlance, Ruthenians were Ukrainians.
23 Deuteronomy 13:16. Belz (Western Ukraine). Rabbi Spira succeeded in having the rabbi of Belz expelled from Czechoslovakia.
24 Săpânța, Romania.
25 Zhydachiv, Western Ukraine.
26 *Ir nidahat*: Deuteronomy 13:1–19.
27 Vyzhnytsia, Ukraine; Sighetu Marmației, Romania.
28 Yosef Tzvi Dushinsky (1867–1948), the first Rebbe of Dushinsky and chief rabbi (*gavad*) of the *Edah HaChareidis* of Jerusalem; Khust, Western Ukraine.
29 Hameiri is sarcastically comparing long sidelocks to horse tails.
30 Deuteronomy 27:26.
31 An untranslatable pun between *meshiach* (messiah) and *meshicha* (spreading, pouring, anointing).
32 When the country of Czechoslovakia was created after the First World War, Munkács became part of the Carpathian region of Eastern Slovakia. At least five political parties vied for power. The position of the Jewish community, especially in Slovakia, was ambiguous and, increasingly, a significant part looked towards Zionism.
33 Hameiri is caustically comparing Rabbi Spira to Girolamo Savanarola (1452–1498), Dominican friar and teacher, who instituted an extreme puritanical campaign enlisting the active help of Florentine youth. He was burned at the stake as a heretic.
34 The ninth day of Av. National day of Jewish mourning and fasting commemorating the anniversary of a number of disasters in Jewish history, including the destruction of the First Temple by the Babylonians, the Second Temple by the Romans, and the 1492 Jewish expulsion from Spain. The First World War began on *Tisha Be'av*.
35 Deuteronomy 25:19.
36 The book of Lamentations is read on *Tisha Be'av*.
37 Yehuda Halevi (c. 1076–1141), Jewish Spanish physician poet and philosopher, died (possibly murdered) shortly after arriving in the Holy Land on a pilgrimage in 1141. Many of his poems express a deep longing for Zion; Hayim Nahman Bialik (1873–1934), Israel's national poet.
38 Isaiah 24:12.
39 The two men lived eight centuries apart.

Chapter 23. The Holy Operetta

1 Rabbi Spira's only daughter Frima's wedding to Baruch Rabinovich took place on March 15, 1933 in Munkács. Over 20,000 guests attended the wedding, coming from all over Europe and even from the US. According to the daily newspaper *Rudý večerník*, "The wedding lasted for seven days." Hungary, Poland and Czechoslovakia opened their borders and no visa was necessary for people who wished to attend the wedding. Special triumphal arches were erected throughout the city in celebration of the joyous event. Film companies came from all over Europe and America to document the historic event. See www.youtube.com/watch?v=8sWe603vHoY. Rabbi

Spira is seen chastising America Jews in Yiddish for not meticulously observing all the minutiae of Sabbath laws.
2. This section must have been added after Hameiri's 1930 trip, but the chapter is written as though he was there. The irony of the lavish celebration a few months after Adolf Hitler assumed the chancellorship of Germany is painful.
3. Baruch Yehoshua Yerachmiel Rabinovich (1914–1997) was born into a distinguished Hasidic dynasty and succeeded to the title Munkacser Rebbe after Rabbi Spira's death.
4. *Mitnaged*: opponent of Hasidism. More sarcasm: *Hilula*—joyous celebration on anniversary of the death of a very pious, learned man; Kiddushin 71a: R. Joshua b. Levi said: money purifies *mamzerim* (bastards).
5. Canaanite god associated with child sacrifice.
6. Jeremiah 22:19.
7. After Proverbs 13:20: "He that walks with wise men will be wise, but the companion of fools shall suffer for it"; and Proverbs 27:17—"Iron sharpens iron, so one person sharpens another."
8. Daniel 3:5, 15.
9. The high priest's breastplate was decorated with four rows of three precious stones.
10. Part of the High Holy Day liturgy.
11. Psalm 147:10.
12. Exodus 15:16.
13. Part of the prayers after reciting the *Shema*.
14. Exodus 13:13.
15. Part of the *asher yatzar* blessing: "Blessed are You, our God, king of the universe, who formed man with wisdom and created within him many openings and hollows"
16. 2 Chronicles, 20:12.
17. Psalms 26:6.
18. K'ritot 6a. Hameiri's multiple citations mock the hypocrisy of the ceremony.
19. Sons of Zevach and Zalmunna (Judges 8).
20. Part of the "Hallel" prayer recited on the three pilgrim festivals and *Rosh Hodesh* (new moon) if it falls on the Sabbath. Also recited in the Pesach Hagadah (ritual prayer book recited at the Seder).
21. Ilya Grigoryevich Ehrenburg (1891–1967), Soviet writer, journalist, translator, and cultural figure. Ludwig Renn (1889–1979), German writer and the founder of German proletarian-revolutionary literature.
22. Literally, "abomination." A derogatory epithet for a non-Jewish woman.
23. Seventh king of Israel after Jeroboam I and husband of Jezebel.

Chapter 24. The Canaanite Servant

1. Modern-day Ukraine.
2. Reference to payment for services rendered makes the meaning of the Hebrew word used—*eved*—servant rather than slave.

Chapter 25. Spain the Healer

1 Miguel de Unamuno y Jugo (1864–1936), Spanish essayist, novelist, poet, playwright, philosopher, professor of Greek and Classics, and later rector at the University of Salamanca.

Chapter 26. Charoset

1 A sweet, dark-colored paste made of fruits and nuts eaten at the Pesach seder. Its color and texture are meant to recall mortar (or mud used to make adobe bricks) that the Israelites used when they were enslaved in Ancient Egypt. The word *charoset* comes from the Hebrew word *cheres* (clay).
2 Many great rabbis were often lauded with this honorific as both a mark of respect and a means to indicate their greatness in the field of Torah learning.
3 *Pardes* is an acronym formed from the initials of the following four approaches to interpretation of Torah text: *Peshat* (literal or direct meaning); *Remez* (a hint, allegorical, hidden, or symbolic meaning beyond just the literal sense); *Derash* (inquire: comparative midrashic meaning, as given through similar occurrences): *Sod* (secret: esoteric/mystical meaning, as given through inspiration or revelation).
4 Leviticus 10:16: "And Moses diligently enquired about the goat of the sin-offering and behold, it was burnt."
5 In 1904, François Coty (1874–1934) founded Coty in Paris with the goal of revolutionizing the fragrance and cosmetics industry. In 1912, Coty opened subsidiaries in London and New York. Coty, Inc. became a publicly traded company in 1925 and acquired a majority interest in the European Coty companies in 1929. Hameiri is being sarcastic: Coty was a fierce antisemite and fascist supporter.
6 Proverbs 31:30; after Job 36:11: "If they obey and serve him, they will spend the rest of their days in prosperity and their years in contentment."
7 The text states: locked in by the Great Wall of China; Bratislava (Slovak Republic).
8 Hayim Nahman Bialik, Israel's national poet.
9 Theodor Herzl (1860–1904), founder of modern Zionism.
10 Fyodor Mikhailovich Dostoyevsky (1821–1881), Russian novelist, short story writer, essayist, journalist, and philosopher.
11 *Brit Shalom*, also called the Jewish-Palestinian Peace Alliance, was a group of Jewish "universalist" intellectuals in Mandatory Palestine, founded in 1925, which never exceeded a membership of 100. The original *Brit Shalom* sought peaceful coexistence between Arabs and Jews, to be achieved by renunciation of the Zionist aim of creating a Jewish state.
12 Socialist-Zionist, secular Jewish youth movement founded in 1913 in Galicia, Austria-Hungary, was also the name of the group's political party in the *yishuv* in the pre-1948 British Mandate of Palestine.
13 After the Treaty of Trianon, most of Carpatho-Ruthenia found itself in the newly formed state of Czechoslovakia.
14 "Upper Hungary" is the usual English translation. *Felvidék* (literally, Upland) is the Hungarian term for the area that was historically the northern part of the Kingdom of Hungary, now mostly present-day Slovakia.

15 Paul of Thebes, commonly known as Paul the Anchorite (d. 341 CE?) is regarded as the first Christian hermit. Paul fled to the Theban Desert as a young man during the persecution of Decius and Valerianus around 250 CE. He lived in the mountains of this desert in a cave near a clear spring and a palm tree, the leaves of which provided him with clothing and the fruit of which provided him with his only source of food until he was forty-three years old, when a raven started bringing him half a loaf of bread daily. He would remain in that cave for the rest of his life, almost a hundred years. Paul is emblematic of the "desert fathers"—those early Christian hermits, ascetics, and monks who lived mainly in the deserts of Egypt and Libya beginning around the third century CE.
16 Auguste Rodin (1840–1917), French sculptor.
17 The palace officially opened on 28 August 1913, and was originally built to provide a home for the Permanent Court of Arbitration, a court created (on the suggestion of Tsar Nicholas II) to end war by the Hague Convention of 1899. Barbara Gould: see chapter 12.
18 Formed from the Cheka, the original Russian state security organization, on 6 February 1922, it was initially known under the Russian abbreviation G.P.U.—*Gosudarstvennoe politicheskoe upravlenie*. Its first chief was the Cheka's former chairman Felix Dzerzhinsky.
19 Probably Nové Mesto nad Váhom (Slovak Republic).
20 Probably Yehoshuah Avizohar, idiosyncratic gymnasium teacher.
21 Home of Carmel winery and vineyard in Israel. Founded in 1882 by Edmond James de Rothschild, and the largest winery in the country.
22 Slovakia.
23 Center for Orthodox Judaism east of Tel Aviv.
24 Leaven, forbidden on Passover.
25 Abraham Isaac Kook (1865–1935), Orthodox rabbi, first Ashkenazi chief rabbi of British Mandatory Palestine, one of the fathers of religious Zionism; Yosef Chaim Sonnenfeld (1848–1932), rabbi, cofounder of the Jerusalem *Edah HaChareidis*.
26 Chapter 7, note 4.
27 Chapter 2, note 2.
28 Untranslatable wordplay: *charoset* and *charoshet* (production, industry) (*beit charoshet*: factory). Thus, a *beit charoshet* for manufacturing *charoset*.
29 Hameiri is parodying Proverbs 17:1: "Better is a dry morsel ate in quiet than a house full of feasting with strife."

Chapter 27. The Legend of Alliance

1 Endre Ady (1877–1919), turn-of-the-century Hungarian poet and journalist. Regarded by many as the greatest Hungarian poet of the twentieth century.
2 Count István Tisza de Borosjenő et Szeged (1861–1918), Hungarian politician, prime minister, and political scientist. The prominent event in his life was Austria-Hungary's entry into the First World War when he was prime minister for the second time. He was later assassinated during the Chrysanthemum Revolution on 31 October 1918. Tisza was against war from the start.
3 The Hungarian peoples originated from an area between the Volga River and Ural Mountains, not from Central Asia.

4   Mór(ic) Jókay de Ásva (1825–1904), known outside Hungary as Maurus Jokai, was a prolific Hungarian dramatist and novelist.
5   Quintus Horatius Flaccus (65–8 BCE), leading Roman lyric poet during the Augustine period.
6   This is incorrect. Titus (39–81 CE), Roman emperor during the destruction of Jerusalem and siege of Masada, was a soldier, not an engineer.
7   Error: this fortress is not related to Count Andrassy.
8   Count Dénes Andrássy de Csíkszentkirály et Krasznahorka (1835–1913) was a Hungarian nobleman, who served as chairman of the Hungarian Heraldic and Genealogical Society. A wealthy, generous, and enlightened patron of the arts, he married the Czech Franciska Hablawetz. After her death he founded Franciska Relic Museum in his birthplace.
9   An untranslatable play on words: *osher* with an ayin means "wealth," *osher* with an aleph means "happiness." Both letters are silent, therefore the words are pronounced the same and the difference is only apparent when written.
10 During the siege of Jerusalem, Rabbi Yohanan ben Zakkai (30–90 CE) argued in favor of peace. According to the Talmud, when he found the anger of the besieged populace to be intolerable, he arranged a secret escape from the city inside a coffin so that he could negotiate with Vespasian (who, at this time, was still just a military commander). Yochanan correctly predicted that Vespasian would become emperor and that the temple would soon be destroyed; in return, Vespasian granted Yohanan the salvation of Yavneh and its sages.
11 Hameiri doesn't mention Romania, which annexed the greatest portion of Hungarian lands, including Transylvania.

Chapter 28. The Rear Echelon

1   The Jewish community of Nitra was, between the wars, second in size only to that in Bratislava, and was the site of a well-known yeshiva. In 1929, Rabbi Eleazar Schweiger became head of the community. He was an enthusiastic Zionist and assistant of Theodore Herzl at the first Zionist Congress.
2   Hameiri sarcastically uses the verb *leharbitz* (to knock in), symptomatic of rigid, loveless rote learning that was (and still is) often the case with the ultra-Orthodox teaching of their sons. Gaon: honorific for someone very learned in Torah and Talmud. For other terms, see chapter 2, note 2; chapter 7, note 4; chapter 9, note 26.
3   Abraham Isaac Kook, Orthodox rabbi, the first Ashkenazi chief rabbi of British Mandatory Palestine, founder of *Yeshiva Mercaz HaRav Kook*, Jewish thinker, halakhist, kabbalist, and renowned Torah scholar; Rabbi Chaim Yehoshua Kasovsky (1873–1960). Kasovsky's reputation rests upon the concordances which he compiled of the *Mishnah*, the *Tosefta*, *Targum Onkelos*, and the Babylonian Talmud (the last of which he was unable to complete). His early works were self-printed on a primitive printing press.
4   God to Moses in front of the burning bush: "Do not come near here; remove your sandals from your feet, for the place on which you are standing is holy ground" (Exodus 3:5); the Pressburg Yeshiva was the most famous in Central Europe.
5   Stare Dadvykovo (Ukraine)

6   "It is good to grasp the one and not let go of the other. Whoever fears God will avoid all extremes." Ecclesiastes 7:18.
7   Moses Schreiber/Sofer (1762–1839), also known by his main work *Chatam Sofer* (Seal of the Scribe), one of the leading Orthodox rabbis of European Jewry in the first half of the nineteenth century; Avraham Shmuel Binyamin Sofer (*Ktav Sofer* [Writing of the Scribe], 1815–187), son of the *Chatam Sofer*.
8   See chapter 26, note 3. Every Jew can remember sermons like this, often in his/her youth. I certainly can!
9   This and the previous citation are taken from "The City of Slaughter (Ba'ir Haharega)"—C. N. Bialik, *Selected Poems by Hayyim Nachman Bialik*, ed. and trans. Israel Efros (New York: Bloch Publishing Company, 1965), 114, 124. This poem was written after the pogroms in Kishinev (Chișinău, Moldova) April 1903 and October 1905, a terrible prediction of things to come. Hayim/Chaim Nahman Bialik (1873–1934), Israel's national poet.
10 Rabbi Mosheh ben Maimon (1135–1204), one of the most prolific and influential Torah scholars of the Middle Ages. In his time, he was also a preeminent physician.
11 Theodor Herzl (1860–1904), founder of modern Zionism.
12 Tomáš Garrigue Masaryk (1850–1937), Czech politician, sociologist, and philosopher, an eager advocate of Czechoslovak independence during the First World War, who became the founder and first president of Czechoslovakia, and thus referred to as "President Liberator."
13 Untranslatable pun: *rav chovel* (skipper); *mechabel* (one who damages).
14 Presumably because of their ability to pronounce letters with glottal stops like *chet*, *ayin*, and *kuf*, so difficult for Ashkenazi Jews.
15 Untranslatable Yiddish use of a German word: upright, decent, honest, and honorable.
16 Joseph Trumpeldor (1880–1920), early Zionist activist and war hero, who lost his left arm to shrapnel during the 1905 Russo-Japanese War. He helped organize the Zion Mule Corps during the First World War and bring Jewish emigrants to Israel. Trumpeldor died defending the settlement of Tel Hai in 1920 and subsequently became a Zionist national hero. According to the standard account, to him are attributed the last words, reminiscent of Horace: "It doesn't matter, it is good to die for our country."

Chapter 29. The Beacon of Light

1   Hameiri doesn't mention the Sudeten Germans, who proved more disruptive to national unity than any of the three groups mentioned. He mentions the danger from Germany a little later in this chapter. Ruthenians and Ruthenes are Latin exonyms formerly used in Western Europe for the ancestors of modern East Slavic peoples, especially the Rus' people with a Ruthenian Greek Catholic religious background and Orthodox believers who lived outside the Rus'. In the Austro-Hungarian context, Ruthenians were equivalent to Ukrainians.
2   Siberian tribe whose belief is shamanism.
3   Hameiri is being needlessly harsh. Ruthenian/Ukrainian folk music is varied and often tuneful.

4   Hameiri may be alluding to the Khmelnytsky Uprising of 1648–1657, which led to the massacre of up to 500,000 or more Jewish civilians.
5   Edvard Beneš (1884–1948), Czech politician who served as the president of Czechoslovakia twice, in 1935–1938 and 1945–1948.
6   Genesis 18:11: "And Abraham and Sarah were old, well stricken in age."
7   Numbers 24:23: the last prophecy of Balaam to Balak after the parable of the talking ass.
8   Karel Čapek (1890–1938), Czech playwright, dramatist, essayist, publisher, literary reviewer, photographer, and art critic, best known for his science fiction, which introduced the word "robot." He also wrote many politically charged works dealing with the social turmoil of his time. Largely influenced by American pragmatic liberalism, he campaigned in favor of free expression and despised the rise of both fascism and communism in Europe.

Chapter 30. The Intoxicating Darkness

1   Genesis 22:13: "A ram caught in the thicket."
2   Isaiah 1:6. "From the sole of the foot even unto the head."
3   Hameiri uses the word *rei'noa*, signifying silent movies. Talking pictures (*kolnoa*) arrived in Europe a few years after their introduction in the United States.
4   The English philosopher, scientist, and historian Thomas Hobbes (1588–1679) stated that "the natural condition of mankind is a state of war in which life is 'solitary, poor, nasty, brutish, and short' because individuals are in a 'war of all against all.'"
5   Untranslatable wordplay between *mukyon* (clown) and *kone* (buy, acquire).
6   Greta Garbo (1905–1990), Swedish American film actress during the 1920s and 1930s.
7   Not found.
8   Eleonora Duse (1858–1924), one of the greatest actresses of all time; Vera Fyodorovna Komissarzhevskaya (1864–1910), one of the most celebrated actresses and theater managers of the late Russian Empire; Sarah Bernhardt (1844–1923), French stage actress who starred in some of the most popular French plays of the late nineteenth and early twentieth centuries.
9   In 1895, Duse met the Italian writer, poet, and playwright Gabriele D'Annunzio (1863–1938), who was five years her junior, and the two became involved romantically as well as collaborating professionally. He wrote four plays for her but, after he gave the lead for the premiere of the play *La Città morta* to Sarah Bernhardt instead of Duse, there was a furious fight and Duse ended her affair with him. Hameiri's interpretation is not true in all aspects.
10 Moritz Stiller (1883–1928), Finnish Swedish film director, best known for discovering Greta Garbo and bringing her to America.
11 None of this is true. Stiller left the United States after an argument with Paramount and died in Sweden of pleurisy.
12 Leonardo da Vinci (1452–1519), brilliant Italian polymath of the Renaissance, whose areas of interest included invention, drawing, painting, sculpture, architecture, science, music, mathematics, engineering, literature, anatomy, geology, astronomy, botany, paleontology, and cartography.

13 Rudolf Valentino (1895-1926), John Gilbert (1897-1936), Maurice Chevalier (1888-1972)—actors.
14 Norma Shearer (1902-1983), Joan Crawford (1906-1977)—American screen actresses.
15 Rudyard Kipling (1865-1936), "The Ballad of East and West."
16 Adolph Zukor (1873-1976), Hungarian-born American film mogul and founder of Paramount Pictures.
17 Hameiri is referring to the Babelsberg film studio of Weimar Germany and the Russian films of Sergei Eisenstein. The term "Christian" is untrue: German movies were replete with Jewish influences and Eisenstein was half-Jewish. Moreover, *The Blue Angel* was a German movie written, scored for music, and directed by Jews.
18 Terrible irony in view of what awaited in both countries. German cinema, purged of its Jews, was turned into a Nazi propaganda tool; Eisenstein was one of the few whose art Stalin didn't attempt to influence; Florenz Ziegfeld Jr. (1867-1932), American Broadway impresario.
19 Untranslatable wordplay between *teva tavua* (submerged nature) and *teva tovea* (demanding nature).

Chapter 31. Conscience

1 Isaiah 11:6.
2 Albert Einstein, German-born theoretical physicist, who developed the theory of relativity, one of the pillars of modern physics, is also known for his influence on the philosophy of science. He was a committed pacifist and one of the few German scientists unalterably opposed to the First World War from the very beginning.
3 A little specious, in view of Einstein's promiscuous relationships with women and his penchant for using people for his own ends.
4 Bamidbar Rabbah 21:4; Midrash Tanhuma Pinhas 3.
5 Esther 7:10.
6 Bronisław Huberman (1882-1947), Jewish Polish violinist known for his individualistic and personal interpretations and his tone color, expressiveness, and flexibility. The bloodshed of the First World War triggered Huberman's interest in politics. Convinced that peace could only be achieved through European unification (modeled on the economic and political integration of the United States), he became involved in the Pan-Europa Movement. He toured the United States repeatedly in the 1920s, explaining his political ideas in *Mein Weg zu Paneuropa* (My Road to Pan-Europa, 1924). Huberman is also remembered for founding the Israel Philharmonic Orchestra (then known as the Palestine Philharmonic), thus providing refuge from the Third Reich for nearly 1,000 European Jewish musicians.
7 Words taken from the second verse of "Hatikvah," the future Israeli national anthem.
8 Formerly Temesvár: annexed by Romania after the Treaty of Trianon, together with a large part of the Banat Region. The other part was awarded to Yugoslavia. The war was between Romania and Hungary (1918-1920).
9 Genesis 1:16-18: "And God made two great lights; the greater light to rule the day, and the lesser light to rule the night: he made the stars also. And God set them in the firmament of the heaven to give light upon the earth, and to rule over the day

and over the night, and to divide the light from the darkness." The order of the text indicates Einstein as the sun and Huberman as the moon.
10   Richard Wagner (1813-1883), German composer of operas and music dramas; Ludwig van Beethoven (1757-1827), German composer and pianist, and crucial figure in the transition between the classical and romantic eras in classical music.
11   An untranslatable play on the two Hebrew words for "why": *madua* (past) and *lama* (future). Nicolaus Copernicus (1473-1543), Renaissance- and Reformation-era mathematician and astronomer, who formulated a model of the universe that placed the Sun rather than the Earth at the center of the universe; Johannes Kepler (1571-1630), German mathematician, astronomer, and astrologer, best known for his laws of planetary motion; Sir Isaac Newton (1642-1727), English mathematician and astronomer, widely recognized as one of the most influential scientists of all time, who laid the foundations of classical mechanics, and made seminal contributions to optics and infinitesimal calculus.

Chapter 32. Homeward Bound

1   Before the First World War (Hameiri was born in 1890).
2   Kyiv (Ukraine).
3   A *moshava* (pl. *moshavot*) is a form of rural Jewish settlement established by the members of the old *yishuv* since late 1870s and during the first two waves of Jewish Zionist immigration—the first and second *aliyah*. In a *moshava*, as opposed to later communal settlements like the *kevutza* (later, kibbutz), all land and property are privately owned. The first *moshavot*, described as "colonies" in professional literature, were established by the members of the Jewish community and by pioneers of the first *aliyah* arriving in Ottoman Palestine. The economy of the early *moshavot* was based on agriculture.
4   Hameiri uses the example of whether the population of Shanipishuk could also belong to the congregation of Vilna, the nearest big town.
5   Ethics of the Fathers 1:12.
6   (Military) review or tattoo. *Proverka* means "inspection."
7   *HaHistadrut HaKlalit shel HaOvdim B'Eretz* (General Organization of Workers in the Land of Israel), known as the *Histadrut*, is Israel's organization for trade unions. Established in December 1920 during the Mandate, it became one of the most powerful institutions of Israel.
8   Theodor Herzl (1860-1904), founder of modern Zionism.
9   Jeremiah 22:19.
10 Yiddish theater actress; untranslatable pun on Rosen and *razon* (thinness).
11 Carl von Ossietzky (1889-1938), German pacifist and recipient of the 1935 Nobel Peace Prize for his work in exposing the clandestine German rearmament. He died in Nazi captivity.
12 Mimi Shorp (1905-1974), Austrian cabaret artist.
13 The text reads in Prussian, but Russian makes more sense.
14 Revisionist Zionism is a faction within the Zionist movement. It is the founding ideology of the nonreligious right in Israel and was the chief ideological competitor to the dominant socialist Labor Zionism.

www.ingramcontent.com/pod-product-compliance
Lightning Source LLC
Chambersburg PA
CBHW051121160426
43195CB00014B/2283